AQA English Language B

A2

2nd Edition

Mark Saunders
Felicity Titjen

Series editor
Mark Saunders

Nelson Thornes

First published in 2009 by Nelson Thornes Ltd

This edition published in 2013 by:
Nelson Thornes Ltd
Delta Place
27 Bath Road
CHELTENHAM
GL53 7TH
United Kingdom

13 14 15 16 17 / 10 9 8 7 6 5 4 3 2 1

A catalogue record for this book is available from the British Library

ISBN 978 1 4085 2201 1

Cover photograph: PhotoAlto/Laurence Mouton
Illustrations include artwork drawn by Harry Venning, Peters and Zabranksy UK Ltd and Pantek Arts Ltd

Page make-up by OKS Prepress, India

Printed in China by 1010 Printing International Ltd

Acknowledgements

The authors and publishers wish to thank the following for permission to use copyright material.

Text: p7 Fig. 4, Taken from the resource 'What's in a name? An introduction to language study at AS level' © 2005 www.teachit.co.uk; p8 Table 5, Pamela Grunwell for material from Pamela Grunwell, PACS: *Phonological Assessment of Child Speech*, NFER-Nelson (1985); p11 Jane Hale for Rachel's first words; p13, Continuum International Publishing Group for an extract from Clare Painter, *Into the Mother Tongue: A Case Study in Early Language Development* (1984); pp16, 17, 19 and 21, Cengage Learning Services Ltd for Tables 11, 12, 13 and 14 from Jean Stilwell Peccei, *Child Language* (1999); p19 Laura Grimes; P20 From Fromkin/Rodman/Hyams. *An Introduction to Language*, 8E. © 2007 Wadsworth, a part of Cengage Learning, Inc. Reproduced by permission. www.cengage.com/permissions; p21 Amanda Coultas; p23 Jess Darby; pp26, 27 and 29, Amanda Coultas; p29 Laura Grimes; p32, Penguin Books Ltd for extract from David Crystal, *Listen To Your Child: A Parents' Guide to Children's Language* (1986). Copyright © David Crystal 1986; p30 Jess Darby; p41 Julia Donaldson and Axel Scheffler, *The Gruffalo*, Macmillan Children's Books, 1999; p45 Oxford University Press for material from Roderick Hunt and Alex Brychta, Oxford Reading Tree: Stage 8: Storybooks (Magic Key): *Victorian Adventure* (1990); pp66, 67 and 68, Jess Darby; p70, Oxford University Press for material from Roderick Hunt and Alex Brychta, Stage 8: More Magpie Workbooks: *Flood!* (2003); p80 Oxford University Press for definition of 'Nice' from *Oxford English Dictionary*, eds J. Simpson & E. Weiner (1989); p82, Penguin Books Ltd for extract from Richard Curtis and Ben Elton, *Blackadder: The Whole Damn Dynasty*, Michael Joseph (1998). © Richard Curtis and Ben Elton 1987; p87, The Random House Group Ltd for material from Ainsley Harriott, *Meals in Minutes*, BBC Books (1998); pp90 and 96, Reproduced by courtesy of the University Librarian and Director, The John Rylands Library, The University of Manchester for material from John Gabriel Stedman, *Narrative of a Five Years' Expedition Against the Revolted Negroes of Surinam, 1796*; p94, Reproduced by courtesy of the University Librarian and Director, The John Rylands Library, The University of Manchester for material from Nicholas Culpeper, *The English Phyſitian Enlarged*, 1676; p97, Darren McClelland, Rodney and Inge for material from www.travelblog.org; p98 Reproduced by courtesy of the University Librarian and Director, The John Rylands Library, The University of Manchester for material from Hester Thrale Piozzi, *Observations and Reflections Made in the Course of a Journey Through France, Italy and Germany*, 1789; pp100 and 101, Cambridge University Press for material from David Crystal, *The Cambridge Encyclopedia of the English Language, 2nd edition* (2003); pp106 and 107 DC Thomson & Co Ltd for material from 'The Cathy and Claire page' from *Best of Jackie Magazine*, Prion Books (2005); p111 Published with the kind permission of the family of John William Mayer; p114 Palgrave Macmillan for material (numbered list) from Dennis Freeborn, *Varieties of English* (1993); p115 DC Thomson & Co Ltd for material from 'The Four Marys' in *Bunty Book* (1963); and 'The Four Marys' in *Bunty Book* (2001); p120, Universal Press Syndicate for Lynn Johnston, 'For Better Or For Worse', 22 April 2007. Copyright © 2007 Lynn Johnston; pp121 and 122, Jean Aitchison, 'The Language Web, The Power and Problem of Words' – The 1996 BBC Reith Lectures (1996); p123, Ingrid Tieken-Boon van Ostade for material from Ann Fisher, *A Practical New Grammar with Exercises of Bad English*, 1789; p124 (top), unable to trace; pp125 and 126, Solo Syndication for material from John Humphrys, 'I H8 text speak', *The Daily Mail*, 24 September 2007; pp128 and 129, Trustees of the Keep Military Museum for Private Honey, 'Camp Before Sebastapol, Nov 20 1854'; p129, Georgina Foss; p140 Pearson Education Limited for Mark Sebba, *London Jamaican*, Longman, 1993; pp158 and 159, Parragon Books Ltd for material from Sue Graves, *Silly Pig Has An Idea* (2004); p159 Fig. 13, Silly Pig, by Sue Graves © Parragon Books Ltd, 2004; p161 Cambridge University Press for material from Jenny Cheshire, *Variation in an English Dialect. A Sociolinguistic Study* (1982); p162 Palgrave Macmillan for Mark Sebba, *Contact Languages: Pidgins and Creoles*, (1997); p161 Joanna Przedlacka for material from www.phon.ox.ac.uk; p178 Beverley D'Silva for material from her article, 'Mind your language', *The Observer*, 10 December 2000; pp179 and 180, British Broadcasting Company with Ian Peacock and Michael Rosen for material from *Word of Mouth*, BBC Radio 4.

Photos: p12 Fig. 6, Fotolia; p18 Fig. 10, iStockphoto; p23 reprinted by permission of Jean Berko Gleason; p27 Fig. 14, Fotolia; p31 Fig. 15, Fotolia; p38 Fig. 16, Fotolia; p39 Fig. 17, Fotolia; p42 Fig 18, Debbie Hepplewhite, www.phonicsinternational.com; p50 Fig. 19, Fotolia; p65 Fig. 21, Fotolia; p77 Fig. 3, iStockphoto; p78 Fig. 4, McPix Ltd/Rex Features; p82 Fig. 6, BBC Motion Gallery; p87 Fig. 8, iStockphoto; p89 Fig. 9, Fotolia; p96 Fig. 12, Fotolia; p97 Fig. 13, Mary Evans Picture Library/Alamy; p116 Fig. 16, Fotolia; p117 Fig. 17, Alamy; p136 Fig. 2, Fotolia; p138 Fig. 3, Fotolia; p143 Fig. 5, Bloomberg via Getty Images; p143 Fig. 6, Getty Images; p144 Fig. 7, Fotolia; p150 Fig.10, Alamy; p164 Fig. 14, Fotolia; p176 Fig. 1, Fotolia; p180 Fig. 3, Lebrecht Music and Arts Photo Library/Alamy.

Every effort has been made to trace the copyright holders but if any have been inadvertently overlooked the publisher will be pleased to make the necessary arrangements at the first opportunity.

Contents

Introduction

Nelson Thornes has worked hard to ensure this book and the accompanying online resources offer you excellent support for your course. You can feel assured that they match the specification for this subject and provide you with what you need to for this course.

These print and online resources together **unlock blended learning**; this means that the links between the activities in the book and the activities online blend together to maximise your understanding of a topic and help you achieve your potential.

These online resources are available on  which can be accessed via the internet at **http://live.kerboodle.com**, anytime, anywhere. If your school or college subscribes to this service you will be provided with your own personal login details. Once logged in, access your course and locate the required activity.

For more information and help visit **http://www.kerboodle.com.**

Icons in this book indicate where there is material online related to that topic. The following icons are used.

💡 Learning activity

These resources include a variety of interactive and non-interactive activities to support your learning.

☑ Progress tracking

These resources include a variety of tests that you can use to check your knowledge on particular topics (Test yourself) and a range of resources that enable you to analyse and understand practice questions (On your marks…).

🔎 Research support

These resources include WebQuests, in which you are assigned a task and provided with a range of weblinks to use as source material for research.

🔖 Study skills

These resources support you and help develop a skill that is key for your course, for example planning essays.

🔍 Analysis tool

These resources feature text extracts that can be highlighted and annotated by the user according to specific objectives.

■ How to use this book

The structure of this book mirrors the specification: it is split into two units (Unit 3 Developing language and Unit 4 Investigating language), each of which is divided into Sections A and B. Each section begins with an introduction to the topics that will be covered and concludes with exam (Unit 3) or coursework (Unit 4) preparation. At the back of the book you will find feedback on the activities and exercises, and a glossary of key terms.

The features in this book include:

Learning objectives

At the beginning of each section you will find a list of learning objectives that contain targets linked to the requirements of the specification.

■ Key terms

Terms that you will need to be able to define and understand.

■ Research points

Linguistic research that has been carried out in the area you are studying.

Thinking points

Questions that check your understanding of the research point.

■ Activities

Starter, Classroom, Language around you and Extension activities all appear throughout. Coursework activities appear throughout Unit 4.

■ Links

Links to other areas in the textbook which are relevant to what you are reading.

■ Data response exercises

Questions based on given data.

■ Further reading

Suggestions for other texts that will help you in your study and preparation for assessment.

■ Looking ahead

Points relating to how English Language skills can be applied in the future outside the classroom, with particular reference to research, finding sources, essay and report writing, problem solving, analysis and critical thinking.

Study tip

Tips to help you with your study and to prepare for your exam.

Practice questions

Questions in the style that you may encounter in your exam. Practice questions are reproduced by permission of the Assessment and Qualifications Alliance.

Nelson Thornes is responsible for the solution(s) given and they may not constitute the only possible solution(s).

■ Transcription conventions

In order to make analysis of transcripts easier and more predictable for you, the AQA specification follows particular conventions that you need to be aware of. This information is provided to help you interpret the data, exploring some of the reasons for these features in the light of the specific contexts of the speech. You should refer to this key for all the transcripts provided in the book.

Key:

(.) indicates a normal pause

(2.0) Numbers within brackets indicate length of pause in seconds

Words between vertical lines are spoken simultaneously

:: indicates elongated sounds

Underlining indicates a stress placed on this syllable

Capital letters indicates volume

Other contextual information is in italics in square brackets

Phonemic symbols are set within square brackets

■ Weblinks in the book

As Nelson Thornes is not responsible for third party content online, there may be some changes to this material that are beyond our control. In order for us to ensure that the links referred to in the book are as up-to-date and stable as possible, the websites are usually homepages with supporting instructions on how to reach the relevant pages if necessary.

Please let us know at **kerboodle@nelsonthornes.com** if you find a link that doesn't work and we will do our best to redirect the link, or to find an alternative site.

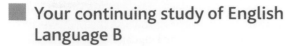

Introduction to this book

Your continuing study of English Language B

Your AS Level studies have, no doubt, whetted your appetite for studying language, and given you a fresh perspective on the language that surrounds you each and every day. You are now a seasoned linguist, and I am sure that you are enjoying your new-found insight: maybe you can't help analysing the differences in the way your male and female friends interact in conversation with you, or perhaps you are now conscious of the orthographical choices you make when you text or message on your phone – the use of punctuation, emoticons and non-standard spellings – and how they might be interpreted. There are many ways in which a wider awareness of language enhances your life – and, at A Level, you are about to extend these horizons even further.

You will now know that the way you approach texts and language at Advanced Level is quite different from your GCSE experiences of textual analysis, original writing, investigation and discussion. You have put your natural interest in language to work on the study of English, and that can indeed be a weird and wonderful world.

Midway along the path from GCSE English, through to AS Level, and then A Level study, you are now much better acquainted with the challenges involved. The AS level course gave you the opportunity to build on your original writing abilities and skills of textual analysis. In the A Level units, you will deepen your knowledge and understanding of these areas and add new approaches, including that of language investigation, and an increasingly academic approach to working with existing research and theory.

At A Level, the skill of textual analysis remains a fundamental part of the AQA GCE English Language B experience. The knowledge of word classes, grammatical structures, semantics, graphological elements and phonology you developed during your AS Level studies will underpin the analytical work that you undertake in the A Level units. Of course, the adverbs, clauses and syllables you can spot in the language remain the same as they were before; only now you will need to bring them into your work with increasing frequency and confidence, and understand the way that these different layers of language interact in complex situations – like those you will encounter in learning about child language acquisition, or in pursuing your own language investigation.

The key difference in the A2 year, in terms of coursework, is the language investigation. In many ways this is the closest thing to an undergraduate assignment that you will encounter on the A Level course. Taking pretty much any area of language as a starting point, you'll be able to ask your own questions, formulate your own methodology and collect your own data, analysing it to produce a piece of research into something that interests you. While this could be drawn from the language topics you have studied in AS, or the new ones you come across in A2, a good starting point can often be the language around you – friends, family, work – and the varied ways in which we use language in different situations. You will be able to take social variables (for example, gender, age, ethnicity, social class) and linguistic variables (for example, tag questions, slang, forms of address) that you have encountered elsewhere in the course, and explore how they are used, and to what effect. The section on ENGB4 coursework will explain this in much more detail and offer you a range of possibilities for further study.

The opportunity to produce some of your own writing is also retained at A Level, although it is now linked to your language investigation, providing a media text to shed new light on the topic you have been investigating. This piece of journalistic writing will need to be aimed at a non-specialist audience, transforming tricky academic ideas into something accessible, engaging and informative for the general public. The editorial know-how that you developed in Unit 2 will stand you in good stead when producing this text, as you work to blend the intellectual quality of your discussion of the topic with a creative eye and ear for what works in the varied and vivid language of the media.

How is English Language B assessed at A Level?

You will already be familiar with the assessment breakdown at AS Level, and there is still coursework at A2 Level, which amounts to 20 per cent of the A Level marks. Again, there is a good balance of the ways in which you will be assessed, and the coursework helps you to embark upon the sort of independent study and exploration that A Level work makes possible.

The Unit 3 examination counts for the remaining 30 per cent of the A Level total. If you are wondering where the remaining 50 per cent comes from, remember that the marks you get in the AS and A Level each count equally towards your overall grade. Therefore, in addition to the A Level units, the marks from your AS Unit 1 exam contribute 30 per cent, and the AS Unit 2 coursework 20 per cent of the final A Level grade you are awarded.

The same four assessment objectives (AOs) used in your AS units continue into the A2 units. The way that your coursework and examinations are marked is governed by these AOs, and you'll find plenty of detail in this book to help you understand exactly what they mean for Units 3 and 4. The four AOs used in 'Spec B Lang' help to emphasise the importance of communicating your ideas clearly, using linguistic approaches well, placing the language examples that you deal with in context, and developing your creative abilities. Just as with your AS Level units, it is a good idea to get to know the way that these AOs are shared out in the A Level units, to help you make sure your work fits them as well as possible.

■ What does each unit cover?

The two units at AS Level, fully covered in the AS Level book, introduced you to a wide range of skills, all of which can be built upon at A Level. The main areas of analytical writing, textual analysis, language debates, and even your own original writing are all developed in the content of Units 3 and 4.

The Unit 3 examination, 'Developing language', looks at two very different ways in which the English language can be seen to develop: the personal, somewhat miraculous development of the way that children acquire language on the one hand; and, on the other, the way that the English language as a whole has changed over time, and is developing still.

You may well remember (or have been told by your parents) anecdotes of how you learned to speak. Your study of language acquisition will help you to grasp some of the fundamentals of how children rapidly develop from pre-verbal babbling to fluent, subtle and creative communication in the space of a few short years. After understanding some of the main approaches adopted by researchers, this unit takes the issue further, tackling the wider issues of literacy and the way in which reading and writing are mastered by children.

On a larger scale, studying language change will take you on a tour of several hundred years of language history and chart the path of English right through to the present day. This added dimension of time will bring you into contact with texts that reveal some of the many different faces of English over time, and the character of a language that has made its ability to morph and adapt a definitive virtue – one that has enabled it to survive and grow so successfully.

In the Unit 4 coursework, you get the chance to investigate a particular area of the language in more detail. To prepare for this unit, look back over the topics that you have studied at AS and A Level, and choose something you have nurtured a real interest in. This can be an excellent way to explore an area that you may want to go on to study further (for example, journalistic writing from your coursework from Unit 2), or even forge a career in (for example, the language of technology from Unit 1, or supporting children's literacy, from Unit 3).

As well as producing an investigative project, Unit 4 also affords the opportunity to add your own voice to the area of language you have chosen to focus on. You will be asked to produce a media text of some kind, designed to communicate ideas related to your investigative topic – be it in the form of an article for a website, an editorial for a newspaper, or an advice and information piece for a magazine.

■ Where could it take you?

So, what *does* the future hold for a linguist? English Language is certainly a subject very well regarded by Higher Education institutions, and because you are studying the thing that you will probably use the most whatever you do in life – your language – it easily complements any educational course you might follow, and provides a new perspective on most conceivable professions.

At university, there is a considerable range of English-related courses available, that directly build on one or more aspects of your work at AS and A Level, from creative writing through to speech therapy. However, outside the wider school of English, your knowledge and skills will share ground with the many subjects within the social sciences, and particularly with psychology, sociology and law-related courses. Even further afield, it is not difficult to see the value of a sophisticated understanding of English in areas of design, business, computer science – in almost anything you could imagine, really.

When you come to begin a career, you will find language study will make you an attractive, skilled and flexible employee in most services and industries. Whether it is the increased insight you can bring to analysing written or spoken language, or your ability to control and shape your own communication, abilities of this nature will prove a real benefit to you. Even some of the specific topics you will have studied may find their niche: maybe the language and technology work you have done at AS Level will give you an overview of the impact of technology as you start out as a software designer. Or perhaps the section on language acquisition will help you get to grips with work in childcare and with very young children. You never know, you might even want to start teaching English yourself and pass your ideas on!

■ The English Language B series

All of which brings me back to a quick reminder about the Nelson Thornes English Language series. This comprises a series of books designed to be an ideal companion and guide to your journey through our language. In addition to these texts, there are support materials for your teachers, and online e-learning resources, which help to create a multi-dimensional and truly blended learning experience. The work that has gone into this collection has been carried out by teachers and subject experts who have taught A Level English Language in schools, colleges and online, for many years, and have just the right mix of experience and subject knowledge to bring the course to life for you.

The English language holds something for everyone, and I am sure that the step you have taken to embark upon AS and A Level English Language is one that you will enjoy and one which will offer you genuine challenge and personal satisfaction. Use this book to help you, but be prepared to follow your nose too – language is such a tremendous and ever-changing thing, it would be impossible for one book to cover everything. Then, maybe, come back to the book to keep you right on track as you prepare for your exams, your coursework, and success. Finally, let me wish you the very best in your life as a linguist – it should be fun.

3 Developing language

- **AO1** Select and apply a range of linguistic methods, to communicate relevant knowledge using appropriate terminology and coherent, accurate written expression (15 per cent of the A Level mark).

- **AO2** Demonstrate critical understanding of a range of concepts and issues related to the construction and analysis of meanings in spoken and written language, using knowledge of linguistic approaches (10 per cent of the A Level mark).

- **AO3** Analyse and evaluate the influence of contextual factors on the production and reception of spoken and written language, showing knowledge of the key constituents of language (5 per cent of the A Level mark).

Key terms

Multimodal texts: texts that combine word, image and sound to produce meaning.

By the time you have reached A2 you already know some key concepts and theories surrounding language study, and you may be wondering how the A2 course uses this knowledge. In Unit 3, this is achieved by focusing on two main topics:

- the acquisition of language by children
- the development of and changes in English over time.

Your study of the language used in particular social contexts and the genres of speech, writing and **multimodal texts** first explored in Unit 1, along with your practical experience of writing in Unit 2, are directed in your second year to questions about language development in specific contexts. Detailed breakdowns of the key knowledge required for each section of the unit are provided in each section and topic of this book, but by concentrating on two specific areas you will engage with some of these important questions about language acquisition and development.

- How do children first acquire spoken language and learn to read and write?
- How and why has English changed in both spoken and written forms?

The focus of your A2 is on synopticity, offering opportunities to look at the English language as a whole through your investigation of language in Unit 4, and here, in Unit 3, building on your existing knowledge and understanding with new theories and concepts to test out and evaluate. Above all, this unit is data-based. You will explore real-life texts to illustrate how children encounter language and develop the sophisticated skills they need in order to become effective communicators, and the ways in which English speakers have changed the nature of English to reflect their society and the influences on it. Enjoy the challenges of interpreting children's skilful use of English as they develop communication abilities, and engaging with English in its different forms and varieties over the last three centuries.

The examination tasks

You will be assessed through one written paper of $2\frac{1}{2}$ hours, where you will answer two questions based on a selection of data relating to the topics: one on Language acquisition (Section A) and one on Language change (Section B). You will be able to choose from two questions for each topic. Remember to keep the assessment objectives in mind as you study each topic. Being aware of these will help you focus on effective ways to approach the texts you study by:

- demonstrating your linguistic awareness
- applying relevant theories and ideas about the language used
- thinking about important contextual factors.

A | Language acquisition

Introduction

- learn the stages of early spoken language development and children's acquisition of literacy skills, focusing on early reading and writing, from birth to age 11

- evaluate the different theoretical views about child language acquisition

- assess the importance of contextual factors in governing early language and literacy development

- apply and select appropriate linguistic methods, key concepts and relevant contextual factors to data about young children's speech and writing.

Key terms

Idiolect: an individual's own 'linguistic fingerprint'.

Register: a variety of language appropriate to a particular purpose and context.

Section A of Unit 3 concerns the acquisition of language by children up to the age of 11 years. The three particular areas of focus are spoken language and the beginnings of reading and writing. The first topic will help you develop your knowledge of early speech development, the second will cover reading, and the third will cover writing.

What is language acquisition and why is it an important area of study? Well, the understanding of how we, as speakers and communicators, first acquired the ability to use words, string them together in a meaningful way and convey our thoughts and feelings to others must be at the heart of all language study. In fact, it might seem strange that you didn't study this at AS. However, all your AS knowledge about speech and writing modes, the social contexts of language use and the concepts of language use, such as **idiolect** and **register**, will underpin your A2 study of child language. Child language acquisition is a truly synoptic topic, combining all the linguistic areas that you are already able to use in analysing texts, and using them to examine children's speech and literacy development.

Above all, language acquisition relates to all of our experiences. We have all acquired language and learned to read and write. You might remember humorous anecdotes about your early speech, and your parents may have kept your early attempts at writing because they found them amusing or touching. This might seem quite remote to you now as a competent, adult user of language, but younger family members, interactions in your job role, or seeing children in the social environment should make you a keen observer of language development.

Surprisingly, language acquisition remains a hotly debated topic amongst linguists. Despite the amount of research on all aspects of language acquisition, linguists can't explain every developmental feature. Many opposing views jostle for acceptance, and evaluating these ideas will encourage you to be inquisitive about language development. You could already be thinking about how children acquire language – is it a 'taught' skill or is it just within all humans to communicate through speech? We record our ideas in written form and enjoy reading what other people have written, but are reading and writing instinctive?

Responding to unseen data involving children's speech and literacy development is a compulsory topic area. A sound knowledge of these areas will assist you in making informed choices about the right question to choose in the examination. Opportunities to practise examination questions and to get advice about what you can do to maximise your mark potential are given at the end of this section, and you might be inspired to investigate children's development further for your A2 coursework (covered in Unit 4).

Developing speech

In this topic you will:

- learn the stages of young children's language development

- consider the ways children interact with others and develop communication skills

- link linguistic methods and concepts to examples of children's speech

- evaluate the theories regarding children's language acquisition and practise applying these.

Key terms

Phoneme: the smallest contrastive unit in the sound system of a language.

Phonetics: the study of the sounds used in speech, including how they are produced.

Lexis: the vocabulary of a language.

Semantics: the study of meaning.

Syntax: the way words are arranged to make sentences.

Morphology: the area of language study that deals with the formation of words from smaller units called morphemes.

Phonology: the study of the sound systems of language and how they communicate meaning.

Discourse: a stretch of communication.

Pragmatics: the factors that influence the choices that speakers make in their use of language – why we choose to say one thing rather than another.

Starter activity

In preparation for studying early language development, it might be interesting to start with your own experiences.

- Share your earliest language and literacy memories with the rest of your group or class.

- Find out what your first word was, whether you always pronounced words as an adult would or whether you used your own made-up words.

- What were your favourite toys and why? What about your favourite books and nursery rhymes?

- What TV programmes did you enjoy watching and why?

You could make a poster collage of images and text to illustrate your early language development or you could give a PowerPoint presentation.

When you discuss this with others, or look at their presentations or posters, can you see any familiar patterns of early language behaviour? Consider what these might suggest about how we learn to talk and what kind of influences are important.

Child language skills

Children learn an enormous amount of language very quickly. While learning to say so much, they are also learning many motor skills, such as walking. Therefore, it's important not to criticise them for not talking like adults.

Look at what they have to learn.

- To create individual **phonemes** and phonemic combinations (**phonetics**).
- To use a vocabulary of words and understand their meanings (**lexis/ semantics**).
- To combine words in a variety of sentence constructions, changing word formations to express different word classes (**syntax/morphology**).
- To use prosodic features such as pitch, loudness, speed and intonation to convey meaning (**phonology**).
- To structure interactions with others (**discourse**).
- The subtleties of speech such as politeness, implication and irony (**pragmatics**).

This demonstrates why language acquisition study is so important. Children's acquisition of language combines all the linguistic methods used throughout the course – it is the start of the synopticity that your A2 study is all about.

What are the main stages of language development?

As a starting point, an outline of the main stages of development will help you to understand how children acquire language and the ways that sounds (phonology) lead to words (lexis) and then to forming sentences

Fig. 1 *Not all children develop speech at the same rate, but most end up as successful adult language users*

(syntax). You can begin to grasp the complex processes involved in language development.

Later on you will evaluate the different theoretical debates; you might agree with some of the arguments more than others. However, to understand what aspects of speech are acquired by the age of 5 it is important to interpret transcripts of young children's speech. Nobody disputes that the ability to acquire language is universal (i.e. possible by all children in all speech cultures), but there is disagreement about the significance and role of certain factors that influence speech development.

Be aware that the stages outlined offer only approximate timescales. Most parents worry about the milestones their children reach, making comparisons between children in all aspects of their development. Obviously a lack of speech development can indicate particular learning difficulties, but most parental worry is unfounded, as children pass all the developmental thresholds and become successful adult language users.

Tables 1 and 2 chart the key linguistic stages of development.

Table 1 *The pre-verbal stage*

Stage	Features	Approx. age (months)
Vegetative	Sounds of discomfort or reflexive actions	0–4
Cooing	Comfort sounds and vocal play using open-mouthed vowel sounds	4–7
Babbling	Repeated patterns of consonant and vowel sounds	6–12
Proto-words	Word-like vocalisations, not matching actual words but used consistently for the same meaning (sometimes called 'scribble talk'). For example, using 'mmm' to mean 'give me that', with accompanying gestures such as pointing, supporting the verbal message	9–12

Table 2 *Lexical and grammatical stages of development*

Stage	Features	Approx. age (months)
Holophrastic/ one-word	One-word utterances	12–18
Two-word	Two-word combinations	18–24
Telegraphic	Three and more words combined	24–36
Post-telegraphic	More grammatically complex combinations	36+

During the post-telegraphic stage the acquisition of the key literacy skills of reading and writing starts to develop. This is covered separately in the Developing reading and Developing writing topics later on in this section.

Classroom activity 1

Think how children's communication skills develop. Using Tables 1 and 2, create a table like the one below to suggest at what stage lexis, grammar, phonetics/phonology, pragmatic and discourse skills might develop. For example:

1 Why might phonology be one of the first skills acquired? What are children practising in the pre-verbal stage?

2 When will syntactical awareness develop and how do you think word order might be important?

Stage	Lexis/ semantics	Phonology	Grammar	Pragmatics/ discourse
Pre-verbal				
Holophrastic/ one-word				
Two-word				
Telegraphic				
Post-telegraphic				

You can see that language is acquired very quickly in a child's life; this is a factor that influences some schools of thought about the ways that children learn to communicate.

Research point

Noam Chomsky, an American linguist, believes that learning takes place though an innate brain mechanism, pre-programmed with the ability to acquire grammatical structures. He calls this the **Language Acquisition Device (LAD)**. To him, it is also significant that human languages, although they might seem different, share many similarities, which he describes as **universal grammar**.

casa/maison/house/haus/huis

mano/main/hand

torta/pie/tarte/tarta/pastel

sacchetto/bag/sac/bolsa/sacola

château/schloss/castelo/castello/castillo/castle

Fig. 2 *Children all round the world are thought to develop language skills in similar stages and at a similar rate*

Supporting this is evidence that children from all around the world develop at a similar rate in similar stages of development. That all children can acquire complex grammars by an early age, regardless of their environment or intelligence, points to an innate learning device – although the actual nature of this has never been pinpointed.

Further reading

As you go through this unit read Marilyn Shatz's book based on her study of her grandson, Ricky, from 15 months old. It is called *A Toddler's Life: Becoming a Person* and focuses on how Ricky's mental, social and language development all combine to help him mature. It's available as an e-book, so you can dip into it as you study typical features of young children's language development. It helpfully summarises and applies to a real child some of the key theories you are going to learn about, just as you will do in the exam.

See http://books.google.co.uk/books/about/A_Toddler_s_Life_Becoming_a_Person.html?id=gmFC_mj1r7cC&redir_esc=y.

Key terms

Language Acquisition Device (LAD): the human brain's inbuilt capacity to acquire language.

Universal grammar: the explanation that all world languages share the principles of grammar despite surface differences in lexis and phonology. Sometimes called linguistic universals.

💡 Developing phonology

Producing sound is crucial for any child's language development. From an early age using their vocal cords gets the attention needed for their basic survival and emotional needs. The 'cooing' and 'babbling' stages mark the beginnings of prosodic features. Pitch and tone encode meaning for a listener/receiver of a verbal message; this links to pragmatic development, as prosody is important for social interaction. Crucially, early developments allow the child to increase the variety of sounds produced (**phonemic expansion**) and then reduce the sounds to only those they need for their own language (**phonemic contraction**), showing that children have, at this stage, the potential to learn any language.

Key terms

Phonemic expansion: the variety of sounds produced increases.

Phonemic contraction: the variety of sounds is reduced to the sounds of the main language used.

Table 3 *Stages of phonological development*

Stage	Features	Examples	Approx. age (months)
Vegetative	Sounds of discomfort or reflexive actions	Crying, coughing, burping, sucking	0–4
Cooing	Comfort sounds Vocal play	Grunts and sighs become vowel-like 'coos' Laughter starts Hard consonants and vowels produced Pitch (squeals and growls) and loudness (yells) practised	4–7
Babbling	Extended sounds resembling syllable-like sequences Repeated patterns	Sounds linking to own language Reduplicated sounds ('ba-ba') and non-reduplicated (variegated) such as 'agu'	6–12
Proto-words	Word-like vocalisations		9–12

Fig. 3 *Early responses to football scores*

Research point

Linguists have been interested in whether young children can understand the effects of intonation. Intonation is important because it gives a listener clues to the meanings of a speaker's message. We often use pitch to signal our feelings (rising pitch might show excitement) or to give the listener notice that we are giving up our turn to speak (a rising intonation indicates a question).

Alan Cruttenden (1974) compared adults and children to see if they could predict football results from listening to the scores, finding that adults could successfully predict winners by the intonation placed on the first team, but children (up to age 7) were less accurate.

How are sounds produced?

Sounds are produced by air from the lungs passing across the vocal cords. The production of **consonant** sounds is affected by:

■ the manner of articulation (how the airstream is controlled)

■ the place of articulation (where it occurs); to make sounds we can use our lips, tongue, teeth and the roof of our mouth, or combine these

■ if the sound is voiced or unvoiced (by vibrating or not vibrating the vocal cords).

Sounding phonemes out loud helps you hear how and where they are produced. The IPA chart shows the types of sounds produced, consonants and **vowels**. However, vowels can be combined into **diphthongs** in

Consonants	Vowels
p as in pet, cap and sport	ɑ: as in bar and father
b as in box and crab	i: as in feet and speak
t as in tap, story and cot	ɪ as in quick
d as in dog and cod	ɛ as in friend and said
tʃ as in champion, feature and catch	ɜ: as in heard and third
dʒ as in germ, jet and dodge	æ as in spat
k as in caravan, kick, sky, queasy	ʌ as in drunk and tough
g as in garden, dagger and log	ɒ as in spot and wasp
f as in fit, cough, phat and beef	ɔ: as in taught, port and saw
v as in vein and give	ʊ as in full
θ as in thimble and fourth	u: as in moon, true, through and grew
ð as in this and smooth	ə as in water and above
s as in sauce, hiss and cinema	eɪ as in pray, sleigh, grey and fade
z as in zero, hose and rows	aɪ as in fry, high and spider
ʃ as in shop, lotion, mash and sugar	ɔɪ as in joy and toilet
ʒ as in leisure and beige	əʊ as in go, blow and toe
h as in hair	aʊ as in cow and Slough
m as in mould, numb and jam	ɪə as in hear, pier and we're
n as in night and loan	ɛə as in care, flair and where
ŋ as in minger and cling	ʊə as in tour
l as in laugh and below	ju: as in beautiful and student
ł as in milk and tell (Cockney)	
r as in ready and corrupt	
w as in wall	
j as in yawn	
ʔ as in butter and bottle (Cockney)	
ʍ as in which (Scottish)	
x as in loch (Scottish)	

www.teachit.co.uk

Fig. 4 The International Phonetic Alphabet *(IPA) symbols for Standard English*

■ **Key terms**

Consonant: a speech sound that is produced when the vocal tract is either blocked or so restricted that there is audible friction.

Vowel: a sound made without closure or audible friction.

Diphthong: a sound formed by combining two vowels in a single syllable, where the sound begins as one vowel and moves towards another.

International Phonetic Alphabet: also known as IPA, this is a detailed system containing over 160 symbols to represent the sounds of spoken language.

Study tip

Becoming familiar with the IPA chart and its phonetic symbols may help you analyse children's phonological development in more depth. However, the IPA will be printed on the exam paper if phonetic transcriptions are present.

English. See the diphthongs used in English at the bottom of the IPA chart in Figure 4, starting with eɪ. The manner in which sounds are produced is also relevant to children's phonological development.

Classroom activity 2

Practise using the IPA and you will see that you can't easily link letters to sounds. This is not surprising as you can see from the chart that there are more sounds than there are letters in the alphabet.

1 Try writing your name using the phonetic alphabet.

2 Record a classmate speaking and then transcribe this phonetically.

3 Check your transcription with those of the rest of the group to see if they match.

If you find the print version of the IPA hard to use, or want to check whether you are transcribing the words accurately, use an online IPA chart where you can hear the sounds being produced. For example, use the British Council's phonemic chart at www.teachingenglish.org.uk/activities/phonemic-chart.

Table 4 *The different types of sounds produced*

Types of sound	Voiced	Unvoiced
Plosives are created when the airflow is blocked for a brief time (also called 'stop consonants')	b, d, g	p, t, k
Fricatives are created when the airflow is only partially blocked and air moves through the mouth in a steady stream	v, ð (as in thy), z, ʒ (as in leisure)	f, θ (as in thigh), s, ʃ (as in ship), h
Affricates are created by putting plosives and fricatives together	dʒ (as in judge)	tʃ (as in church)
Approximants are similar sounds to vowels	w, r, j	
Nasals are produced by air moving through the nose	m, n, ŋ	
Laterals are created by placing the tongue on the ridge of the teeth and then air moving down the side of the mouth	l	

Table 5 *Phonological acquisition sequence*

Age (months)	Phoneme
24	p, b, m, d, n, w, t
30	k, g, h, ŋ
36	f, s, j, l
42	tʃ, dʒ, v, z, ʃ, r
48+	θ, ð, ʒ

Pamela Grunwell's *sequence from* Phonological Assessment of Child Speech, *1987*

Classroom activity 3

Table 5 shows the sounds acquired by age.

Use this sequence and the information you have on the types of sounds produced to answer these questions.

1 In what order do the sounds appear?

2 What reasons can you find for this order?

Types of early phonological 'mistake'

One feature of child language acquisition is that children master language by making mistakes until they fully acquire the skills. This 'trial and error' approach is taken by some linguists as evidence that learning is taking place, but as you have seen, phonological development seems also to depend on physical ability to produce sounds.

In phonology the following patterns have been observed.

Table 6 *Early phonological errors*

Term	Explanation	Examples
Deletion	Omitting the final consonant in words	do(g), cu(p)
Substitution	Substituting one sound for another (especially the 'harder' sounds that develop later, such as ʃ)	'pip' for 'ship'
Addition	Adding an extra vowel sound to the ends of words, creating a CVCV pattern	e.g. doggie
Assimilation	Changing one consonant or vowel for another (as in the early plosive sounds 'd' and 'b')	'gog' for 'dog'
Reduplication	Repeating a whole syllable	dada, mama
Consonant cluster reductions	Consonant clusters can be difficult to articulate, so children reduce them to smaller units	'pider' for 'spider'
Deletion of unstressed syllables	Omitting the opening syllable in **polysyllabic** words	'nana' for 'banana'

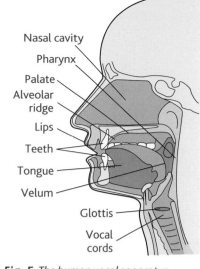

Fig. 5 *The human vocal apparatus*

Nasal cavity
Pharynx
Palate
Alveolar ridge
Lips
Teeth
Tongue
Velum
Glottis
Vocal cords

■ **Key terms**

Polysyllabic: words that contain three or more syllables.

■ **Extension activity 1**

Find nursery rhymes or books for young children.

1 Survey the types of phonological devices they use, especially alliteration and onomatopoeia.

2 Label the features using the technical terms you have just learned for the types of sounds being used.

3 How do they help young children learn about speech and writing?

■ **Research point**

Researchers have looked at children's phonological errors to see how they link to their understanding of words and ideas, as well as their ability to imitate the language surrounding them. In a famous study Jean Berko Gleason and Roger Brown (1960s) found that a child who referred to a plastic inflatable fish as a 'fis', substituting the s sound for the sh, couldn't link an adult's use of 'fis' with the same object.

Child: A fis **Adult:** Is this your fis? **Child:** no

Child: A fis **Adult:** is this your fish? **Child:** yes, my fis

Thinking points

1 Why do you think that the child only responded to the adult's correct pronunciation of the noun 'fish'?

2 What does this suggest about a child's ability to imitate adult speech?

Classroom activity 4

This task will test whether you can apply your knowledge of phonological development to data and explain how this links to theory (AO2).

Use some past data sets for AQA exam questions, particularly those featuring younger children.

Survey the data for any phonological errors made by the children speaking. Also look at the adults' responses to these errors and take a note of the child's age.

1 Label the phonological error that the child makes. For example, is it deletion?

2 Is there a pattern for each child? For example, is it mainly deletion of the same sound?

3 Explain the type of sound being pronounced wrongly or not used by labelling it with the correct term for the type of consonant. For example, is it a fricative being deleted?

4 Link the sounds pronounced wrongly or not used to Grunwell's sequence. Can you make a link between her sequence and the data?

5 Does the adult correct the child either by telling them the correct pronunciation or by subtly just repeating the word correctly? If they do, does the child say the word correctly next time?

6 Apply the 'fis' example to your data. Can it be used to support or challenge the findings in your data?

7 Write this up into a paragraph of analysis. Swap this with another student. Give feedback by checking each other's use of terminology and whether the theories have been applied relevantly.

To evaluate how others handled the same examples, return to the AQA website for student responses (as they are usually the strongest answers to the questions). Find the sections where they have analysed phonology.

Developing lexis

Once children can produce sounds effectively they can use these skills to form 'real' words that others can recognise. By the first-word stage (usually around 12 months) they have already contracted their sounds to those of their main language. Initially, **proto-words** have meaning for the child and their carers, but are less effective with others. So a child needs to acquire the vocabulary that will help them be understood by a wider audience. Together with vocabulary building, a child needs to learn the meanings (semantics) of words in order to link objects and ideas.

Key terms

Proto-word: an invented word that has a consistent meaning.

Holophrase: a single word expressing a whole idea.

Table 7 *Rate of lexical development*

Age	Number of words
12 months	50
24 months	200
36 months	2,000

Holophrases and one-word utterances are likely to develop either alongside or after proto-words. The differences between one-word utterances (usually a label for objects) and holophrases (where a word contains an entire sentence meaning) will be covered in more detail when investigating grammatical development.

The first 50 words

Here is a data set of one child's first 50 words.

Data set: Rachel's first words

Jasper	no	my	cuddle
socks	yes	toast	biscuits
Daddy	yeah	Marmite	cat
shoes	ta	jam	wassat
juice	poo	ball	bubbles
bye-bye	book	hot	Laa-Laa
more	duck	cup	jump
hello	quack quack	spoon	nice
hiya	woof	bowl	two
Nana	please	Mummy	eyes
Grandad	bot-bot	bang	weeble

Jane Hale, AQA June 2007

💡 Categorising first words

Katherine Nelson (1973) identified four categories for first words:

- ■ naming (things or people)
- ■ actions/events
- ■ describing/modifying things
- ■ personal/social words.

She found that 60 per cent of first words were nouns (the naming group). Verbs formed the second largest group, and were used with actions or location words like 'up' and 'down'. Modifiers came third. Personal/social words made up about 8 per cent of the sample. Recategorising your earlier list of Rachel's words according to Nelson's groups would probably produce the following.

Naming		Action	Social	Modifying
Jasper	woof	more	bye-bye	more
socks	bot-bot	poo	hello	my
Daddy	Marmite	book	hiya	hot
Shoes	jam	quack-quack	no	nice
juice	ball	woof	yes	two
Nana	cup	bang	yeah	
Grandad	spoon	cuddle	ta	
poo	bowl	jump	please	
book	Mummy		wassat?	
duck	cuddle			
quack-quack	cat			
biscuits	Laa-Laa			
bubbles	weeble			
eyes				

■ Looking ahead

Being able to look at data in different ways will develop your critical-thinking ability as well as your analytical skills. Deciding how you can analyse data first rather than following set approaches given by others will make you more independent. Independence is something you will need at university and it is also valued by employers. Applying a methodology to data analysis, then checking your findings or the validity of your methods by referring to other studies, will make you more critical and self-reflective.

■ Classroom activity 5

Before you look at the categories identified by researchers, try to group the words in different ways. For example, group the references to people or animals, or group by word classes such as proper nouns. What conclusions can you draw from the types of words used by Rachel?

■ Further reading

Deb Roy has been studying how children learn language and has used his own child in order to do this. His interest lies in using technology to record and research patterns in young children acquiring their first words. Watch him talking about his research and see how this supports or challenges Nelson's findings from the 1970s: http://ed.ted.com/lessons/deb-roy-the-birth-of-a-word.

You can also read a summary of his research at http://news.bbc.co.uk/1/hi/sci/tech/8127804.stm.

■ Key terms

Vocative: a form (especially a noun) used to address a person.

Content word: a type of word that has an independent 'dictionary' meaning, also called a lexical word.

Function word: a word whose role is largely or wholly to express a grammatical relationship.

Social interactionists: those who believe that child language develops through interaction with carers.

Positive reinforcement: when a behaviour is rewarded, including verbal praise to encourage this behaviour to be repeated.

Negative reinforcement: when an undesirable behaviour is unrewarded with the intention that it will not be repeated.

Behaviourists: those who believe that language is acquired through imitation and reinforcement.

Overextension: a feature of a child's language where the word used to label something is 'stretched' to include things that aren't normally part of that word's meaning.

Underextension: a feature of a child's language where the word used to label is 'reduced' to include only part of its normal meaning.

■ Link

There is more information about positive and negative reinforcement on page 44.

Fig. 6 *Some experts believe that language is acquired through social interaction*

This data shows that first words are often proper or concrete nouns. Children can link a word and the referent (the object it describes) quite easily as they can usually see it, or see a visual representation in a book. The social and interactive nature of many of these words also indicate the importance of interacting with others, suggesting that pragmatic awareness (see page 24) is vital to early language development. The reduplicative ('quack-quack') and diminutive **vocative** ('Mummy') show the bridge between phonological and lexical development.

Early vocabulary contains **content words** (from word classes such as nouns, verbs and adjectives). **Function words** (determiners, prepositions and auxiliary verbs) have a grammatical rather than a semantic function, and are acquired later.

■ Research point

You have already considered some theories about language acquisition. Chomsky's focused on grammatical development and doesn't explain children's acquisition of words and their associated meanings. Some psychologists and linguists believe that language is acquired through **social interaction**, and this would seem true with lexical and semantic development. This view started from B.F. Skinner's views that children imitate and copy adults and, as they get either positive or negative reinforcement for their verbal behaviour, they are conditioned into using the right language. Attention and praise are often given as **positive reinforcement** for the right naming word or for politeness, with **negative reinforcement** resulting from their frustration at not being understood or being denied positive comments. However, recent researchers have looked at the role and importance of interaction to help children acquire language, rather than simply taking a **behaviourist** standpoint.

Thinking points

1. What do Rachel's first words show about her early social experiences?

2. How might her first words encourage the view that other people help children to acquire language?

Developing meanings

It is common for children to **overextend** a word's meaning. Children link objects with similar qualities and may, for example, apply the word 'dog' to all four-legged household pets. Less frequently children **underextend** a word by giving it a narrower definition than it really has, for example a child might use 'duck' for fluffy cartoon ducks, and not for the brown ones in the local pond.

Eve Clark's study of first words found that children base overextensions on:

- the physical qualities of objects
- features such as taste, sound, movement, shape, size and texture.

Children's first words connect to their experiences of the world, dominated by the senses. Think how babies and toddlers delight in touching objects and putting them in their mouths.

In other research, Leslie Rescorla divided overextensions into three types, as set out in Table 8.

Table 8 *Types of overextension*

Type	Definition	Example	% of overextension
Categorical overextension	The name for one member of a category is extended to all members of the category	Apple used for all round fruits	60%
Analogical overextension	A word for one object is extended to one in a different category; usually on the basis that it has some physical or functional connection	Ball used for a round fruit	15%
Mismatch statements	One-word sentences that appear quite abstract; child makes a statement about one object in relation to another	Saying 'duck' when looking at an empty pond	25%

Another linguist, Jean Aitchison, connects children's lexical and semantic development. Her developmental stages are shown in Table 9.

Table 9 *Aitchison's stages of children's linguistic development*

Number	Stage	Description
1	Labelling	Linking words to the objects to which they refer, understanding that things can be labelled
2	Packaging	Exploring the labels and to what they can apply Over/underextension occurs in order to eventually understand the range of a word's meaning
3	Network-building	Making connections between words, understanding similarities and opposites in meanings

Once children expand their vocabulary they use network-building to sort the words. An aspect of this stage is an understanding of **hyponymy**, the links between lexical items that divides into **hypernyms** and **hyponyms**. If you take 'clothes' as the hypernym, you could list all the hyponyms a child could use for specific items of clothing they wear: socks, shoes, coat, vest, pants, T-shirt, jumper, jeans, trousers, top, gloves, hat, wellies, etc. When they have a larger vocabulary (18 months onwards), they may use these more accurately and precisely to identify individual items of clothing. Synonymy appears too, offering different ways to name the same object. Rachel (page 10) used the noun 'duck' and the onomatopoeic 'quack-quack' to refer to the same animal.

This example of overextension demonstrates the child's exploration of labels. The child uses the word 'moon' for 'stars' as a categorical overextension – both being bright objects in the night sky. The adult provides a new word ('stars') and the packaging process begins. In a few months this child may know a host of words associated with outer space.

Transcription conventions are given on page v.

Context: adult and child are looking at a night scene in a picture book.

Child:	moon
Adult:	moon yes
Child	moon (.) moon (.) more (.) more
Adult:	more
Child:	more moon
Adult:	[*suddenly realising that he is pointing at stars in picture*] oh these are stars (.) these are little stars (.) stars in the sky

5

Clare Painter, Into the Mother Tongue: A Case Study in Early Language Development, *1984*

> ■ **Key terms**
>
> **Hyponymy:** the hierarchical structure that exists between lexical items.
>
> **Hypernym:** a superordinate, i.e. a word that is more generic or general and can have more specific words under it.
>
> **Hyponym:** a more specific word within a category or under a hypernym.

As in this interaction, it has been found that parents are more likely to use the specific words for objects (hyponyms) than the general word (hypernym); this encourages children to network-build and increases their vocabulary as they acquire new words for particular objects.

Classroom activity 6

Explore the lexical and semantic development of children and select the words they use that might:

■ show overextension or underextension

■ provide evidence of labelling, packaging or network building.

Write up your analysis, building in contextual factors that might influence a child's lexical and semantic development.

Collect the data from previous AQA exam questions and data or from resource-sharing sites such as Teachit (www.teachit.co.uk) and CHILDES (Child Language Data Exchange System – http://childes.psy.cmu.edu/). Revise the key terms used earlier in this topic to describe different types of lexical and semantic development, and make a list of these. Then, match the data examples to these terms.

Find relevant theories and concepts in this book to discuss and evaluate the features. Discussing the features involves explaining your findings, whereas evaluating them means weighing them up. For example, evaluating means exploring how your examples support or challenge the theories.

Use the data you have collected to identify relevant contextual factors, or there might be factors you can infer from the child's language use. You might find evidence that the child is learning words based on their cultural experiences (such as TV or book characters), or repeated activities (such as shopping or bath time, etc.), or from their immediate environment (house, toys), or from adults (local dialect words, for example).

Ask another student to give feedback on your work and to assess its strengths and weaknesses. From this feedback, suggest what you need to include next time and set this as your personal target.

Link

Definitions of the assessment objectives are shown on page 1 as well as in the Examination preparation and practice section.

Research point

Jean Piaget was a 20th-century Swiss psychologist whose views about children's cognitive development have been very influential.

He emphasised that children are active learners who use their environment and social interactions to shape their language. Rachel's use of 'wassat' (page 10) shows that she wanted more labels to describe the objects around her and used this word to be an active learner.

Piaget linked linguistic development with an understanding of the concepts surrounding the word's meanings, suggesting that children cannot be taught before they are ready. His four developmental stages are shown in Table 10.

Table 10 *Piaget's stages of children's linguistic development*

Stage	Age (years)	Key elements
Sensorimotor	Up to 2	The child experiences the physical world through the senses and begins classifying the things in it; lexical choices, when they appear, tend to be concrete rather than abstract Object permanence develops – the concept that objects exist when out of sight
Pre-operational	2–7	Language and motor skills develop and become more competent Language is egocentric – either focused on the child or used by the child when no one else is around
Concrete operational	7–11	Children begin thinking logically about concrete events
Formal operational	11+	Abstract reasoning skills develop

Eve Clark's more recent research found that common adjectives ('nice', 'big') are among children's first 50 words, but spatial adjectives ('wide'/'narrow', 'thick'/'thin') are acquired later. Try explaining what 'wide' means, and you will see why a child might have difficulty with its meaning!

Wide

Narrow

Thick

Thin

Fig. 7 *Why might a child have difficulty in learning to use spatial adjectives?*

Thinking points

1 Using Piaget's ideas, what reasons can you give for the adjectives that children use first?

2 Why do you think children find spatial adjectives more difficult to understand and use?

Developing grammar

Acquiring greater lexical and semantic understanding requires grammatical skills to combine words into complete and increasingly complex utterances. A 24-month-old with a 200-word average vocabulary, in the two-word stage, is limited in the ways those words can be joined. Compare this with a 36-month-old, with a 2,000-word vocabulary, and you can see the connection between grammatical progression and the number of words at a child's disposal.

Study tip

One of the biggest leaps from AS to A2 is the shift in focus from context (AO3) to language methods (AO1). What this means in practice is that you need to be much more accurate in your application of linguistic terms and use a wider variety with more precision and accuracy. So, you need to become good at identifying grammatical features. Brush up or improve your skills by trying out these websites:

■ The Internet Grammar of English: www.ucl.ac.uk/internet-grammar/exlist/list.htm.

■ English Grammar Online: www.ego4u.com/en/cram-up/grammar.

■ BBC Skillswise: www.bbc.co.uk/skillswise/english.

Fig. 8 *First word 'duck'*

The two areas of grammar are syntax and morphology.

■ Syntactical advances allow children to:

1) order words into phrases and clauses

2) make different types of utterances (simple, compound, complex) for different functions apart from declarative (interrogative and imperative require different word order).

■ Morphological advances allow children to:

1) add inflections to words creating tense, marking distinctions between adjectives, showing possession and making plurals (**inflectional morphology**)

2) experiment with language by adding prefixes and suffixes to make up words and to convert words from one word class to another (**derivational morphology**).

When linguists calculate the **mean length utterance (MLU)** for children, they look at the individual morphemes that children use rather than adding up the number of words. Why do you think this is a more effective way to analyse children's grammatical development?

💡 **Table 11** *Stages of children's grammatical development*

Stage	Descriptors	Grammatical constructions	Age (months)
One-word/ holophrastic	One-word utterance		12–18
Two-word	Two words combined to create simple syntactical structures	Subject + Verb Verb + Object	18–24
Telegraphic	Three or more words joined in increasingly complex and accurate orders	Subject + Verb + Object Subject + Verb + Complement Subject +Verb + Adverbial	24–36
Post-telegraphic	Increasing awareness of grammatical rules and irregularities	Instead of saying 'runned' using 'ran'	36+

From a theoretical perspective, it is useful to look at Chomsky here. His view of acquisition is built on the universal features of all language (for example nouns and verbs) along with phonological aspects (vowels and consonants). These are termed 'linguistic universals'. Children, to Chomsky, are equipped to discover the grammar of their language because they have an innate grammar. This, to him, means that acquiring language must be about more than just imitating adult speakers.

One-word/holophrastic stage

The one-word stage provides the building blocks for syntax to develop. You saw that first words are mainly nouns used to label and name objects. The term 'holophrastic' means 'whole phrase' and is used to describe words that don't simply fulfil the naming purpose, but behave more like a short utterance. To show the variation between young children's first words, here are two siblings' first words.

The child in Figure 8 said 'duck' first because it was linked to a favourite picture book. For a few months the mother and child had been reading over and over again an interactive book where a yellow duck could be found hiding on each page. Before finally saying the word the little girl has been pointing to the hidden duck when asked to by her mother, eventually using the noun 'duck' to describe it. So this child's first word named an object.

Figure 9 shows the child whose first word was 'stuck'. What did 'stuck' mean to him? It could have been a statement, as he used it when sitting in his highchair. However, it was often accompanied by actions as he struggled to climb out of the highchair. It probably meant 'I want to get out!' Rising intonation on the word 'stuck' could indicate that it was a request to be lifted out, or stress on the word could show his frustration at being trapped. At first he used this word only when in his highchair, but later used it when shut in anywhere he did not want to be, so it could be described as a holophrase.

Fig. 9 *First word 'stuck'*

Having only one word makes meaning a matter of interpretation, relying on others successfully decoding your meaning. At this stage the carer's role is important as they try to make sense of early words through trial and error ('Are you hungry?', 'Did you want this teddy?'). Context, too, is central to understanding children's needs; the meaning of proto-words or holophrases can be deduced from the fact that the child uses them in a particular place or when holding a certain toy. Children also use other linguistic clues, such as prosodic features ('juice?'), to make their intentions clearer, showing the importance of having acquired and practised phonological skills early on.

Do you know what your first word was? If so, did it name an object or was it a holophrase? Why did you use this word?

Two-word stage

This stage marks the beginning of syntactical development. Once two words are joined the child can explore different combinations and learn correct English word order. Roger Brown's 1970s study of two-word sentences found that children from all cultures and countries make the same relationships between grammatical concepts.

Table 12 *Types of meaning relations in two-word utterances*

Meaning relation	Explanation	Example	Context
agent + action	Did someone (the do-er) perform an action?	Daddy kick	Dad kicks ball
agent + affected	Does someone do something to an object (done-to)?	Me ball	Child kicks ball
entity + attribute	Is a person or object described?	Kitty big	Sees tigers in zoo
action + affected	Does an action affect an object?	Throw stick	Child throws stick
action + location	Does an action occur in a place?	Sit chair	Child sits on chair
entity + location	Is an object located?	Spoon table	Spoon is on the table
possessor + possession	Does an object have a possessor?	Daddy coat	Points to dad's coat
nomination	Is a person or object labelled?	That cake	That is a cake
recurrence	Is an event repeated?	More ball	Finds second ball
negation	Is something denied?	No ball	Has lost her ball

Classroom activity 7

Use these examples to practise applying Brown's findings. Copy and complete the table below, matching each two-word utterance with the correct meaning relation. Contextual information to help you match the example to the meaning relation is given in brackets.

Example	Meaning relation
More cat (the second family cat arrives in the room)	
Daddy sit (father sits down at the kitchen table)	
No dolly (not finding a favourite toy)	
Brush hair (child brushes hair)	
Mummy key (child points to mother's car keys)	
Ball big (picking up a ball)	
There Jack (on seeing baby brother)	
Biscuit floor (child sees her biscuit on the floor)	
Sit buggy (child sits in his pushchair)	
Drop juice (child throws cup to the floor)	

■ Key terms

Copula verb: a verb used to join or 'couple' a subject to a complement, e.g. Mummy is nice.

Fig. 10 *Children's questions tend to develop in the order 'what', 'where', 'why' and 'when'*

Telegraphic stage

Once a child can combine three or more words they are starting to make their meanings more explicit. This is the telegraphic stage; utterances are similar to the style and construction of a telegram (or even like a text message) in that function words are left out but content words are retained. Early in the stage, verb inflections, auxiliary verbs, the **copula verb**, prepositions, determiners are all omitted. As the child moves towards the post-telegraphic stage, these function words appear accurately in utterances. Key developments take place in the construction of questions, negatives and pronouns.

Questions

Questions are a feature in early speech but, in the one- and two-word stages, they are formed by rising intonation alone ('juice', 'have book'). Only later can children successfully create yes/no interrogatives because these involve changing word order and using auxiliary verbs ('can I have book?').

Other questions require the words 'what', 'where', 'when', 'why'. These too appear fairly early on in development and are frequently used correctly at the beginning of a sentence ('where mummy?'). They appear to be acquired in a certain order.

- ■ What – subject or object
- ■ Where – location
- ■ Why – reason
- ■ When – time

If you think about it, you can see why this order is typical. Knowing 'what' is happening ('what doing?' or 'what that?') gives a child more words. The 'where' stage ('where teddy?') pinpoints where objects can be found, with the 'why' stage showing some cognitive awareness (relevant later when you consider different theories about language development) and the desire to learn about their environment. 'When', the temporal aspect, is more abstract and any parent knows that children do not acquire a sense of the constraints of time until much later!

Negatives

The ability to use negation also needs syntactic awareness; researcher Ursula Bellugi identified three stages of negative formations in young children.

Table 13 *Stages of negative formation*

Stage	The child:	Example
1	uses 'no' or 'not' at the beginning or end of a sentence	No wear shoes
2	moves 'no'/'not' inside the sentence	I no want it
3	attaches the negative to auxiliary verbs and the copula verb 'be' securely	No, I don't want to go to nursery I am not

David Crystal, a respected contemporary linguist, adds another way of learning to say 'no' to Bellugi's stages. This is a more pragmatic than grammatical method of expressing what you don't want to do, as it does not use a negative word at all. It can be observed when adults don't want to be direct in disagreeing with their children – for example, using 'maybe' to mean 'no' – and is a skill that children will develop.

Pronouns

Pronouns can be difficult words to use accurately. This is because they express many things: for example, person (the people involved in a communication, I/you, and the subject/object positioning with an utterance, I/me); number (the singular or plural, I/we); gender (s/he); possession (mine).

Ursula Bellugi found three stages.

1 The child uses their own name (for example, 'Tom play').
2 The child recognises the I/me pronouns and that these are used in different places within a sentence (for example, 'I play toy', 'Me do that').
3 The child uses them according to whether they are in the subject or object position within a sentence (for example, 'I play with the toy', 'Give it to me').

In the following extract, two 4-year-olds are playing. Children of a similar age can be at different stages of pronoun development. As you have already looked at negation, look too at Ewan's stage of pronoun development.

Transcription conventions are given on page v.

> *Ewan:* no me shopkeeper (2.0) Hollie Hollie playing
> *Hollie:* yes (.)
> *Ewan:* don't go home yet Hollie (.)
> *Hollie:* I'd like to buy all these please (.)
> *Ewan:* right (.) me

Laura Grimes, AQA June 2007

Ewan still uses the object pronoun ('me') in the subject position but is in Stage 2 of Bellugi's model as he uses pronouns rather than nouns. Hollie is in Stage 3 as she opts for the subject pronoun ('I'd like'), although this is at the beginning of her sentence. She is clearly well into the telegraphic stage with her ability to create a long and accurate sentence using **deixis** correctly ('these'). However, Ewan is in Stage 3 of negation with his use of the auxiliary verb ('do') and the attaching of the negative ('not') in the contracted form to it. His use of the negative in his opening utterance ('no me shopkeeper') suggests he is either responding to a yes/no question or asserting the role he wants to take in the play.

Determiners

Determiners are another function word acquired later in development. Determiners are attached to nouns and are: articles ('a', 'the'); numerals ('one'); possessives ('my'); quantifiers ('some', 'many'); or demonstratives ('this'). Look at this child's struggle to use determiners accurately, despite valiant attempts.

Transcription conventions are given on page v.

Child:	want other one spoon Daddy	
Adult:	you mean you want the other spoon	
Child:	yes I want other one spoon please Daddy	
Adult:	can you say the other spoon	
Child:	other (.) one (.) spoon	5
Adult:	say other	
Child:	other	
Adult:	spoon	
Child:	spoon	
Adult:	other spoon	10
Child:	other spoon (.) now give me other one spoon	

Victoria Fromkin, Robert Rodman and Nina Hyams, Introduction to Language, *2002*

Classroom activity 8

Earlier you read some different perspectives on language acquisition.

- Skinner's view was that children acquire language through conditioning and imitation. How does the father attempt to correct the child? Does correcting children's language work?
- Piaget's ideas centre on the understanding of concepts coming before language. How does the 'spoon' extract support his views of language acquisition?
- Chomsky suggests that children learn the rules of language. What evidence is there here that the child has learned some syntactical rules?

Post-telegraphic stage

This is when the remaining function words are acquired and used appropriately. The child can:

- combine clause structures by using coordinating conjunctions ('and', 'but') and subordinating conjunctions ('because', 'although') to make complex and compound utterances
- manipulate verb forms more accurately, for instance using the passive voice ('The car was followed by the lorry')
- construct longer noun phrases ('the two big red buses').

Key terms

Deixis: lexical items that 'point' to the time, place or situation, e.g. words like 'now' and 'there'.

Here is Olivia, who is in the post-telegraphic stage. How would you identify that she has reached this? Focus on the complexity of her utterances and verb usage.

Transcription conventions are given on page v.

> *Olivia:* I never get a chance to be the leader (.) but I got to be today
>
> *Mother:* you were the leader today
>
> *Olivia:* yeah (.) oh yeah (.) I so so I been there (.) actually I need a present
>
> *Mother:* you've had a good day (1.0) you've been the leader and you were star of the week   5
>
> *Olivia:* I know but (1.0) I need someone to get me a PRESENT
>
> *Mother:* what sort of present
>
> *Olivia:* my daddy
>
> *Mother:* what (.) your daddy's going to   10
>
> *Olivia:*   I had a nosebleed |today|
>
> *Mother:* |oh no| (.) did you (2.0) when
>
> *Olivia:* when I was playing out after dinner time

Amanda Coultas, *Prudhoe High School, AQA June 2005*

Olivia uses compound sentences, using the coordinating conjunction ('but') to structure her utterances. She also uses subordinate clauses ('when I was playing out after dinner time') as an adverbial to give her mother extra information. She uses the past progressive ('I was playing') and expresses future actions ('I need someone to get me'). Pronouns ('I' and 'me') in the correct subject/object positions also indicate her competence. Her sophistication is shown with her MLU: she constructs long utterances. Obviously, some development is needed as her meanings are not entirely clear ('I so so I been there'). But even adult speech, as you know from your study at AS, is not always grammatically accurate.

Morphological development

Moving from the telegraphic to post-telegraphic stage involves understanding that not only can word order be changed but so too can words themselves. A useful starting point is to look at the two types of **morphemes**: **free** and **bound**.

Roger Brown found that morphemes are acquired in a particular order.

Table 14 *Stages of morpheme acquisition*

Present tense progressive	–ing
Prepositions	in, on
Plural	–s
Past tense irregular	run/ran
Possessive	's
Uncontractible copula	is, was
Articles	the, a
Past tense regular	–ed
Third person regular	runs
Third person irregular	has
Uncontractible auxiliary verb	they were running
Contractible copula	she's
Contractible auxiliary	she's running

*Adapted from **Jean Stilwell Peccei**, Child Language, 1999*

■ Key terms

Free morpheme: one that can stand alone as an independent word, e.g. apple.

Bound morpheme: one that cannot stand alone as an independent word, but must be attached to another morpheme/word (affixes, such as the plural '–s', are always bound, as is the comparative adjective inflection '–er').

■ Key terms

Cognitive theorists: those who believe that language acquisition is part of a wider development of understanding.

Virtuous error: syntactic errors made by young children in which the non-standard utterance reveals some understanding, though incomplete, of standard syntax.

Overgeneralisation: a learner's extension of a word meaning or grammatical rule beyond its normal use.

■ Research point

Piaget's **cognitive theory** is useful to apply to Brown's findings as the increasing complexity of the morphemes acquired suggests a link between cognitive development and language acquisition. Adding '–ing' to verbs and working out that more than one of a noun requires the plural '–s' seems more straightforward than using the correct form of 'to be', which needs more understanding of tense and number.

Piaget believed that children will only acquire more complex forms of language when their intellectual development can cope, so trying to teach children before they are ready will fail because they cannot grasp the ideas involved. He advocated 'discovery learning' (learning by doing), theorising that language doesn't shape thought but that thought shapes language.

Thinking points

1. What play activities could parents and carers use that would help 'discovery learning'?

2. What toys might help children learn about language rules?

3. What links are there between children's language development and the ages they attend playschool, nursery or infant reception class?

Fig. 11 *'Virtuous errors' are mistakes made by children as they develop grammatically – their choices are often logical even though incorrect*

'Virtuous errors' and overgeneralisations

The phrase '**virtuous error**' is usually applied to the mistakes children make as they develop grammatically. It implies that children make choices from a linguistic basis, and therefore are logical. Because English has many irregularities, these seem 'wrong'. If you listen to children around age 3 or 4 you often hear them say 'I runned' instead of 'I ran'. A good way to respond to this virtuous error is to think how clever they are to have worked out that most verbs end with the –ed inflection. Linguists call some virtuous errors **overgeneralisations**. Another common overgeneralisation is to add the plural –s inflection to nouns ('house'/'houses') but there are of some irregular plurals ('mouse'/'mice', 'foot'/'feet'). Children go through the process of applying rules and then learn the exceptions.

Overgeneralisations are often used to support Chomsky's views about acquisition, as they show that children produce language that they have never heard an adult say. Using 'goed' instead of 'went' shows that children have worked out a syntactical rule. You have seen from the data extracts that adult correction doesn't seem to work and that children repeat their errors. However, they do learn irregular verbs, suggesting that hearing correct versions or having adults correct them might be needed as well.

In the following transcript, Tom talks to his mother about stroking a chicken at a friend's house. The conversation demonstrates how children overgeneralise and why virtuous errors might happen.

Transcription conventions are given on page v.

Mother:	what did it feel like	
Tom:	it feels shy (2.0)	
Mother:	it felt shy	
Tom:	yeah	
Mother:	did you feel shy or did the chicken feel shy	5
Tom:	the chicken feeled shy (2.0)	

J.A. Darby, AQA January 2005

Tom uses the present tense ('feels') to describe a previously completed action. The mother models the correct irregular past tense verb ('felt'). Later, when the mother asks Tom his feelings, and uses the present tense verb (feel) Tom now places his ideas in the past tense but overgeneralises the –ed ending and concludes that 'the chicken feeled shy'. You can see why Tom might be confused as in this context even the word 'feel' is used ambiguously as it is both an abstract concept (a **stative verb**) and a tangible action (a **dynamic verb**).

■ **Key terms**

Stative verb: verb that describes a state; stative verbs are not usually used in the progressive aspect, which is used for incomplete actions in progress.

Dynamic verb: a type of verb that expresses activities and changes of state, allowing such forms as the progressive.

■ **Research point**

These overgeneralisations were famously proved by Jean Berko Gleason who, in the 1950s, conducted a study into children's pronunciation and morphological development. Part of this study was into the use of the –s plural. She gave children a picture of an imaginary creature called a 'wug' and asked them what more than one wug would be called. Three-quarters of the 4- and 5-year-olds surveyed formed the regular plural 'wugs'.

Thinking points

1 Why do you think she chose an imaginary creature?

2 What does this study suggest about how children acquire grammatical skills?

3 Could you devise a test for other morphemes acquired?

Fig. 12 *The 'wug' test*

Possession

The concept of possession is another aspect of inflectional morphology that children need to acquire. Here you can see Tom (aged 2 years) grapple with the idea of 'dad's bike'.

Transcription conventions are given on page v.

Tom:	OH PLEASE	
Mother:	so what are you doing Tom	
Tom:	I sitting on the bike (.) it make noises	
Mother:	it makes noises	
Tom:	yeah	5
Mother:	what sort of noises	
Tom:	the bike (.) the dad bike	
Mother:	dad's bike	
Tom:	yeah (.) the dad (.) dad's bike (.) dad's bike mum (.) dad's bike	
Mother:	you're not on dad's bike (.) you're on your bike	10
Tom:	I am on dad's bike but I not on dad's bike	

J.A. Darby, AQA January 2005

First he terms it 'the dad bike'. After his mother's correction, he seems to copy her correctly, following a false start and self-correction ('dad's bike'). When he says that he is 'on dad's bike but I not on dad's bike' he seems to be struggling with some concepts of ownership. His dad has been mending Tom's bike and so, to Tom, has some responsibility towards it. Ideas about possession still have to be worked through; this is perhaps a limitation of his understanding rather than a linguistic one, as he copies his mother's words and uses the –s inflection accurately.

💡 Developing pragmatics

Pragmatic understanding, especially with regard to conversational skills, is crucial to children's successful language development. As a reminder, pragmatics is about:

- implicature (what we mean rather than what we say)
- inference (interpreting what others mean)
- politeness (using the right words and phrases to be polite)
- conversational management and turn-taking (knowing when to speak).

A good starting point is to use Michael Halliday's 'taxonomy'. His functions of speech are shown in Table 15.

Table 15 *Halliday's functions of speech*

Function	Where language is used to:
Instrumental	fulfil a need (e.g. 'want milk')
Regulatory	influence the behaviour of others (e.g. 'pick up')
Interactional	develop and maintain social relationships (e.g. 'love you')
Personal	convey individual opinions, ideas and personal identity (e.g. 'me like Charlie and Lola')
Representational	convey facts and information (e.g. 'it hot')
Imaginative	create an imaginary world and may be seen in play predominantly (e.g. 'me shopkeeper')
Heuristic	learn about the environment (e.g. 'wassat?')

John Dore offers another way of describing language functions that focuses more on speech acts as individual utterances (Table 16), rather than Halliday's broader approach to pragmatic functions.

Table 16 *Dore's language functions*

Function	Description
Labelling	Naming a person, object or thing
Repeating	Repeating an adult word or utterance
Answering	Responding to an utterance of another speaker
Requesting action	Asking for something to be done for them
Calling	Getting attention by shouting
Greeting	Greeting someone or something
Protesting	Objecting to requests from others
Practising	Using language when no adult is present

Both provide useful models for analysing children's utterances, explaining why a child uses language. However, it is often hard to apply them accurately without information on the context of the utterance. Imagine a child at the one-word stage using the noun 'mummy'. In Dore's categories this could be labelling. But 'mummy' could also be repeating an adult utterance as a statement, or it could be used as a greeting.

Classroom activity 9

Practise applying Halliday and Dore. Copy and complete the table below, deciding which categorisation model seems to be the most helpful in identifying language functions.

Utterance	Context	Halliday's function	Dore's function
Look at me, I superman	Child playing		
Mummy	Mummy returns home from work		
Want juice	Child is thirsty		
Put down	Father is holding child		
Me like that	Child looks at toy in a shop		
Why?	Child asks why she has to get her shoes on		
Night night daddy, love you	Being put to bed		
No	Child wants to stay at the park		

For some, pragmatic development is a key aspect of language that has to be learned from others and supports those theorists who believe that social interactions lead to language advances rather than the 'innate' view. However, as you have seen from Halliday and Dore's model, the focus is on the child's use of language as a way to discover the world and so draws on Piaget's ideas. Indeed, where Dore sees children practising with language without needing adults present, Piaget coined the phrase **egocentric speech** to describe his observations of children talking when alone, seeing it as their way to classify their experiences and environment.

How important is politeness?

Politeness is encouraged by parents from an early age. Your own experiences of being instructed to say 'please' and 'thank you' suggest how important these words are for social interaction – these words also featured in Rachel's first 50. Politeness extends to the ways conversations are maintained, encompassing the face theory proposed by Penelope Brown and Stephen Levinson. They suggested two main aspects of face in communicative interactions.

Key terms

Egocentric speech: the running discourse style of speech used by children where no listener is directly addressed and the talk is focused on the child's activities.

Study tip

Synoptic assessment is built into this course and the topic of language acquisition has been carefully selected to allow you to make connections between all aspects of the specification. You are expected to further your knowledge and understanding of key concepts and theories about language at this level.

■ **Positive** – where the individual desires social approval and being included.

■ **Negative** – where an individual asserts their need to be independent and make their own decisions.

Fig. 13 *Politeness strategies in action*

The following transcript, documenting a child's first visit to a friend's house, demonstrates young children's pragmatic awareness. Note the efforts to be polite and accommodate others' needs.

Transcription conventions are given on page v.

Context: the children are playing downstairs and Anya has said she needs to go to the toilet.

Keri's mother:	Keri will show you where it is Anya (.) in case you don't know
Keri:	okay Anya (.) that a deal
Anya:	I remember where it is
Keri:	no (.) I show you
Anya:	I know where mine is (.) mine's upstairs (.) cos you're supposed to have toilets upstairs aren't you
Keri's mother:	mmm
Anya:	my nan (.) em has one toilet <u>down</u>stairs
[*they go upstairs to the bathroom*]	
Keri:	yes (.) that's it (.) it's nice my toilet (1.0) do you want a step (.) Anya
Anya:	yeah
Keri:	I get you one (.) oh (.) there one in my bedroom
[*Keri goes to get a step which will enable Anya to climb up onto the toilet*]	

5

10

15

Amanda Coultas, AQA January 2003

The mother's modelling of politeness directs Keri to show Anya the toilet with a face-saving phrase ('in case you don't know'); this makes

Anya feel good about herself by not pointing out the obvious – that she won't know where the toilet is because it's her first visit. Keri adopts the helpful host role in her declaratives ('I show you') and ('I get you one') and in the polite interrogative ('do you want a step'). The mother's minimal response ('mmm') shows her unwillingness to correct Anya's assumptions about downstairs toilets, viewing this as rudeness. This, too, provides Keri with a politeness model. Anya, however, is demonstrating some aspects of negative face by asserting her independence and her own point of view, justifying the accuracy of her assertion that houses only have toilets upstairs with her tag question ('aren't you') to prompt agreement from Keri or her mother.

How important is context?

First, what is meant by the context? As it refers to the situation of an interaction, you should ask these questions when examining data.

- ■ Who participates? (one or more speakers, gender)
- ■ What relationship exists between speakers? (family members, friends, carer and child, teacher and student)
- ■ What is the setting? (domestic, nursery, local environment, etc.)
- ■ In what developmental stage is the child? (age)
- ■ What other factors might affect the data? (cultural influences such as books, television, social experiences)

Look at the following transcript. The supporting contextual information provided is:

- ■ this is the first time that they have played together outside their shared time at nursery
- ■ they are playing at Keri's house
- ■ Keri is 38 months old and Anya is 44 months old.

How does this contextual knowledge affect your linguistic analysis of the language choices and the structure of the discourse?

Transcription conventions are given on page v.

Context: the children are sitting at the top of the stairs and Keri is showing Anya the contents of her jewel box.

> **Keri:** look at my necklace grandma oh (.) look at my necklace (.) Anya
>
> **Anya:** I have a necklace (.) a duck one and I lose my glasses (.) you know
>
> **Keri:** I lose MY glasses (.) that's only mine [pointing at necklace] 5 (.) but we can share them
>
> **Anya:** well I lose mine (.) mummy's going to get another ones (.) and then I'll share them (.) right
>
> **Keri:** yeah
>
> **Anya:** when I come again I'll wear them (.) and then I'll share them 10
>
> [Anya stands up]
>
> **Keri** you can hold my hand you want (1.0) when you jump (.) jump
>
> **Anya:** no I can't (.) I want to walk
>
> **Keri:** you want to hold my hand when we go downstairs
>
> **Anya:** no 15
>
> **Keri:** you can go in my bedroom you want

Amanda Coultas, AQA specimen paper

Fig. 14 *Children often role-play adult behaviours*

Keri appears quite assertive in her control of the role-play with her choice of imperatives ('look') and assigning Anya with the role of 'grandma'. She also refuses to accept Anya's attempt to take control of the game through the suggestion that Anya loses her glasses by stressing her ownership of the role-play object ('glasses') with the possessive pronoun ('MY'). She could be making these linguistic choices because she feels it is her right to do this in her own house and extends her possession to claiming ownership of her bedroom, magnanimously allowing Anya access to it (because this is polite).

Because this is the first time they have played together in a domestic context, they negotiate frequently about roles and activities. Indeed, playing at each other's houses for the first time is a social development and the sign of an emerging friendship; the use of the inclusive plural pronoun ('we') indicates they are sharing experiences and want to play together. Their given ages pinpoint the likely features you could expect from children in the telegraphic stage with subject pronouns ('I'), possessive pronouns ('my') and the second person pronoun ('you') used accurately. The children are competent in using auxiliary verbs ('want' and 'can'). The number of words in utterances combined with subordinate clauses ('when we go downstairs') indicates syntactic competence and places them in the post-telegraphic stage.

■ Play and language acquisition

Lev Vygotsky, an early child development researcher, observed children's play and linked it to both cognitive and social development. Young children often use props as 'pivots' to support their play but, when older, use their imagination instead. Vygotsky also observed how children role-play adult behaviours as part of exploring their environment, which has interested more recent researchers.

Catherine Garvey's study of pairs of children playing found that children adopt roles and identities, acting out storylines and inventing objects and settings as required in a role-play scenario. This is termed pretend play and fulfils Halliday's imaginative language function. Children play together because it is enjoyable, but it also practises social interactions and negotiation skills, with players' roles and responsibilities often decided as they play. Sometimes called sociodramatic play, it involves both social and dramatic skills, with explicit rules and reflecting real-world behaviour.

Sociodramatic play usually begins when children are around 4 years old, possibly linking to their cognitive understanding as they understand the different roles people have and how these affect language. In their re-enactments they use field-specific lexis and structure them in some of the formulaic ways that adults use in precisely these situations, suggesting that they can observe and imitate adult behaviours. To illustrate children's real-world imitation, look at the transcription below of two children playing shops.

Transcription conventions are given on page v.

Context: two 4-year-olds, Hollie and Ewan, playing shops at Ewan's house, while their aunt, Laura, watches.

[*Till sounds*]
Hollie: I've got loads of scans one at the top
Ewan: I'm gonna put all of them on (1.0) me got real one
Hollie: this is a real one an' all (1.0) would you like cashback
Ewan: no but Laura does

■ Further reading

Read Unit 3: Play and talk from Julia Gillen's book from the Intertext series *The Language of Children*. Not only is it a very accessible read, explaining these ideas clearly for you, it supports this section on language development and play. It also models an excellent analysis of real data in the Childphone project, showing how to interpret data by linking linguistic discussion with an evaluation of the meanings deduced from these features.

Gillen, J. *The Language of Children*, Routledge, 2003

5

Hollie: Laura can you play please

Ewan: it's two pounds then that

[*Till drawer opens*]

Hollie: and then you say would you like cash back

Ewan: do you like cash back   10

Hollie: no not yet

Laura Grimes, AQA June 2007

The lexis reflects a modern shop ('scans', 'cashback') and they are clearly undertaking the activity of putting objects through a till. Even the politeness is linked to the formulaic utterances made within customer transactions when Hollie gives Ewan the correct phrase to use ('would you like cash back') and the request for payment ('it's two pounds then').

Transcription conventions are given on page v.

Context: the children are dressed in fairy outfits and are playing in Keri's bedroom.

Anya: here's a lovely thing (.) a lovely princess thing

[*pointing at Keri dressed up in a fairy outfit*]

Anya: I can be the (.) I can be the mother (.) right

Keri: I can be a princess

Anya: lie in your bed now princess (.) it's too late (1.0) right (.)   5
straight to bed (.) mummy has to go to bed too

[*Keri gets into bed*]

Keri: your had to kiss me Anya

Anya: right (.) you want me to read a story

Keri: no (.) your had to kiss me   10

Anya: okay then

[*Anya kisses Keri on the forehead and Keri laughs*]

Anya: go to sleep now

[*Keri shuts her eyes for a few seconds then gets up*]

Anya: not morning yet baby   15

Keri: I not a baby

Anya: it's still bedtime (.) go to sleep fairy (.) fairy

Keri: I going to play in mummy's bedroom

Anya: no (.) go back to sleep now fairy (.) go to sleep (.) what mum
says (.) right (1.0) mums says (.) right (1.0) go to bed (.) let's   20
go back to bed now (.) go to sleep (2.0) hum (.) this is my bed
(.) I go to sleep (.) shh (.) shh

Amanda Coultas, AQA specimen paper

Research points

You might remember from your AS gender study that theorists such as Lakoff and Tannen asserted that men and women use language differently. Some studies have been conducted on young girls and boys to see if this difference is still true in the early stages of language acquisition. Here is a summary of a few of these that seem to suggest that pre-school boys tend to be more forceful and demanding in their conversational style, whereas girls tend to be more polite and cooperative.

- Thompson (1999) found that girls are more likely to ask an adult for help in play activities such as assembling a jigsaw puzzle.
- Sachs (1987) found that boys are more likely to use simple imperatives with their playmate in pretend play. In contrast, girls use fewer imperatives and use language that involves the other child in the planning.
- Amy Sheldon (1990) found that girls try to negotiate a settlement to any play disputes, whereas boys make threats and issue directives.
- Killen and Naigles (1995) found that children used less gender-stereotyped language in mixed-sex groups than in same-sex groups.

Thinking points

1. Why do you think young girls and boys use language differently?

2. How could you set up a short investigation to test these theories?

The role of parents

Although you will be evaluating language acquisition theories later, the role of parents cannot be overlooked. They are the main communicators with their children. The terms used to describe the non-standard form of language used by adults with young children have changed over time: baby talk (the traditional term used by non-linguists) became 'motherese', then changed to 'parentese'. The current preferred term used by linguists is **child-directed speech (CDS)** because it focuses on the child rather than the specific role of the adult.

What do you think these examples of English baby talk highlight?

| beddy-byes | jim-jams | din-din | ickle | bic-bic |
| oopsie-daisie | wee-wee | yum-yum | pussy | doggie |

Baby talk seems to rely on reduplication ('din-din', 'bic-bic'), deletion and substitution ('ickle') and addition ('doggie') with the adult speaker adopting child-like characteristics. When you learn about acquisition theories, evaluate what the linguistic theorists might think about the value of baby talk. Baby talk focuses on simple lexical features and exaggerated prosodic features, such as sing-song intonation.

Features of child-directed speech (CDS)

Parents are likely to use some (or all) of the following:

- repetition and/or repeated sentence frames
- a higher pitch
- the child's name rather than pronouns
- the present tense
- one-word utterances and/or short elliptical sentences
- fewer verbs/modifiers
- concrete nouns
- **expansions** and/or **recasts**
- yes/no questioning
- exaggerated pauses giving turn-taking cues.

Key terms

Child-directed speech (CDS): any of various speech patterns used by parents or care givers when communicating with young children, particulary infants, usually involving simplified vocabulary, melodic pitch, repetitive questioning, and a slow or deliberate tempo.

Expansion: the development of a child's utterance into a longer, more meaningful form.

Recast: the commenting on, extending and rephrasing of a child's utterance.

Child-directed speech has a far broader reach than baby talk. The benefits of CDS, some argue, are in teaching children the basic function and structure of language. Not all cultures use CDS, either not speaking to their children until they have reached a certain age (as in Samoa and Papua New Guinea), or not simplifying adult language for children.

Chomsky maintained that language structures cannot simply be acquired by repeating language from varieties such as CDS, because of its 'impoverished' and 'random' nature – using incomplete grammatical utterances. However, this now seems to be less valid, as studies of CDS features suggest that this register is more structured and regular than previously thought.

Some people have also looked at whether men use a different language register to their children. This has been dubbed 'fatherese'. Men seem to use more direct questioning styles, seek more information and use a wider vocabulary than women.

Some of the evidence about the effects of CDS appears contradictory. In her 1970s research, Alison Clarke-Stewart found that children had a larger vocabulary if their mothers talked to them a lot. However, Roger Brown found that children were rarely corrected for grammatical mistakes, though they were for their lexical errors or for the content of their speech. So child-directed speech alone cannot explain children's acquisition of language, but may affect their linguistic competence.

■ Research point

Just as Chomsky thinks language occurs from an inbuilt processing device (LAD), others, like Jerome Bruner, think that there must also be a **Language Acquisition Support System (LASS)**. He particularly looked at ritualised activities that occur daily in young children's lives – mealtimes, bedtimes, reading books – and how carers make the rules and meanings of these interactions explicit and predictable so that children can learn.

Bruner cites the game of 'Peek-A-Boo' as an example of these educational rituals. In this game, parents hide their faces and then seem to reappear. As well as the non-verbal actions, this is accompanied by such phrases as 'bye bye', 'where am I?', 'here I am' and prosodic indicators such as pitch and intonation. So, for Bruner, this teaches children important linguistic aspects such as turn-taking, formulaic utterances and syntax.

Piaget would also use this game to test **object permanence**, where children understand that an object still exists even when it is no longer in sight. Some also link object permanence with the lexical growth from 36 months, as well as the emerging ability to use personal pronouns, distinguishing between 'I', 'me' and 'you'.

Thinking points

1 What might nursery rhymes and songs encourage children to learn about language (some suggestions are 'One, two, three, four, five, once I caught a fish alive' or 'Hickory, dickory, dock')?

2 Why is it important to understand the difference between 'I', 'you' and 'me'?

■ Key terms

LASS (Language Acquisition Support System): this refers to the child's interaction with the adults around them and how this interaction supports language development.

Object permanence: the awareness that objects continue to exist even when they are no longer visible.

■ Further reading

If you are interested in how gender identity and play might link to language development, read Lise Eliot's 2010 book, *Pink Brain, Blue Brain: How Small Differences Grow Into Troublesome Gaps and What We Can Do About It*. Read chapter 3, Learning through play in the pre-school years.

Eliot, L. *Pink Brain, Blue Brain: How Small Differences Grow Into Troublesome Gaps and What We Can Do About It*, Houghton Mifflin Harcourt Publishing Company, 2010

Fig. 15 *Games like Peek-A-Boo can teach a child many things*

Study tip

Be open minded with your conclusions. Don't suggest that your data conclusively 'proves' or 'disproves' particular theoretical viewpoints. Using words like 'could' and 'might' implies links between features of child language and certain theories, and helps to avoid sweeping judgements about the soundness of Chomsky's or Skinner's theories.

Classroom activity 11

What child-directed speech techniques do the parents use in the interactions in Texts A and B? Use the list from page 30 to help you find specific features. Or, if you want to practise for the exam, revise them first and apply them from memory to examples in the data. Share your list with another student to see if you have found the same CDS strategies or add to your list. Evaluate the CDS strategies to see whether you can find evidence that these vary according to the children's ages.

Transcription conventions are given on page v.

Text A

Michael: [3 months; loud crying]

Mother: [enters room] oh my word (.) what a noise (.) what a noise [picks up baby]

Michael: [sobs]

Mother: oh dear dear dear (.) didn't anybody come to see you Let's 5
have a look at you [looks inside nappy] no (.) you're all
right there aren't you

Michael: [sputtering noises]

Mother: well what is it then Are you hungry Is that it Is it a
long time since dinner-time 10

Michael: [gurgles]

Mother: [nuzzles baby] oh yes it is a long time

Michael: [cooing noise]

Mother: yes I know (.) let's go and get some lovely grub then

David Crystal, Listen to Your Child: A Parent's Guide to Language, *1989*

Text B

Mother: how many chickens are there

Tom: (2.0) there's many chickens (.) one (.) two (.) three (.) four
(.) five (.) six (.) seven (.) eight (.) nine (2.0)

Mother: hmm (.) shall I count them now

Tom: yeah 5

Mother: one (.) two (.) three (.) four (.) five

Tom: yep

Mother: and we saw chickens this morning didn't we

Tom: we did

Mother: at Pascale's house (.) she's got some pet chickens 10

Tom: has (.) have (.) has (.) has she I (.) stroke one chicken

Mother: you did (.) didn't you You stroked it

Tom: yeah

Mother: Pascale had to hold it still and then you stroked the
feathers didn't you 15

J.A. Darby, AQA January 2005

■ Research point

Interesting views have developed about the role of parents in providing linguistic support. Vygotsky, again, was influential in this area. His phrase 'zone of proximal development' describes how adults and children work together to move children towards independence, knowledge and competence. Jerome Bruner, with other researchers, introduced the concept of '**scaffolding**' to refer to the ways adults help children advance cognitively. He observed that adults withdraw support as children's skills develop.

The 'scaffolding' metaphor relates the support offered to children's language development with that offered by scaffolding around a building. Once the building or the child can support themselves independently, scaffolding is no longer required. Likewise, the carer plays an important role in early development, and the nature of their support changes with the child's needs and understanding.

■ Key terms

Scaffolding: the process of transferring a skill from adult to child and then withdrawing support once the skill has been mastered.

Thinking points

1. How might parents encourage children to reach 'the zone of proximal development' in activities such as completing jigsaws or with other practical toys?

2. What verbal support could adults withdraw as children's speech develops? (For example, think back to typical features of CDS.)

🔍 ✐ 💡 Competing language acquisition debates

You have already read about many of the important theorists' views as you have studied children's linguistic development, and have seen how it applies to data of real children speaking and interacting with others. Knowing the theories is important as it makes up AO2, for which you will be awarded marks. But having an open mind and evaluating the diverse perspectives will help you in the examination as you interpret data that you have never seen before.

So, to summarise, the key debates are whether:

- children learn language from imitation
- language is inbuilt, with humans pre-programmed to acquire it
- children need input from others to communicate effectively
- children use cognitive skills to develop language by themselves.

Debates over language acquisition really started from a simple nature vs nurture perspective. These opposing stances were taken by two theorists, Noam Chomsky and B.F. Skinner, in the 1950s and 1960s. The nature view foregrounds the ability to use language as innate, whereas the nurture argument suggests that language acquisition is affected by others. Other linguists and psychologists challenged that either of these was capable of completely explaining language acquisition. Some, like Jean Piaget, took a cognitive approach, linking thought and language development, and others were interested in the role of other people and the social interaction needed to make children successful speakers. What has happened now is that many of these ideas have come together in order to explain the very complex process of acquisition and the factors needed to make it happen successfully.

■ Extension activity 2

Using a style model from parenting magazines like *Practical Parenting*, write an informative article for parents, advising them about effective ways to speak to their children. If you are planning a child language investigation, this will help with the media task.

Table 17 *Language acquisition theories*

Theory	Definition	Key theorist
Nativist	Humans have an inbuilt capacity to acquire language	Noam Chomsky, Eric Lenneburg
Behaviourist	Language is acquired through imitation and reinforcement	B.F. Skinner
Social interactionist	Child language is developed through interaction with adults	Jerome Bruner, Lev Vygotsky
Cognitive	Language acquisition is part of a wider development of understanding that develops	Lev Vygotsky, Jean Piaget

Noam Chomsky and nativist theory

Chomsky has changed his ideas over the years, although not from the core concept of children's innate ability to learn language (**nativism**). His focus is useful to explain grammatical development, but you can see that it does not go all the way to explaining other aspects of language.

Table 18 *Arguments for and against nativist theory*

For	Against
Children:	**Children:**
■ experience the same stages of development and at the same pace ■ resist correction ■ create forms of language that adults don't use (overgeneralisations) ■ make their own rules for language use that seem to understand that all languages have grammatical rules ■ produce correct language when surrounded by 'impoverished' faulty adult-speech, i.e. with false starts, incomplete utterances	■ stop overgeneralising and learn to use language correctly, as with irregular verbs ■ need input to give them more skills than grammar, for example pragmatic understanding ■ children who have been deprived of social contact can't achieve complete communicative competence
Relevant studies:	**Relevant studies:**
■ 'wug' test suggests children apply grammatical rules	■ studies of Genie (a girl deprived of social contact until she was 13 and then unable to learn speech beyond a very basic level) and feral children support the 'critical period' hypothesis that says that language needs to be acquired within a certain time frame. This challenges Chomsky's early argument that the ability to acquire language is simply innate within us as it shows that some interaction is needed for language completency.

Eric Lenneburg (1967) furthered the nativist argument by proposing that language has to be acquired within a critical period – really within the first five years. Case studies of feral ('wild') children, where human input has been limited, show that although some language processes can be acquired, full grammatical fluency is never achieved.

However, feral children who have grown up outside human society are not able to acquire language effectively when they return to live alongside others. Their individual stories, although sad, have allowed linguists and psychologists to test their theories about whether language is innate or if nurture is important too.

Extension activity 3

Use a recognised search engine to find case studies of feral children. Read their stories, focusing on their language development. What does the children's development, or lack of it, suggest about the importance of human interaction to acquiring language? Do their experiences support any other theoretical views?

Looking ahead

Being able to use resources critically will be very important when developing your research skills at university or in further education. Using key terms to make online searches effective is a good start to finding the most relevant sources. Then think about the reliability of these and who has produced the source. Finally, make a note of the source you have used and create a bibliography so you can show that you are able to reference secondary sources when you use them.

B.F. Skinner and behaviourist theory

Skinner's views have been largely discounted as a way of explaining language acquisition, although you might see that parents do use reinforcement when speaking to children and that children do copy language heard around them.

Table 19 *Arguments for and against behaviourist theory*

For	Against
Children: ■ imitate accent and dialect ■ learn politeness and pragmatic aspects of language ■ repeat language they have heard around them and incorporate it into theirs – lexical knowledge must be gained from being told the right labels	**Children:** ■ do more than just imitate language and can form sentences that they have never heard before ■ hear ungrammatical spoken language around them but can still learn correct language ■ do not seem to respond to correction ■ aren't negatively reinforced for language use ■ aren't always corrected by parents for incorrect grammar ■ corrections might actually slow down development ■ imitate but don't necessarily understand the meanings **Other limitations:** ■ 'fis' phenomenon suggests that children can hear and understand the correct pronunciation but simply can't produce it themselves at that stage ■ research was conducted on rats and pigeons, not on humans

Social interactionist theory

This is an appealing explanation for children's development in some key linguistic areas, foregrounding the roles of both carers and children. Clearly humans are sociable creatures and gain much from communicating with others. Increasingly, linguists have seen how important the help and 'scaffolding' given to children is, but it is still debated whether a greater adult linguistic input gives children an advantage.

Table 20 *Arguments for and against social interactionist theory*

For	Against
■ Routine/rituals seem to teach children about spoken discourse structure such as turn-taking ■ Pragmatic development suggests that children do learn politeness and verbally acceptable behaviour ■ Role-play and pretend play suggest that more interaction with carers can affect vocabulary	■ Children from cultures that do not promote interaction with children (e.g. Samoa) can still become articulate and fluent language users without adult input
Relevant studies: ■ Halliday's research into the functions of language supports the importance of social interaction ■ Vincent, a hearing child born to deaf parents, learned to communicate using sign language. As a hearing child he enjoyed watching televison, but he ignored the sounds. He did not start to speak until he went to school, where people talked to him.	

Cognitive theories

Today cognitive theories go hand in hand with social interactionist theories, as people see how adult input helps children's understanding. Much of the research into children's developmental stages provides a convincing argument to explain the maturing of their language. These theories emphasise the active role of children themselves, seeing them not as passive beings in an adult-controlled linguistic world, but as humans who want to discover their surroundings and who use language to reflect this.

Table 21 *Arguments for and against cognitive theory*

For	Against
Children: ■ can't grasp aspects of language until they are ready; stages of development support this ■ produce utterances which increase in complexity as they work towards mastering a rule	**Children:** ■ with cognitive difficulties can still manage to use language beyond their understanding ■ acquire language without having an understanding of it, especially in the early stages of development
Relevant studies: ■ Brown's morphemes ■ Bellugi's stages for pronoun and question formation	■ 'fis' phenomenon suggests children's cognitive understanding can be present but their physical development still impacts their ability to use language

On a final note, there are many arguments and researchers' case studies apart from the ones cited here, offering evidence for and against aspects of all theories, especially the earlier ones – Skinner and Chomsky. Recent linguists have focused on the whole picture and concluded that:

■ the ability to produce language is within all humans

■ cognitive skills develop and link to language development

■ all children exposed to language acquire it naturally, without deliberate teaching but social input is needed and sought by children to help them communicate effectively and explore their environment.

💡

F:	Dora are you making tea (1.0) are you (.) Dora (.) can you make daddy a cup of tea
D:	there aren't any cup of teas
F:	there aren't any cup of teas
D:	no 5
F:	can you make daddy a cup of tea
D:	yes (2.0) I get one (1.0) [*goes back to tea set and picks up a plastic teapot*] look here's a cup of tea (2.0) this is a cup of tea [*brings it to her father*]
F:	mm (.) that's not a cup of tea (.) that's (.) a teapot 10
D:	do you want a teapot (.) do you want a tea (.) cup (.) cup
F:	teapot
D:	do you want a teacup (1.0) here [*hands over teapot*]
F:	say teapot

Personal communication from Marcello Giovanelli

■ Classroom activity 12

Selecting theories, concepts and research carefully and applying these relevantly to data is important to your success in this unit. Practise these skills by using this extract of Dora (aged 2 years, 4 months) with her father pretend-playing in the family living room with a plastic tea set.

You can decide which theories might be supported or challenged by the data extract or, if you would like some suggestions, choose from the list below. All of these can be evidenced from the data.

- Social interactionist ideas such as role-play and rituals
- Behaviourism – imitation and reinforcement
- Bellugi's negation stages
- Stage of question formation
- Halliday's functions of language
- Chomsky's ideas of innateness/LAD
- Virtuous errors/overgeneralisation/'wug' test
- Telegraphic stage of development
- CDS strategies
- Gender ideas
- Cognitive theory

Create a paragraph exploring a selection of these. Ensure you link the concepts to a language feature precisely and explain how the example supports or challenges the data. Swap with another student and see if you can suggest to each other how the responses could be developed further.

Don't worry if you cannot apply all of these the first time. Sometimes it just takes practice analysing lots of data before it becomes second nature. Also, applying only some theories but developing your discussion, is better than just saying 'X' is an example of overgeneralisation and moving onto the next theory. Remember, this unit is data led not theory led.

Here is a model to help you approach this task.

- Pick an aspect of the data that you think you could link to a theory. For example, Dora's 'any cup of teas' could be explored.
- Identify the linguistic features. For example, Dora's noun phrase includes the non-standard pluralisation of 'teas' in this context.
- Select a relevant theory. For example, you could use Dora's pluralisation to support 'virtuous errors' or Chomsky's LAD.
- Write it up ensuring that you identify the features precisely, link to the concept and, if you can, a contextual explanation, such as setting, roles and relationships.
- Look at all of the data before coming to conclusions. Check if there are other examples that would support your application of LAD.
- Evaluate the concept as you write. For example, Dora's response seems to show innateness and to support Chomsky's LAD, but it is also clear that she does not yet understand what a 'cup of tea' is, perhaps introducing the concept of cognition or overgeneralisation.

Developing reading

Starter activity

Search YouTube for children learning to read English and look at the list of possible videos. List some of the key words you can see in the titles such as 'phonics' and 'sight words'. Once you have compiled your list and watched some of the videos, share with others what you think are the main ways that young children are taught to read and what methods are used to help children. For example, you might see that many of the videos use bright colours.

Fig. 16 *Early story books are designed to be read to children*

When does reading start?

Literacy differs from oracy in that reading and writing skills are explicitly taught to young children, as an established part of formal schooling (from age 4). However, for young children, as for adults, reading books is just one literacy experience as they encounter the written word in other aspects of daily routines and cultural experiences. All around are words and symbols to interpret, not always written in strings of words or in the narrative structure of story books: PUSH and PULL on the doors of buildings provide information about how to use them, as does the word STOP alongside a picture on a pedestrian crossing. Even company logos and names of shops become a way to interpret their environment. Children also absorb information from television and computer sources (including games), and these have become part of the young learner's literacy environment.

Research point

S.B. Heath, in the 1980s, studied three different American communities' use of both spoken language and writing/reading practices within the home. Comparing two working-class areas – one predominantly black, the other white – with a middle-class suburb, she found that early school literacy experiences reflected middle-class values, with activities based around shared books/reading and creative writing.

The other communities' cultural activities were more oral. Storytelling, singing and rhymes were part of daily experiences. Actions, gestures and visual images played a more active part, perhaps resulting from community gatherings. She argued that, because early literacy is shaped by the community and the home, schools should recognise children's literacy experiences instead of imposing their own.

Thinking points

1. Did your own pre-school or family experiences shape your attitudes to reading and writing and your confidence at school?

2. Technologies (interactive television, the internet and video games) offer a new kind of literacy. What literacy skills do you need to use these?

3. Should other cultural practices (such as video games) be valued within schools?

Different types of reading books

First, recognising the variety in the types of books written for young children highlights their different functions. Many baby and toddler books aim to help with speech development by providing pictures for children to label objects and package/network build. These are often based around themes or topics using hypernyms (weather, clothes, animals) to provide children with relevant hyponyms (rain, socks, dogs). Nouns and adjectives are the most common word classes in early books that contain only a few words. These link children's literacy experiences with the equivalent stage of speech acquisition, by giving labels for objects and increasing children's knowledge of their immediate environment.

Early story books are designed to be read to children, not by them. They contain complicated words and grammatical structures that children can understand, even though they cannot read them or use them in their own speech. Children's understanding of words and structures is ahead of their ability to use them.

Books for young children aim to be enjoyable and act as a shared experience; such books introduce children to stories and storytelling, as well as often being instructional. Reading schemes for school-age children are slightly different in that, although entertaining, they have been created to help in the formal learning process, being graded to assist children in acquiring fluency skills.

And then what? Well, children become independent readers around the age of 8. Books for older children are still entertaining, informative and instructive, but are centred on them as active, solo readers.

Research point

Jerome Bruner's LASS (Language Acquisition Support System) theory explains how adults encourage children's speech by using books to interact with babies and young children.

He saw parent–child interactions with books as four-phased:

1. **gaining attention**: getting the baby's attention on a picture
2. **query**: asking the baby what the object in the picture is
3. **label**: telling the baby what the object in the picture is
4. **feedback**: responding to the baby's utterance.

Bruner was inspired by Vygotsky, who believed that children learn not by being told how to do something but by being helped to do it when they are ready – and part of the 'scaffolding' process (see page 33). Both Bruner and Vygotsky see children as active learners and believe that the social contexts of their experiences are very important.

Fig. 17 *Children become independent readers around the age of eight*

Thinking points

1. How might early exposure to books help children's language skills?
2. In what ways do children use books to become active learners?
3. Apart from books, what other toys might help their speech development?

Classroom activity 13

Collect a selection of children's first books. Categorise them: for example, lift-the-flap, touch/feel, press/sounds, characters (Spot the dog), etc. Investigate key linguistic features and their effects. Think about how the texts:

- interact with their audience
- suggest values (e.g. behaviour/politeness/morals)
- use rhyme and other phonological devices
- depict characters (animal or human)
- use spoken language features

- proportion the amount of text to pictures; use pictures; use colour
- use hypernyms/hyponyms and semantic fields (what typical word classes are there?)
- use rhetorical devices (repetition, parallel sentence structures, etc.)
- create textual **cohesion** (lexical repetition, syntactical repetition, connectives)
- vary sentence moods (declarative, exclamatory, interrogative or imperative).

What do young readers need to know?

Children need to understand that written texts:

- reflect the relationship between written symbols (**graphemes**) and sounds (phonemes)
- have cohesion, with different parts interconnecting
- are organised in particular ways, with chapter headings, page numbers, etc.
- differ in their organisation according to genre (e.g. fiction and non-fiction books are organised in different ways)
- represent the original culture, following its rules and conventions (e.g. English is read from left to right; narratives are organised in particular ways; certain 'characters' are well known in English-speaking cultures, etc.).

🔍 Analysing early books

An interesting feature of books written for young children is the use of animals, rather than human characters, as the central focus of fictional narratives in English-speaking cultures. *The Gruffalo*, by Julia Donaldson and Axel Scheffler, a popular and well-known story, exemplifies typical features of the genre.

Focusing on these four aspects of the text will show you how effective writing for children can be:

1 the significance of the characters of a mouse and a fox
2 the kinds of phonological devices
3 the use of direct speech
4 the types of pictures and layout chosen.

Choosing a mouse (usually the prey) as the hero of the tale and a fox (usually the predator) is significant, with breaking of stereotypes suggesting a moral or implied meaning for children to absorb. Here the mouse is the bravest animal, outmanoeuvring other animals, revealing their cowardly natures when confronted with the idea of a fierce-sounding unknown animal, the Gruffalo. These stereotypes are probably already recognisable to children, from fairy tales or television cartoons. Even the monster's name ('Gruffalo') is interesting, with hints of the invented terms and names used in Lewis Carroll's 'Jabberwocky'. It echoes a real animal name (buffalo), and the adjective (gruff) has semantic connotations of grumpiness or badness.

Poetic phonological devices are used, as in the line-end rhymes ('wood'/'good'). This typical characteristic helps young children to remember words when hearing the text read aloud. Young children enjoy having the same book read to them repeatedly, responding to the repetitive nature and familiarity in a very different way from adult readers, who are more likely to search for new reading matter. Aside

A mouse took a stroll through the deep dark wood.
A fox saw the mouse and the mouse looked good.
*"Where are you going to, little brown mouse?
Come and have lunch in my underground house."*
"It's terribly kind of you, Fox, but no —
I'm going to have lunch with a gruffalo."

"A gruffalo? What's a gruffalo?"
"A gruffalo! Why, didn't you know?"

"He has terrible tusks   and terrible claws,

And terrible teeth in his terrible jaws."

"Where are you meeting him?"
"Here, by these rocks,
And his favourite food is roasted fox."

"Roasted fox! I'm off!" Fox said.
"Goodbye, little mouse," and away he sped.

"Silly old Fox! Doesn't he know,
There's no such thing as a gruffalo?"

Julia Donaldson and *Axel Scheffler*, The Gruffalo, 1999

from predictability, rhyme is a common feature of nursery rhymes and songs, where the emphasis is on the interactive and multimodal nature of the experience (actions and words) and on sharing these. The rhythmic pattern is another poetic feature, linking the written word with oral storytelling; the sound effects in the plosive alliterative choices ('terrible tusks', 'terrible teeth') are reminiscent of poetry or descriptive literature. Repeated structures emphasise phrase structure, helping to extend vocabulary; the placing of a new word ('tusk') makes sense in the parallel structure to a near **synonym** ('teeth').

Most of the text is a dialogue. Direct speech, as a narrative feature, creates interesting variations of animal voices, but also becomes a grammatical and rhetorical patterning device. Syntactical structures used by the fox, and the other would-be eaters of the mouse, are repeated; only different lexical choices signal the places where the mouse might be enticed to be the predators' next meal. For example, the next creature to suggest to the mouse that they have a meal together, the owl, replaces 'underground house' with 'treetop house'.

Extension activity 4

Select two books of different types (i.e. interactive and a more traditional narrative) or for slightly different age groups. Use linguistic methods to compare the language in the books, such as lexis/semantics, grammar and graphology. Within these methods, find specific features to explore such as adjectives, sentence complexity and text–image ratio. Present these under headings, being systematic in your approach to the comparison, and explain why you think these features have been chosen. The 'why' is really important in making sure that you always consider contextual factors.

Graphologically, placing the picture on the left of the page draws the child's attention to the images of the animals and the woodland context, before attention shifts to the text on the right. Already the child is encouraged to 'read' from left to right. Facial expressions can be interpreted – the mouse's innocence and naivety decoded from its smiling face, contrasting with the rather evil smile of the fox. Another recurrent feature is the placing of pictures both within the page and between passages of text, providing text–image cohesion. The pictures either link to the action, giving context to the dialogue, or help children understand the meanings of words – as where the adjectival material ('terrible claws') is pictured to give a visual impression. The **typographical** device of italics to present the speech of the fox is aimed at the adult reader of the text, who can create a different voice for the animal speaker.

How are children taught to read?

All this may have triggered memories of your first school reading books. Can you remember how you were taught to read words and produce the sounds that they represent? Changes in literacy strategies have changed some teaching methods within the classroom, but the main teaching approaches haven't altered significantly. Recently, debate has been fierce about the most effective methods for teaching reading. While you won't be asked in an examination to evaluate the different approaches, it is helpful to be aware of the strategies children apply and the support parents and teachers offer to advance their skills.

The 'look and say' and **phonics** methods are the two used in British classrooms.

'Look and say' or whole-word approach

Children learn the shape of words, not breaking them down phonologically. With the 'look and say' method, children learn to recognise whole words or sentences rather than individual phonemes. Flashcards with individual words written on them are used for this method, often accompanied with a related picture so that children can link the object and the referent.

Phonics

Children learn the different sounds made by different letters and letter blends and some rules of putting them together. Emphasis is on developing phonological awareness and on hearing, differentiating and replicating sounds in spoken words. The two main approaches to teaching phonics are analytic and synthetic (Table 22).

Fig. 18 *The many ways that 'n' and 'k' can be pronounced*

■ Research points

Some theorists have found that children who are sensitive to rhyme are much better at reading. Learning phonological patterns in language is key to reading successfully, as is learning that orthography does not always match phonology in English.

■ Dombey (1999) says that rhyming (and rhyming games) help children to relate sound patterns to letter clusters, which assists both reading and spelling.

■ Konza (2011) makes phonemic awareness one of the most important skills for reading successfully. Phonemic awareness is the ability to hear, separate and manipulate individual sounds and phonemes.

Thinking points

Look at the alphabetic code for the sounds /n/ and /k/.

1 What complexities of the English alphabetic code can you see?

2 How might this make learning to read difficult?

■ Further reading

Gunther R. Kress has been interested in literacy in its broadest sense for many years and has written several books, mainly focused on written literacy. His book *Literacy in the New Media Age* features a chapter on reading as a way of interpreting and ordering the world around us. It takes reading beyond just a skill of early childhood development and is about the way we use reading all our lives to make sense of experiences.

Kress, G. R. *Literacy in the New Media Age*, Routledge, 2003

Table 22 *The key features of the analytic and synthetic phonics approaches*

Analytic phonics	Synthetic phonics
Children learn: ■ to break down whole words into phonemes and graphemes, looking for phonetic or orthographic patterns. ■ to decode words by separating them into smaller units: – *onset* (the vowel or syllable at the start of a word) – *rime* (the rest of the word, always beginning with a vowel) ■ to use rhyme or analogy to learn other words with similar patterns, e.g. c-at, m-at, p-at ■ to recognise one letter sound at a time, seeing pictures showing words beginning with the same letter sound Children learn initial letter sounds first, then middle sounds, followed by the final sounds of words and consonant blends. Children are competent readers within three years, breaking down and sounding out unfamiliar words. This phonics method runs alongside whole-word approaches and reading-scheme books.	Children learn: ■ to remember up to 44 phonemes and their related graphemes (one phoneme can be represented by different graphemes, for example 'ough', 'ow' and 'oa') ■ to recognise each grapheme, sound out each phoneme in a word, blending the sounds together to pronounce the word phonetically ■ to memorise phonemes quickly (up to five or six sounds a week) ■ often through a multi-sensory approach whereby they: 1) see the symbol 2) listen to the sound 3) use an action (such as counting phonemes on fingers or using magnetic letters to correspond to the phonemes) Children learn in whole-class teaching groups. Reading schemes are not used in the early stages of learning synthetic phonics, as the method can be taught in a few months.

■ Classroom activity 14

Use the following rime examples and add onsets to create words.

■ -ow

■ -ake

■ -ove

■ -ough

Phonics is currently viewed as the most effective teaching method, but encouraging and motivating children to read independently outside school also ensures confident readers. This extract from a seven-year-old's reading shows how parents support school literacy programmes.

Transcription conventions are given on page v.

Context: Oliver is reading his school book to his mother at home.

C: the horse needs a new shoe (.) got any jobs mister (.) asked Vicky I'll give you a penny to jump

M: not jump

C: pump

M: yeah   5

C: the pi b-billows

M: not (.) not (.) billows what does that say what does that part of the word say [*mother covers up the end of the word to leave 'bell'*]

C: bell [*mother takes hand off word*] ows

M: yes bellows   10

Author's own data

Already a confident reader, the child reads most words easily. The mother helps him to read an unfamiliar word ('bellows') by separating the syllables visually. Here phonics seems to help him decode syllables as, even prior to his mother's help, he uses his knowledge of rhyme to guess the word ('pi b-billows'). She also confirms he is reading accurately ('yeah', 'yes bellows'), repeating words for reinforcement.

Research point

Skinner's ideas about reinforcement could be useful to link to literacy acquisition. His view that learning takes place through positive reinforcement is perhaps evident in the way parents and teachers correct children's reading. The mother here limits her positive reinforcement to affirming the child's correct reading of words ('yeah') but you could equally see an adult using praise words, such as 'well done' or 'good boy/girl', congratulating children's successful pronunciation or interpretation of words. Negative reinforcement in this interaction is limited to the mother telling the child when they have read a word wrongly ('not billows').

Classroom activity 15

Using the information provided on the previous couple of pages about the various methods of teaching children to read (whole-word, phonics, analytic and synthetic phonics), list some of their advantages and disadvantages.

Thinking points

1. What other kinds of positive reinforcement are teachers/parents likely to offer to children learning to read?

2. Do you think negative reinforcement would be effective as a teaching method?

Extension activity 5

Write a magazine article or a section of a website aimed at parents evaluating the different strategies. Before you do this:

■ Research style models. Collect these from printed magazines and websites. Note where you found them and identify the intended audience.

■ Annotate them for specific linguistic features, such as the use of pronouns, and highlight where they have explained some of the complex ideas about child development to parents who are not language experts.

■ Evaluate the ways they have adapted ideas and used specific features to suit their audience. Practise adapting a linguistic idea of your own, and compare it to your style model before writing it down.

■ Create a list of stylistic devices (language features and genre conventions) that you want to use to make your article convincing.

Link

This activity is good practice for writing the media text that is part of your A2 coursework. You will study this more in Section B Media text, but being aware that writers can adapt language acquisition theories for non-linguists such as parents to understand will help you to prepare for this skill later in your course.

When you have finished, swap articles with another student.

- ■ Did the article explain the reading methods clearly?
- ■ Was it lively and engaging to read?
- ■ What improvements could you suggest?

The cues children use

So far we have concentrated mainly on phonological methods, but an early reader acquires many tools to interpret the written word, using **cues** to decode words and meanings within texts. Writers of children's reading books build cues into their texts. You will see this when you look at reading schemes.

■ **Key terms**

Cueing: the strategies used to help decode written texts successfully.

Table 23 *Types of reading cues*

Cue	Activity
Graphophonic	Looking at the shape of words, linking these to familiar graphemes/words to interpret them
Semantic	Understanding the meanings of words and making connections between words in order to decode new ones
Visual	Looking at the pictures and using the visual narrative to interpret unfamiliar words or ideas
Syntactic	Applying knowledge of word order and word classes to work out if a word seems right in the context
Contextual	Searching for understanding in the situation of the story – comparing it to their own experience or their pragmatic understanding of social conventions
Miscue	Making errors when reading: a child might miss a word or substitute another that looks similar, or guess a word from accompanying pictures

Text A is an extract from the opening of *Victorian Adventure*. Text B is a transcript of Oliver, aged 7, reading from the book. These texts show Oliver's use of cueing to read accurately.

Transcription conventions are given on page v.

Text A

Biff and Chip had been to
  London with Gran.
They had some pictures which
  they put into a scrapbook.
They wanted to take the book to school.

Gran came into Biff's room to
  look at the children's scrapbook.
'We had a great time in London,' said Biff.
'Thank you, Gran.'
Gran was pleased.

Roderick Hunt and *Alex Brychta*, Victorian Adventure, *1990*

Text B

M: okay are you going to read your book to me Ollie (2.0) what's it called

O: Victorian Adventure

M: yes

O: Biff and Chip had been to (.) London (1.0) with Gran (,) they   5
had some pictures which (.) they put into a scrapbook (.) they
wanted to take the book to school

M: it's like when we went to London isn't it

O: Gran came into Biff's room to look at the children's
scrapbook(.) We had a great time in London said Biff (1.0)   10
thank you Gran (.) Gran was pleased (2.0) suddenly the magic
(.) key glowed it was time for an adventure (.) the magic took
the children into the (.) little house (.) but didn't it take Gran

M: no no what does it say

O: but did it take Gran   15

M: that's right good boy [*sound of pages turning*]

O: the magic took them back in time to a street on a foggy day
(1) a boy was standing under a (.) gas lamp (.) he looked at
the children in surprise (.) excuse me (.) said Biff do you know
where we are (.) don't you know said the boy (.) this is London   20
(.) he took his cap off it wasn't a boy it was a girl

M: [*laughs*]

Author's own data

Oliver appears to have little difficulty using graphophonic cues; he reads
the words in this opening section accurately with his only error being a
miscue ('didn't' for 'did'). This 'virtuous' error reveals his understanding
of syntax, although the two words have opposite meanings. His
pauses before the nouns ('gran', 'gas lamp') suggest that his semantic
understanding is not as confident; perhaps Oliver does not usually use
the word 'Gran' to address his grandmother, needing the visual clue to
connect the white-haired woman with the word 'gran'. Regular pauses
vary in length from a micro-pause to two seconds. In some cases these
show his uncertainty with a word. The pauses before the proper noun
('London') suggest it is unfamiliar and he looks for prompts from picture
clues. The pictures of Big Ben and Buckingham Palace in the text provide
a cultural context.

The prosodic features, with stresses on words ('great', 'know' and 'girl'),
show that Oliver has semantic awareness. By stressing what he thinks
are key elements of the story ('it was a girl'), rather than particular word
classes, he engages with the listener's needs. When reading to his mother,
he seems to understand that dialogue creates a character's voice. He tries
to inject emphasis and stress into key words when reading aloud ('Don't
you know, said the boy').

Oliver's use of syntactical cueing is influenced more by line breaks than
the grammatical sense of sentences, as in the pauses after 'to' and 'which'
on the first page of the book. More sophisticated grammatical awareness
is apparent when he uses pauses to show a completed clause ('he looked
at the children in surprise'). Although inconsistent throughout the
transcript, this confirms that his reading ability is developing.

His awareness of context is not really tested here. Despite the unfamiliarity of the 'Victorian' context, the book actually focuses on a London trip. That he can relate to this experience is reinforced by his mother's unacknowledged interrogative ('it's like when we went to London isn't it'). Because this is a staged reading scheme, he has encountered the 'magic key' before and does not question this narrative device ('the magic took the children into the little house').

■ The stages of reading development

Jeanne Chall identified six stages from her studies with children (Table 24). Although your focus is on children reading from toddlerhood to age 11, it is interesting to see how our reading motivations change, and the types of texts we choose alter, as we become accomplished readers. As with all stages, remember that these offer simplified guides and not definitive judgments about all children's development at these ages.

Table 24 *Chall's stages of children's reading development*

Stage	Description	Age (years)	Key characteristics
0	Pre-reading and pseudo-reading	Up to 6	'Pretend' reading (turning pages and repeating stories perhaps previously read to them) Some letter and word recognition, especially letters in own name Predicting single words or the next stage of a story
1	Initial reading and decoding	6–7	Reading simple texts containing high-frequency lexis (this happens when children start to learn the relationship between phonemes and graphemes) How many written words understood? Chall estimated around 600
2	Confirmation and fluency	7–8	Reading texts more quickly, accurately and fluently, paying more attention to the meanings of words and texts How many written words understood? Chall estimated around 3,000
3	Reading for learning	9–14	Reading for knowledge and information becomes the motivation
4	Multiplicity and complexity	14–17	Responding critically to what they read and analysing texts
5	Construction and reconstruction	18+	Reading selectively and forming opinions about what they have read

Returning to Oliver, you can see that he is in the 'confirmation and fluency' stage; he reads quickly with few pauses or inaccuracies. Confident with high-frequency words, he struggles only with unfamiliar ones. Each book he reads adds to his word bank, in both lexical and semantic terms. But he is still reading to learn that skill rather than for the content of a text, i.e. reading for knowledge and enjoyment.

■ Looking ahead

This activity will introduce you to some of the ethics involved with research and primary data gathering that may well affect you depending on your choice of degree course. It is important that you gain consent from the people that you are recording as it is illegal to record people without their knowledge. You will encounter many other types of ethical considerations related to research and data gathering, and being aware of these will help you to make sensible decisions.

Study tip

You will need written parental consent before you record young children. Explain to the parents why you are conducting the research and what you will be doing with the data you collect. Be polite and get this checked by someone else before you send it.

Schools may also require background checks before they allow you to enter them, so do not assume that you can get data immediately. Forward planning and polite communication with parents and schools might be necessary before you can actually go and record children, so don't leave this until the last minute.

■ Link

Ethical issues that you need to be aware of when planning your research are discussed further on page 148.

■ Extension activity 7

Look back at the data extracts in this topic and evaluate how they link to these acquisition debates.

1 Can you apply the nature versus nurture debate to literacy acquisition? Is learning to read an innate skill (Chomsky) or does it have to be acquired through imitation (Skinner)?

2 Is there evidence that the methods used to teach children reading support the interactionist viewpoint?

3 How far to you think cognitive acquisition theories relate to reading development? Do children have to understand concepts before they can read words, or is reading different from spoken acquisition?

■ Extension activity 6

Record and transcribe children who are learning to read. (You could use younger siblings or friends' families, or visit schools or nurseries.)

Compile a list of CDS strategies and miscues before analysing the data. Transcribe data using the usual conventions for pauses (.) and contextual information [], etc. Copy the pages of the book that the child was reading if you can, as this will make it easier to explore the reasons for miscues. Annotate the data, looking for the miscues and CDS strategies that you listed. Match your examples to the miscue/CDS strategy.

Present your findings either in a written answer or as a brief presentation to the class covering:

■ CDS strategies used by the adult

■ miscues

■ reading strategies used by the child or the adult

■ reading stages.

You could also evaluate your findings by looking at what the children did not miscue and what they did accurately.

■ Reading schemes

References have already been made to graded reading schemes designed to help children's development. You might recall characters from your school reading-scheme books and the types of narratives they involved, such as Biff and Chip and the 'magic key' genre. This genre is used in the Oxford Reading Tree scheme and uses the narrative structure of a magic key that begins to glow and transports children back to the past for an adventure. Reading schemes are deliberately staged in difficulty to help children acquire and extend lexical and semantic knowledge, as well as developing grammatical understanding. Familiarity is established through character-based and narrative approaches as the aim is to build confidence through the stages. Like early reading books, texts designed for teaching purposes often offer opportunities for developing pragmatic understanding through modelling good behaviour and politeness conventions, and by using multicultural and gender representations to negate stereotyping. Recently the value of non-fiction books has been recognised, especially to motivate and encourage boys to read.

Reading-scheme books use different linguistic choices from the kinds in *The Gruffalo*, because their primary purpose is to teach reading skills rather than to entertain.

Key features of reading schemes are:

■ **lexical repetition**: especially the new lexis introduced in each book but also proper nouns

■ **syntactical repetition of structures**: usually subject-verb-object order and simple sentences containing one clause (in early books)

■ **simple verbs**: single verbs used (i.e. is) rather than verb phrases

■ **one sentence per line**: helping children to say complete phrases

■ **anaphoric referencing**: pronouns (she/he) refer to the names of characters already used

■ **limited use of modifiers**: this makes graded reading schemes different from imaginative stories where adjectives add detail and description

■ **text-image cohesion**: the picture tells the story of the text on the page.

Training for the race

It was Sports Day at Waterloo School.
Ben's Dad had come to see him run.
Ben was a good runner.
He was in the 200 metres and
he wanted to win.
Kevin was also in that race.
He was a good runner and
he wanted to win the race too.
Kevin and Ben lined up with
the other runners.
'Ready, steady, go!' shouted Mr March.
Everyone ran very quickly but
Kevin and Ben finished first.
They finished the race together.
'Well done!' shouted Mr Belter.
'Well done!' shouted Mr March.
Ben's Dad was very pleased.

4

5

Tessa Krailing, Keith Gaines, Wendy Wren, Shirley Tully, Going for Gold, *1993*

> **Classroom activity 16**
>
> Look at the extract from *Going for Gold*, part of the Wellington Square reading scheme.
>
> Using the list of key features of reading schemes, identify the language devices chosen by the writer to help develop children's reading skills.

Developing writing

In this topic you will:

■ consider the main functions of writing

■ understand the key developmental stages

■ recognise the importance of genre conventions and register in children's written development

■ develop a critical understanding of the key concepts surrounding children's writing development

■ apply linguistic approaches to a range of children's texts.

> **Starter activity**
>
> Discuss in a group your memories of learning to write. Did you start writing at home or at school? What sort of problems did you have? What sort of writing did you do? How were you helped to write? Compare your ideas with others in the class.

■ What is writing and why do we need it?

A useful starting point is to remind yourself of the main differences between speech and writing modes (a key part of your AS study). Other questions to ask yourself are as follows.

■ Why do we write? What are the functions and purposes of writing?

■ How do our writing skills develop and how do we personalise these?

■ How do we adapt our style of writing for different genres and in different registers?

You may believe that writing can be used:

■ to communicate with others for social, interactional and phatic purposes (text messages, letters, birthday cards)

■ referentially to record information (notes, lists, reminders, official forms)

■ expressively (diaries, creative writing).

Fig. 19 *Writing can be used to communicate, to record and to express yourself*

■ Key terms

Cursive handwriting: handwriting in which the characters are joined in rounded and flowing strokes.

Convergence: a process of linguistic change in which people adjust their dialect, accent or speech style to those of others, often occurring to express solidarity and understanding.

Sociolect: a defined use of language as a result of membership of a social group.

Orthography: the study of the use of letters and the rules of spelling in a language.

Writing often supports or replaces oral communication; for example, you can text a message to a friend to arrange a meeting, or give bad news that you would rather not deliver in person.

Before looking at children's writing development, think back to your own. How did your writing style and skills develop? Were you excited when you were allowed to use a pen in your schoolwork instead of a pencil, as this meant that you were now a competent writer? Another milestone may have been when you joined up your **handwriting cursively** and made decisions about your writing style (sloped, upright), letting you personalise your work and define your identity.

You might also remember your pride at having your work displayed on the classroom walls. If you find your old exercise books, your spellings might make you laugh, as might your phrasing of ideas. These sound odd to you now because of your knowledge of grammatical structures and spelling rules. What might surprise you is how creative with language you were as a child.

As an adult writer, you have learned to manipulate register. In text messaging you probably adapt standard spelling, punctuation and grammatical rules to conform to text conventions, and to **converge** to the **sociolect** of your audience. By doing this you can also display your idiolect, creating a style that others recognise as yours (a little like your handwriting). You do this because you know the 'rules' of written language and choose to break them.

So you can see that children have much to learn. It's not just about mechanical and physical control of the pen or pencil, it is as much about:

■ combining words and sentences to convey ideas

■ recognising that writing generally has an audience

■ using recognisable discourse and genre conventions

■ manipulating language to achieve specific purposes.

It's also about being an active learner, discovering that writing can do all these things.

Recent research into children's literacy emphasises the effects of home cultural and social practices on their reading and writing development. But children don't just experience the written word in books, they also find it through computers and television.

Writing is one of the key communication modes, acquired after speech and having its own separate system. In any language, writing uses a common and agreed code of symbols. Individual graphemes combine to make words that a language user can recognise. But writing is only effective when the order is right; this order can be syntactical and in the spelling and **orthography** of words.

To summarise, writing means being able to use:

■ the vocabulary system and associated meanings of words and phrases (lexis and semantics)

■ sentences to create meaning (grammar)

■ graphemes that relate to phonemes, and other devices to create prosodic effects, for example in punctuation choices (phonology)

■ social conventions within certain types of written texts (pragmatics)

■ cohesive structures (discourse)

■ the layout of texts, the use of graphemes and images to create semiotic meaning (graphology)

■ variations in language to suit audience, purpose and context (register).

Orthography too is important. It's the part of language study to do with spelling and the graphemes used. For some linguists, orthography also includes the use of capital letters.

The list above should remind you how complex writing is. Written texts are often constructed far more deliberately than speech. As children have so much to learn, it is unsurprising that it takes a long time to learn to write effectively in all areas. As you know from your own experience, writing is far more prescriptive than speech and follows established rules. Schooling, too, places emphasis on children becoming literate, with national literacy strategies and initiatives like the 'literacy hour' encouraging a focus on successful reading and writing development.

A major difference between reading and writing is that the latter requires motor and mechanical skills; children have to hold pencils and pens, controlling them in order to transfer their thoughts and ideas onto paper. Increasingly, access to computers means that children can combine the letters and symbols on a keyboard to make words and sentences into meaningful texts. Using computers also introduces graphological and typographical choices that are unavailable when writing by hand.

Stages of writing

To introduce writing development, the list below outlines the stages:

- drawing
- letter-like forms
- copied letters
- child's name and strings of letters
- words
- sentences
- text.

Children's skills start with putting a writing instrument on paper (usually crayons and paints). Images and shapes become words, sentences and whole texts. Put like this it seems rather mechanical, but, of course, writing is also about conveying ideas and meanings and so both thought and planning have to apply to any written text.

Early writing

The term **emergent writing** is used to describe children's early scribbles or representations of the written word. On page 52 is Oliver's early attempt, aged 3, at writing his thoughts down on paper. This accompanied a picture he had drawn at nursery school.

Oliver's message would have been impossible for others to interpret without the teacher asking what he had written, and recording this message using recognisable words. He clearly has meaning for his scribbles, indicating semiotic understanding. But he needs to learn mechanical skills to make his graphemes recognisable.

Typically for a 3-year-old, the letters in his name are written clearly. The rest resemble scribbles, but Oliver is aware of directionality (working from left to right) and that English is written from top to bottom of a page. A sense of authorship is already present in the placing of his name at the top left of the text. The teacher reinforces this by writing Oliver's full name. Spaces between the scribbles show that Oliver is aware that individual words have discrete meanings. Letter shapes resemble some of the alphabet ('w', 'm') and **ascender/descender**

> **Key terms**
>
> **Emergent writing:** children's early scribble writing, a stage of their literacy development.
>
> **Ascender:** the typographical feature where a portion of the letter goes above the usual height for letters in any font.
>
> **Descender:** where part of a letter goes below the baseline of a font.

graphemes ('p') suggest an emerging orthographical awareness. For Oliver, however, there seems to be no separation yet between words and pictures. The text is multimodal, conveying his message in both the picture and the scribble writing.

Author's own data

From this early writing, you can see that Oliver has achieved the first four stages of writing development. His writing still resembles a drawing, yet within it are letter-like forms, written in strings, and his name is clearly evident. Oliver's next stage is to create words, sentences and texts. This will be encouraged during his school experiences within a more formal framework of literacy teaching.

Classroom activity 17

Look at this story by Cameron, aged 5.

■ How has he developed from Oliver's stage?

■ What does Cameron understand about constructing texts?

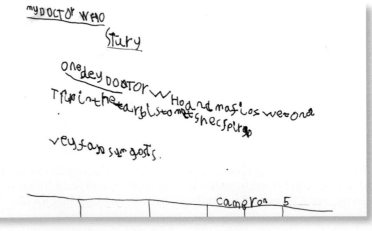

Transliteration:

My Doctor Who story

One day Dr Who and Martha Jones went on a trip in the Tardis to meet Shakespeare and they found some ghosts.

Cameron 5

Author's own data

Kroll's four phases/stages of development

Barry Kroll (1981) identified four phases of children's development, and further work by other researchers, such as Katherine Perera, added suggested age ranges for these stages (Table 25).

Table 25 *Kroll's stages of development*

Stage	Age (years)	Characteristics
Preparation	Up to 6	Basic motor skills are acquired alongside some principles of spelling.
Consolidation	7/8	Writing is similar to spoken language (including a more casual, colloquial register, unfinished sentences and strings of clauses joined by the conjunction 'and').
Differentiation	9/10	Awareness of writing as separate from speech emerges. A stronger understanding of writing for different audiences and purposes is evident and becomes more automatic.
Integration	Mid-teens	This stage heralds the 'personal voice' in writing and is characterised by evidence of controlled writing, with appropriate linguistic choices being made consistently.

Looking at Oliver's 'I painted a box full of numbers' (page 52) and Cameron's 'Dr Who story' (page 52), which stage would you place them in? What support would you give for your decisions?

Later you will see evidence of children's writing in later stages; compare their development with Kroll's stages.

Understanding genre

From an early age children see specific writing genres, usually ones related to their own experience. Think of key events when you were younger, such as parties, and recall the invitations sent out on your behalf and the birthday cards that you first signed and then wrote using genre conventions (dear Emily, happy birthday, love Jenny). Other early home writing experiences might have been writing a list for Father Christmas or a note for the Tooth Fairy.

Understanding register is important in order to meet genre conventions, and children have to learn that vocabulary choices and grammatical constructions contribute to the overall tone. Also significant is the purpose of the text as well as the audience and the relationship between reader and writer. As writing matures, pragmatic awareness becomes more sophisticated, with references to shared experiences and the use of either a humorous or serious tone reflecting the personality of the writer. These pragmatic skills make writing less mechanical and more engaging.

Here are some pieces of writing in specific genres. The first text is a 7-year-old boy's letter to Santa. The second is a 4-year-old girl's invitation for her teddy to attend a tea party celebrating the end of her Reception year.

Transliteration:

Dear Santa

Please may I have a PSP. Please can my dad have some computer stuff. Please can my mum have a new ironing board.

Author's own data

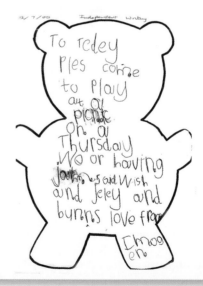

Transliteration:

To Teddy

Please come to play at a picnic on Thursday. We are having jam sandwiches and jelly and buns

Love from Imogen

Author's own data

Both children show the pragmatic understanding that politeness is needed in invitations and certain types of letters, notably those in which you make a request. In the letter to Santa, the child repeats words ('please'), foregrounding this at the beginning of each sentence, as well as using modal auxiliary verbs ('can', 'may') to reinforce the polite tone. This repetition of sentence structure also makes the text cohesive. Although careful to put his own wish first, the child also refers to his parents and identifies items that they may (or may not in the mother's case) be grateful to receive. You might perceive some gender-stereotype issues here! His use of the possessive pronoun ('my') could be an acknowledgement that Santa needs to know the recipients of the presents.

Within the letter to Santa, the child understands letter conventions, choosing 'Dear' to address Santa formally. In the tea invitation the child also demonstrates strong awareness of generic conventions with the address ('To Teddy') and the sign-off ('love from Imogen'). Imogen is also aware of certain conventions associated with invitations in her request for 'Teddy' to join her at an event (a picnic), offering a time, but not a venue, which shows that she has still to learn all the information that Teddy logically would need to know in order to attend. Not only does she show an awareness of genre conventions, she also demonstrates an understanding of the persuasive nature of an invitation, tempting Teddy with promises of jelly and buns. Both texts display an understanding of the correct register, and both have a formal tone.

How are genres used in children's early writing at school?

A useful way to help you evaluate children's writing is to use Joan Rothery's categories, identified from investigating young children's writing in Australian schools (Table 26). She found that early writing within school fell into some distinctive groupings: observation/comment, recount, report and narrative.

Table 26 *Rothery's categories for evaluating children's writing*

Category	Features
Observation/ comment	The writer makes an observation ('I saw a tiger') and follows this with either an evaluative comment ('it was very large') or mixes these in with the observation ('I saw a very large tiger').
Recount	Usually a chronological sequence of events. A typical example would be a recount of a school trip, which children are often asked to do as a follow-up activity. It is written subjectively ('I').
	The structure of a recount usually follows a set pattern: Orientation – Event – Reorientation.
	The orientation sets the scene, perhaps the journey to the place or the name of the place visited. The reorientation at the end of the recount completes the writing.
Report	A factual and objective description of events or things; it tends not to be chronological.
Narrative	A story genre where the scene is set for events to occur and be resolved at the end. It also has a set pattern: Orientation – Complication – Resolution – Coda.
	The coda, which identifies the point of the story, is not always added.
	Because of the structural complexity few children will achieve the whole structure early on, despite their experience of reading stories that follow this narrative structure.

■ Classroom activity 18

Apply Rothery's categories to the three texts on the following pages.
- ■ Which text exemplifies each category?
- ■ What evidence is there in the texts to support your choices?

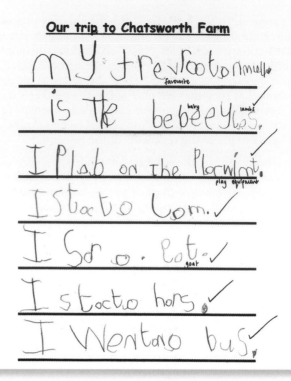

Our trip to Chatsworth Farm

Transliteration:

My favourite animal is the baby lambs. I played on the play equipment. I stroked a lamb. I saw a goat. I stroked a horse. I went on a bus.

Thursday 10th April

My favourite place

Transliteration:

My favourite place

Where is it

Portugal is a warm place in summer. It has lovely restaurants and delicious food. I like to go there with my family. It is a cheerful place.

What is it like

Portugal has delightful beaches and in some beaches there are rock pools. It has the most wonderful villas with good pools.

What happens there.

Author's own data

wednesday 10th seblember

Hedgehogs

I am doing a report on hedgehogs.

Hedgehogs have sharp spines. often on there back and they can prick you when you tuch them. Hedgehogs will curl up into balls when they smell danger.

Most hedgehogs live under leaves and some live in Peoples gardens.

Some hedgehogs eat foul things like dead toads but some just eat snails and worms.

Most hedgehogs wander around and some just stay in thier nests.

I wrote this report on hedgehogs because i like them

Transliteration:

Wednesday 10th September

Hedgehogs

I am doing a report on hedgehogs.

Hedgehogs have sharp spines on their back and they can prick you when you touch them. Hedgehogs will curl up into balls when they smell danger.

Most hedgehogs live under leaves and some live in people's gardens.

Some hedgehogs eat foul things like dead toads but some just eat snails and worms.

Most hedgehogs wander around and some just stay in their nests.

I wrote this report on hedgehogs because I like them.

Author's own data

Other genre perspectives

Britton proposed three modes of writing used by schoolchildren: expressive, poetic and transactional (Table 27). These modes focus more on stylistic choices than on the content of the writing, as with Rothery's categories.

Table 27 *Britton's three modes of children's writing*

Mode	Features
Expressive	The first mode to develop because it resembles speech.
	Uses the first person perspective and the content is usually based on personal preferences.
Poetic	Develops gradually, requiring skills in crafting and shaping language, but is encouraged early on because of its creativity.
	Phonological features such as rhyme, rhythm and alliteration, as well as descriptive devices such as adjectives and similes, are common.
Transactional	Develops last, around secondary school age, once children have finally dissociated speech from writing. It is the style of academic essays, as it is more impersonal in style and tone. The third person is used to create a detached tone. Formal sentence structures and graphological features are used to signpost sections and ideas and structures tend to be chronological.

■ Research point

Katherine Perera suggested an alternative framework for classifying texts: chronological and non-chronological. Chronological texts rely on action words (verbs) and on linking ideas using connectives. Non-chronological texts are considered harder to write because they rely on logical connections between ideas.

This framework complements Rothery's genre categories, focusing also on the importance of the discourse structure of the writing task as a way of assisting children to become competent and confident writers. It is interesting that non-chronological texts are considered harder to write, but Britton suggests that children are encouraged to tackle these early on because of their creative aspect; for example, poetry is a writing activity that children accomplish early in school.

■ Classroom activity 19

Look at Imogen's 'Trees' poem (written at age 4) and Oliver's poem about animals (written at age 7). First, list key poetic conventions (for example, rhyme) and use your list to find examples in the children's poetry to answer the following questions.

■ What do the children know about the genre conventions of poetry?

■ How is this awareness displayed in their writing?

■ How have the children been 'scaffolded' graphologically with the activity?

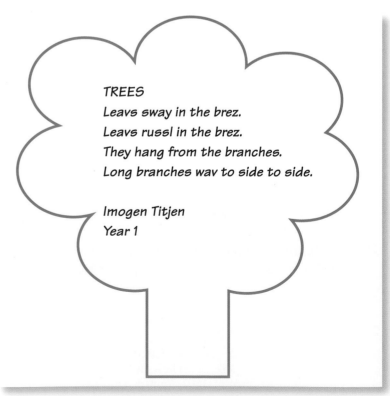

TREES
Leavs sway in the brez.
Leavs russl in the brez.
They hang from the branches.
Long branches wav to side to side.

Imogen Titjen
Year 1

Author's own data

Transliteration:

Animal poem

Lions roar
Eagles soar
Rhinos tramp
Elephants trump
Jaguars leap
And we sleep

A poem by Oliver

Author's own data

Thinking points

1   Why might children write chronological texts first?

2   What kind of genres fit with chronological approaches?

3   What genres might encourage children to practise non-chronological text skills?

Extension activity 9

Return to the texts used in Classroom activity 18. Apply Britton's writing modes to these texts. To what extent can you classify each text as expressive, poetic or transactional? Evaluate the differences you can find when you apply Rothery, Perera and Britton's classifications.

Spelling

How do you spell a word you haven't heard before? We all use various strategies to help us spell accurately, including many we learned as children. The main ones are:

- sound clues, sounding out words to stress the sounds and separate syllables
- clues from the word's meaning to make links with similar words
- writing it down until it 'looks' right
- using grammatical knowledge to predict spelling (such as patterns in affixing to change word class and the common inflections/morphemes that are added to English words)
- a dictionary or a computer spell-checker.

Children become like detectives looking for clues and making guesses but, as they become more experienced, they rely less on guesswork and more on their knowledge of spelling patterns.

Difficulties arise with spelling despite the alphabetic principle (in which a symbol represents a sound or unit of sounds) because there is not a one-to-one correspondence between sound and symbol; in English, 26 letters represent 44 phonemes. Decisions need to be made about whether individual graphemes represent the sound or whether a **digraph** (two letters produced as a single sound, for example 'sh') is needed to create a single sound. The sounds of letters are often affected by their position in the word or by the surrounding letters, so phonetic strategies are insufficient for accurate spelling. To demonstrate the potential pitfalls of spelling, say the following words out loud.

careful   rat   favour   ball   was

Possible problems also occur because of the number of **homophones** in English. Here are some examples of homophones beginning with the letter 's'.

sea/see   sale/sail   stare/stair   son/sun   some/sum   steak/stake

Children have to learn and practise homophones so that they can use the right one in their written work. Another difficulty is created by the addition of inflections, which can affect the phonology of a word, as in 'house' and 'houses'.

The five spelling stages

Research has pinpointed five spelling stages (Table 28) but, again, remember that individual children can reach these at different ages.

Table 28 *Spelling stages*

Stage	What can a child do at this stage?
Pre-phonemic	Imitate writing, mainly scribbling and using pretend writing; some letter shapes are decipherable
Semi-phonetic	Link letter shapes and sounds, using this to write words
Phonetic	Understand that all phonemes can be represented by graphemes; words become more complete
Transitional	Combine phonic knowledge with visual memory; an awareness of combinations of letters and letter patterns, including the 'magic e' rule
Conventional	Spell most words correctly

🔆 Categories of spelling error

Table 29 shows the main types of spelling error. It is often interesting to consider the errors made and how many or few there are within a text. This could link with analyses of other linguistic competencies, building a picture of a child's overall understanding of writing. Remember that children might overgeneralise rules in the same way they do when acquiring speech, which is not always helpful with irregular spelling patterns. Another factor to consider is the effect of accent on some phonetic choices and that some spelling choices might vary according to where children live.

Table 29 *The main types of spelling error made by children*

Term	Definition
Insertion	Adding extra letters
Omission	Leaving out letters
Substitution	Substituting one letter for another
Transposition	Reversing the correct order of letters in words
Phonetic spelling	Using sound awareness to guess letters and combinations of letters
Over/undergeneralisation of spelling rules	Overgeneralising of a rule where it is not appropriate to apply it, or undergeneralising it by only applying it in one specific context
Salient (key) sounds	Writing only the key sounds

Classroom activity 20

The table below shows a selection of spelling errors made by children aged 7 and 8. Copy and complete the table, identifying:

■ what the actual spelling is

■ what types of errors the children have made.

You might put some words into more than one category.

You can then go on to consider:

■ why these might have occurred

■ what effect accent might have on spelling.

Child's spelling	Actual spelling	Type of spelling error(s)
suddnly		
peculier/perculiar		
cloke		
kitchin		
discusting		
(golf) corse		
shale (shall)		
exspensis		
twincling		
butifull		
kitins		
fraindly		
becuase		
correg (meaning bravery)		
bissnis		
chearful		
intelgent		

■ Punctuation and grammatical development

What is punctuation and why is it important? It marks boundaries between units of language: words, phrases, clauses and sentences. These boundaries are marked by spaces, capital letters, full stops and commas. Certain sentence moods, specifically exclamatory and interrogative moods, are indicated by exclamation and question marks. Punctuation also makes meaning clear to a reader.

These typed extracts written by the same child were produced two years apart. Although not in the child's handwriting, the texts have been reproduced using the original spelling and punctuation. Note the differences between the punctuation of each text and the effect this has on the overall success of the narrative for an audience.

A terrible day (child, aged 8)

It all started one morning when the alarm clock rang very loud and I fell out of bed and bumbed my head. I got dressed and had breakfast my sister got a toy in her breakfast and I got nothing. and I lost my toothbrush so my Mum told me of. when I was brushing my hair my brush broke. when I was on my way to school my car broke down and I had to walk to school. Then I dropped my bag and its strap broke in half. when I got into school I had to do a hard test and I got all my spellings wrong. in the playground I had a fall out with my best fraind, and I fell over and hurt my knee.

Author's own data

A Space Adventure (child, aged 10)

Fig. 20 *'Suddenly the ship made a sudden jolt …'*

Somewhere in deepest, darkest space travelled a team of explorers on board. No one could of predicted the mayhem and misfortunate happenings lying ahead. This was only the beginning…

The crew inside the spaceship wasn't a big crew, there was only 4, but they were always arguing; they could never agree on anything! They were called Katie, Jessica, Tom and James and all they thought about was themselves. Nevertheless, they were stuck together.

Suddenly the ship made a sudden jolt and everyone was thrown of their feet and fell with a bump to the floor.

'What was that?' asked Katie

'It wasn't me!' replied Tom

Author's own data

The 'terrible day' writing contains full stops to show the end of ideas, but some are non-standard, such as the full stop before the conjunction ('and I lost my toothbrush'). As stylistic awareness develops, writers learn to break rules for effect. Yet here the child is trying to think of another terrible event to describe, so the connective ('and') simply acts as a continuation, rather than trying to make this sentence stand out to a reader. This is typical of Kroll's consolidation stage (see page 53), where writing is similar to speech; look at the number of times 'and' is used as a connective. The child still uses capital letters inconsistently after full stops and, interestingly, tends to not capitalise sentences starting with the subordinating conjunction ('when') and coordinating conjunction ('and'), perhaps because of their roles as conjunctions.

The one comma in the passage suggests the addition of another terrible event ('I had a fall out with my best fraind, and I fell over') showing some development in punctuation.

When reading this story, or imagined account, of a bad day you might have noticed some sophistication emerging in the grammatical structure; the child is using subordinate clauses to create complex sentences, and uses the subordinating conjunction at the start of a sentence to create clarity and interest for a reader. Adverbial phrases ('in the playground') are important, rather than description, and lexical choices are mainly limited to nouns ('alarm clock', 'toothbrush').

Two years later the same child has advanced to Kroll's differentiation stage. There is a strong narrative, and stylistic choices are used deliberately to entertain an audience and sustain their interest. A range of punctuation is used for effect: ellipsis creates tension (…); commas provide parenthesis, showing grammatical understanding that the ideas contained within the commas provide additional information to the main clause; and semicolons add further information. Direct speech is now punctuated (' ') and separated, so the child distinguishes between represented speech and continuous prose. Question marks and exclamation marks add prosodic effects, illustrating the writer's desire to craft an interesting story. Although complex sentences were used when the child was 8, here the same child uses simple sentences for dramatic effect. More sophisticated adverbs ('suddenly') make cohesive links or change direction in the narrative. Another significant development is the use of paragraphs to structure the narrative, again highlighting greater control of discourse structure and graphological understanding of the right layout of a text. Superlatives ('deepest', 'darkest') and other descriptive adjectives set the scene, with elision used to create a casual register.

As children grow older they also develop skills in checking, editing and correcting their work. If writing is considered a process, this might be separated into thinking and reflecting about their ideas, planning and composing how best to convey them, then writing down, revising and editing them. You can see in children's writing from different stages how the latter skills begin to appear.

Finally, we need to consider the role of the teacher in giving feedback to the children. Remember, teachers are working within the National Literacy Strategy and have guidelines and targets for children's achievement at each Key Stage. Here are some examples of the written feedback given to children.

Text A

1) *What a super description Imogen! Well done for using the present tense. I think I want to go!*

Text B

2) *Good work Jack!* ☺
   Your story was interesting and includes details!
   Paragraphs ✓
   Detail ✓
   Logical order ✓
   What do you think you could have described more? The caravan?

Further reading

Knowing what primary teachers have to teach and assess in young children's literacy development may be helpful in exploring writing produced by children in schools. There are some useful publications and research papers available from the Department for Education that describe learning methods and achievement descriptors.

Go to https://www.gov.uk/government/publications and select Department of Education in the drop-down menu for more information.

Classroom activity 21

Look at the examples of teacher feedback and consider the following questions.

■ How do they support the children's learning?

■ What devices do they use to give positive feedback?

■ How do they give advice to improve?

■ What theories from spoken acquisition could you apply relevantly to children's writing development? Revisit the summaries at the end of the Developing speech topic.

If you prefer to take a more structured approach, then follow these steps.

1. Find at least one linguistic feature used supportively by the teacher for each piece of written feedback.

2. Make sure that you use linguistic terminology, e.g. exclamatory.

3. Analyse these by applying Skinner's ideas about positive and negative reinforcement.

4. Evaluate by explaining why teachers give all feedback positively and how they achieve this.

Examination preparation and practice

Assessment

As part of the $2\frac{1}{2}$ hour examination you will spend half of the time allowed on Section A Language acquisition and half the time allowed on Section B Language change. You need to answer one question from each section.

You will have the choice of two questions for Section A Language acquisition. There can be some mix/matching between the topics, for example a spoken transcript accompanied by written texts, so make sure you revise all topics. All questions are data-based, meaning that you will have to analyse transcripts of real interactions or facsimiles of written material produced for, or by, children.

Assessment objectives

AO1: Select and apply a range of linguistic methods, to communicate relevant knowledge using appropriate terminology and coherent, accurate written expression (7.5%).

AO1 is worth up to 24 marks. Aim to be systematic in your approach to the data in front of you. Read the question carefully, note the main parts of it and annotate the exam paper before you start writing. Focus particularly on identifying relevant linguistic features, using the linguistic methods you are familiar with from your English Language study (grammar, phonology, etc.). Make sure you write clearly and accurately, as this shows that you are able to use English language yourself effectively.

AO2: Demonstrate critical understanding of a range of concepts and issues relating to the construction and analysis of meanings in spoken and written language, using knowledge of linguistic approaches (5%).

This is worth 16 marks. It is testing what you know about the theories and concepts you have studied in English Language. Try to be selective in your choice of theories and theorists to discuss. Choose examples that are relevant to the data in front of you. Don't forget that using your own observations of younger family members' language use, or your Unit 4 child language investigation findings, might be just as pertinent to the data as recognised theorists.

AO3: Analyse and evaluate the influence of contextual factors on the production and reception of spoken and written language, showing knowledge of the key constituents of language (2.5%).

This is worth 8 marks. Read both the question and the data carefully, noting down the significant features of context you can see. Such information could include that the setting of the children's conversations was a home context, or that the written texts were produced in school. Look also for who the participants are and their relationship to each other. Context on its own is not enough to discuss. Try to link the contextual points to your interpretation of features within the data. So consider how the context affects the language used and don't make a discussion of context separate from your analysis of the data.

■ Practising for the exam

In this section you have the opportunity to practise some of the types of questions that you could see in the Unit 3 examination. Practising small tasks, as you have done throughout the topics, was important to ensure your understanding of all the different linguistic areas and methods you can use in your analysis. However, practising extended writing tasks is the most useful thing you can do, as it tests your ability to look at data in a detailed manner, and assesses your ability to apply what you know about language acquisition.

Write your answers to the questions below, keeping the assessment objectives and mark scheme in mind. Check your answers against the sample responses that follow and read the comments, matching these to the mark scheme extracts provided. Add these to your own ideas to see what a comprehensive answer for each question could have contained. Evaluate your own answers to identify what you could have done differently.

You have one spoken acquisition question and one literacy-style question to practise.

Fig. 21 *A thorough knowledge of the topic area will be the biggest help to you in the exam*

Preparing wisely

Knowing the topic area thoroughly will be the biggest help to you, giving you confidence when you face previously unseen data. You know what revision methods work best for you but remember the assessment objectives, and their weightings, when you are revising and, in the examination, when you are constructing your answer:

Transcription conventions are given on page v.

↖ Practice question: spoken

Q1)   **Texts A** and **B** are transcripts of a child, Tom, aged 2 years and 7 months, talking with his parents. **Text A** is a transcript of the conversation which occurred as he helped mend bikes with his mother and father. **Text B** is a transcript of a conversation while he did a jigsaw with his mother.

Referring in detail to the transcripts, and to relevant ideas from language study, explore the language used by Tom and his mother.

You may wish to comment on **some** of the following: the initiation and development of topics; the lexical and grammatical choices made; interactions with caregivers.

AQA January 2005

Text A

	[Tom is sitting on his bike outside in the garden]	
Tom:	oh please	
Mother:	so what are you doing Tom	
Tom:	I sitting on the bike (.) it make noises	
Mother:	it makes noises	5
Tom:	yeah	
Mother:	what sort of noises	
Tom:	the bike (.) the dad bike	
Mother:	dad's bike	
Tom:	yeah (.) the dad (.) dad's bike (.) dad's bike mum (.) dad's bike	10

Mother:	you're not on dad's bike (.) you're on your bike	
Tom:	I am on dad's bike but I not on dad's bike	
	[Tom notices tape recorder]	
Mother:	don't touch (.) don't touch	
Tom:	no (.) can I put it on	15
Mother:	in a minute	
Tom:	please	
Mother:	please (.) where are you gonna go are you going for a ride	
Tom:	*[giggles]*	
Mother:	you	20
	[Tom moves over to father's bike and sticks screwdriver down the handlebar]	
Tom:	me (.) I need to fix dad's bike OK	
Mother:	you need to fix dad's bike	
Tom:	I need to fix dad's bike (.) go (.) on (.) oh (.) I need to fix dad's bike again	25
Father:	my bike	
Tom:	yeah	
Father:	really	
Tom:	an	30
Mother:	oops	
Tom:	I just get the bits out OK	

J.A. Darby

Data response exercise 1

First, read the student's answers to Text A and discuss the following.

1 Does this answer address all three assessment objectives?

2 Does it address the AOs with the right weighting?

3 Is the response systematic in its approach? (This could be by either exploring language methods together, or by having themed paragraphs based around a specific topic.)

4 Does it develop all of the points it makes?

5 How could you improve it?

Then gather together your feedback from the questions and rewrite sections of the essay.

The final stage is to check your own response.

■ Have you used terminology accurately and precisely (AO1)?

■ Have you referred to theories (AO2), linked to the data and developed the discussion of what these suggest about CLA?

■ Have you made connections to contextual factors, where relevant (AO3)?

Highlight the AOs in different colours. This will show you if you have given the right amount to each AO and you will see if you have not made links between the AOs. Write targets for yourself for your next exam practice based on your self-reflection.

Student answer

Tom appears to be in the telegraphic stage as he can create a complete sentence consisting of a subject, verb and complement 'it make noises', although he hasn't acquired the third person singular inflection.

The mother uses an interrogative, 'so what are you doing Tom?' to begin the conversation and Tom has learned that in conversation if you are asked a question it is polite to answer and he can take his turn in an adjacency pair. Tom's mother is using child-directed speech (CDS) as interrogatives are a feature of this and CDS is often used by parents to aid their child in their language acquisition. The mother begins the conversation with a question, illustrating that she has the power in the conversation.

Tom's mother attempts to correct Tom's grammar, 'dad's bike', which provides support for Piaget's cognitive theory as Tom needs to understand possession. By the end of the transcript, however, Tom does understand this and has grasped the concept of dad's bike.

As he is in the telegraphic stage, Tom has acquired some use of auxiliary verbs and can use these to construct interrogatives, 'can I put it on?'. However, when constructing an utterance in the progressive aspect he doesn't use the auxiliary verb 'am', but says 'I sitting'. This virtuous error shows that although Tom is at Stage 4 in his auxiliary verb usage he is still struggling with the progressive, which is often acquired later in the telegraphic stage.

Tom knows what to do with a screwdriver '[*sticks screwdriver down the handlebar*]', which suggests he has used one before. This is a stereotypical game which fathers play with their sons. There is a semantic field of DIY which reflects the male gender.

Tom uses tag questions, 'I just get the bits out OK?' in his speech. This is typically a feature of female speech, suggesting he is imitating his mother's speech, which supports Skinner's behaviourist view that children learn through imitation.

Response starts with focus on the data, selecting an appropriate linguistic method of analysis (grammar) and using relevant and precise terminology (AO1).

Here the grammatical exploration of the data is continued in a systematic manner, along with development into discourse analysis.

AO1 is linked to ideas about language development (AO2) with some development of points.

Again clear connections are being made between the data and concepts surrounding language development, showing evident AO1 and AO2 strengths.

References to theory are implicit and bedded into the detailed analysis.

References to gender stereotypes and theories highlights awareness of the synoptic nature of the question; these are linked to theories showing that the student has begun to take a more conceptual view of linguistic approaches.

Text B

Mother:	where do they go	
Tom:	it goes (2.0) here	
Mother:	pop it in (.) fantastic (.)	
Tom:	ha (.) ha [*laughs*] I put (.) I put (2.0)	
Mother:	what animal's that	5
Tom:	[*looking at the logo on mother's coffee cup*] is these drawing Cartoon Network cup of tea mum	
Mother:	um (.) no (.) it's a moving shadow mug (.) it looks like the Cartoon Network logo (.) but it's actually something else	
Tom:	it is [i:s]	10
Mother:	OK (1.0) and another piece	
Tom:	is (.) is dat your talker	
Mother:	my talker? yeah (.) that's a tape recorder	
Tom:	hello	
Mother:	hello (.) I'm recording you	15
	[*Tom laughs*]	
Mother:	you stood on my fingers (.) [*Tom pushes the piece in the puzzle quite forcefully*] well done (.) can you find the other bit	

Tom:	I (.) I killed it (.) I (.) killed the sh (.) sheep (.) mum (.) yeah	20
Mother:	did you? what you squashed it	
Tom:	yeah (.) I squashed it	
Mother:	poor little sheep (.) oh (.) oh (.) oh	
Tom:	did I kill [ki:l] you	25
Mother:	um (.) did you kill me	
Tom:	I didn't	
Mother:	how many chickens are there	
Tom:	(2.0) there's many chickens (.) one (.) two (.) three (.) four (.) one (.) two (.) three (.) four (.) five (.) six (.) seven (.) eight (.) nine (2.0)	30
Mother:	hmm (.) shall I count them now	
Tom:	yeah	
Mother:	one (.) two (.) three (.) four (.) five	

J.A. Darby

Student answer

Another linguistic method (phonology) is applied relevantly to the data, and linked to an apt example.

In Text B Tom uses substitution, 'is dat your talker'. As Tom is in the telegraphic stage it is surprising to find substitution in his speech as it typically occurs in early phonological development. This shows that language acquisition is an ongoing process. However, this utterance does reveal that Tom is using language to explore his environment, which fulfils Halliday's heuristic function of the pragmatics of language.

Here an open-minded and critical appreciation of the data is demonstrated with the clustered observations on typical stages of child development and the developed point about the function of language (AO2).

Tom's mother is using CDS in this extract also, as when Tom asks if it's a 'talker' she corrects his lexical choice calling it a 'tape recorder'. Like many parents she corrects his lexical choices rather than errors in grammar, as previously Tom made a virtuous error using the plural rather than the singular 'is these drawing'. The fact that children learn the correct grammatical rules without being corrected indicates that language is innate within us, as Chomsky believed.

An exploration of contextual factors (AO3) has been integrated here in the discussion of the data, showing awareness of how contextual influences can be combined with and support the interpretation of the data.

In this text the jigsaw is being used as a tool for learning. Many children's toys have an educational purpose and in this case the purpose is counting, 'there's many chickens one two three four five'. Tom's mother directs the educational part of the conversation asking 'how many chickens are there?' After her interrogative there is an extended pause until Tom realises that it's his turn to speak. Extended pauses are a feature of CDS as parents teach their children the pragmatics of conversation and turn-taking.

As Tom is in the telegraphic stage he has learned the '–ed' rule to create the past tense, 'I killed the sh (.) sheep (.) mum (.) yeah'. He is able to create a grammatically accurate correct sentence using a subject, verb and object.

Overall comments

The student takes a very systematic approach to the data and shows accurate linguistic knowledge, especially when discussing grammar (AO1). A range of theoretical perspectives are discussed (AO2) and challenged in the response to the data. Above all the examples chosen are judicious and discussed thoroughly (AO2). More could have been made perhaps of the different roles taken by each parent (seen later in the data for Text A) but a perceptive and thoughtful engagement with the data is in evidence throughout. The comments are completely led by the data in front of the student and for AO2 (15–16) all the references to theories are relevant, including some synopticity with the discussion of gender. Context (AO3) is integrated insightfully into the essay, especially with the comments on how toys are used, the roles taken by parents encouraging their children's speech and the understanding of the key developmental stages. Overall, this is an excellent response.

◤ Practice: reading

Q2) **Text C** is a transcript of George, aged just 7 years, reading his school reading book to his mother. **Text D** shows the pages that George is reading.

By reference to the texts and to ideas from language study, explore how George is being helped in his reading development.

AQA specimen paper

Text C

George:	in (2.0) the street it was (.) [lə] loaded	
Mother:	that's it	
George:	with (2.0)	
Mother:	sound it out	
George:	[sə] (.) [æ] (.) [nə]	5
Mother:	[də]	
George:	sandbags	
Mother:	well done	
George:	people were taking the s (.) sanbags	
Mother:	sand	10
George:	sand	
Mother:	bags	
George:	bags	
Mother:	good boy	
George:	to their house	15
Mother:	[e] [z] (2.0) watch the endings (3.0)	
George:	we never	
Mother:	nooo	
George:	no we need	
Mother:	that's it	20
George:	all to help said Mum (.)	
Mother:	what's happening (.) what do you think's happening (2.0)	
George:	look at that flood (.) you'll have to get loads there and one there (.) and one there and one there	
Mother:	what are they doing with the sandbags	25
George:	pile them up (.) so it can't get in (.) but it can get up to here but it isn't here (.) but he's letting them get inside is he	

Mother:	no
George:	Biff and Chip (.) helped to carry (.) the sandbags (.) they 30 were very heavy (.) Dad put them in (.) front of the doors (.) I just hope the water doesn't come up (.) this (2.0) far said Dad
Mother:	well done
George:	(3.0) Mum looked upstairs 35
Mother:	no (.) it looks like upstairs doesn't it (.) but look at the word
George:	up [sə] (.) [et] (.) upset
Mother:	that's it
George:	the floods made 40
Mother:	may
George:	may get worse she said so there's (2.) only one thing to do (.) she picked up a chair (.) we'll have to take things upstairs said Mum (4) now where they going

Text D

When the children got home, they saw a lorry in the street. It was loaded with sandbags. People were taking the sandbags to their houses.
"We need you all to help," said Mum.

Biff and Chip helped to carry the sandbags. They were very heavy. Dad put them in front of the doors.
"I just hope the water doesn't come up this far," said Dad.

Mum looked upset.
"The floods may get worse," she said. "So there's only one thing to do."
She picked up a chair.
"We'll have to take things upstairs," said Mum.

Rod Hunt and *Alex Brychta*, Flood!, *2003*

Student answer

Response is immediately grounded in the contextual factors of teaching methods (AO3) and references to concepts and issues from language development study (AO2).

Perceptive and critically aware comments show an engagement with the topic of reading development.

George is being helped to learn reading by an array of techniques, including the mother's use of feedback, correction and positive reinforcement. There is also evidence of the synthetic phonics teaching method which has been used to teach the child. There has been much recent debate regarding the correct methods to teach young children to read. This is mainly due to a strong emphasis on synthetic phonics and there is evidence supporting this style of teaching showing children's reading ability to be far greater than children taught reading by other methods.

Within the text it appears the child uses phonics. This method is also taught to George by his mother who, when he is unsure of a word, tells him to 'sound it out', which George does based on the individual phonemes of the word 'sandbag': [sə] (.) [æ] (.) [nə]. George omits the phoneme [də] which is corrected by his mother. This error, which is clearly virtuous as it will later aid his learning, occurs later in the text in which he reads 'sanbags'. With his mother's emphasis (through her intonation) on 'sand', George corrects his error. However, it is arguable that through use of the 'look and say' method this mistake may not have been made as he would have seen the letter 'd'.

Another virtuous error occurs in line 17 in which George omits the plural for 'houses' and merely says 'house'. This is corrected by the mother saying 'watch the endings'. This error could have been caused by two things, either that George is trying to read on from one line to the next too quickly and therefore fails to notice the plural, or that George is not yet fully aware how words are plural and needs to learn the rule. The speed he is reading seems to be the most likely explanation as he makes a further three errors in a similar way. These include 'never' rather than 'need', 'upstairs' rather than 'upset' and 'made' rather than 'may'. These errors are made by George seeing the first two letters of the word and pronouncing words he knows which begin with the same letters and may fit syntactically into the sentence. This basis for predicting words is shown by his mother's statement 'it looks like upstairs, doesn't it'. However, this may also be a reference to the 'look and say' method in which George has registered that the word resembles 'upstairs'. George's error with 'upstairs' may also suggest that George is reading for reading's sake rather than for actual meaning.

The mother's role in the process is vital in aiding her child's development. This is not just in the form of correcting any mistakes, but in the form of positive and negative reinforcement, a behaviourist approach proposed by Skinner. George's mother uses positive reinforcement in abundance through the use of praise words, 'well done' and 'good boy'. Such statements encourage George to keep reading and to do so using the techniques he is already employing. Even corrections are done in a friendly and positive way, shown by the elongated vowel cluster in 'nooo'; it is likely her intonation would rise at this cluster making the reinforcement friendly whilst simultaneously aiding development. Any corrections are followed with more positive reinforcement, 'that's it', to avoid discouraging him. The mother also invites George to interact with the book by the use of interrogatives 'what do you think's happening'. This enables her to check that George understands the plot and what he has just read.

The book George is reading also aids his development. Such books contain pictures for visual input into the plot. An action in a picture can help a child decode the text underneath and this might be why George said 'upstairs' rather than 'upset'. The language of such texts also aids reading development. The sentences are short and simple, often only containing one clause. Speech is minimal so that the child can keep track of who is speaking and at what point. The lexis is often monosyllabic, making phonetic decoding easier. Full stops are used to teach children when to pause. This is effective in George's reading but is sometimes ignored, showing he still needs to learn the function of punctuation.

General observations about phonics are now firmly rooted in examples from the data, linking AO1 and AO2 effectively.

Again AO2 strengths are evident, with the issues around children's reading development linked to salient examples from the data.

Examples from the data are clustered together from the data, demonstrating close reading and annotation before writing the response; this helps to meet the 'systematic and evaluative' aspect of AO1.

Coverage of the data is full, looking at the language of the mother and the child, as well as the book itself.

The range of linguistic methods (AO1) applied to the data is impressive here with lexical choices linked to discourse features and phonology.

Here sensible observations are made evaluating the influence of context on George's language choices (AO3).

■ Further reading

Crystal, D. *Listen To Your Child*, Penguin, 1982

Crystal, D. *The Cambridge Encyclopaedia of the English Language*, CUP, 1995

Gee, J.P. *Language, Literacy and Learning*, Routledge, 2004

Gillen, J. *The Language of Children*, Routledge, 2003

Heath, S. *Ways with Words: Language, Life and Work in Communities and Classroom*, CUP, 1983

Myszor, F. *Language Acquisition*, Hodder Education, 1999

O'Grady, W. *How Children Learn Language*, CUP, 2005

Peccei, J.S. *Child Language: A Resource Book for Students*, Routledge, 2005

Perera, C. *Children's Reading and Writing*, Blackwell, 1984

Pinker, S. *Words and Rules*, Basic Books, 1999

Overall comments

This is a fluent answer with a clear focus on the question. It meets AO1 criteria at a high level because of the controlled and accurate expression. Evidence of secure linguistic knowledge is demonstrated in the terminology used. The approach to the data is systematic, and there is evidence of a linguistic methodology applied. Critical understanding (AO2) is apparent in the discussion of the different reading methods. Exploration of the concepts and issues surrounding teaching methods is developed and perceptive; examples provided from the data show that this student has not only engaged with the debates but can apply them successfully to unseen texts. There is some consideration of context (AO3) integrated into the essay, although further consideration of context could have included the influence of home literacy practices. Contextual awareness is implicit in the discussion of attitudes to the phonics debate but more explicit links need to be made to specific language features in the data.

■ Data response exercise 2

The comments identify some criticisms of the student answer. These are that context (AO3) could have been included more. (Although context is worth the fewest marks, it is still important to explore a range of factors and it helps you to interpret and evaluate the data.) You might also take the final paragraph of the answer and rework this to include examples of all the features they discuss to ensure that you have a PEA approach (point, evidence, analysis).

Identify where this could have been included in the student response and/or revisit the data to see what you would have said about the situational context (setting, roles, relationships and home literacy) and how you could link this to the language used by George and his mother.

Once you have written your answer focusing on context, review your success with another student to see if:

■ a range of contextual factors were discussed

■ contextual factors were linked to language features and not discussed generally

■ all linguistic features contained exemplification and textual support.

Feed back and note down for the future what you have learned and how this will help you next time.

B Language change

Introduction

Key terms

Standardisation: making all variations of language conform to the standard language.

Mixed-mode: features of printed text combined with features expected in conversation.

Diachronic change: refers to the study of historical language change occuring over a span of time.

Synchronic change: refers to an approach that studies language at a theoretical point in time without considering the historical context.

Section B of Unit 3 focuses your language study on the historical and contemporary changes that have taken place in the English language from 1700 to the present day (Late Modern English). It covers two main areas:

■ the main linguistic changes occurring since 1700 and some contextual influences on these

■ the **standardisation** of English, the reasons for this and various attitudes to the changes in English usage.

So, what is language change and why is it important to study it? If you have already studied acquisition, you have learned about the beginnings of spoken language in children – acquiring lexical and grammatical skills, along with the social pragmatics of communication. Focusing on language change will demonstrate how English has been shaped over time, but will also show that a language doesn't simply stand still. English, as a rich mixture of different language influences, fascinates linguists who both chart its development and discuss its contemporary use, theorising about its spoken and written forms. You won't be tested on a detailed historical knowledge, but an awareness of some of the key factors and attitudes affecting speakers' and writers' language choices in a given period of history is important to interpreting texts perceptively.

What debates surround language change? Well, you might have been corrected for 'improper' use of spoken language, and no doubt your written literacy has been assessed and corrected throughout your schooling. The reason for this lies in the prescriptive attitudes to language use that emerged as the English language was standardised. Society's views of English have always been as important in shaping English as the linguists who note the changes and consider their impact. These sometimes conflict because linguists seek to describe, rather than prescribe, language use; society is often more judgemental than the 'experts' and sees these changes as evidence of declining standards. In your lifetime, you have probably been part of a very significant change in English. Text messaging and instant messaging have affected writing styles, spelling and punctuation, greatly influenced by the spoken word. The boundaries between speech and writing seem to be blurring as **mixed-mode** styles become popular and the ways we use language transform.

Don't forget that Language change is a synoptic topic, so exploring again the social contexts of AS (power, gender and technology) relevant to texts from 1700, as well as investigating different text varieties and applying concepts of language study (such as register) are all still important. But added at A2 is a focus on major changes to English in the linguistic areas you have already studied, and the learning of new terminology to describe your knowledge.

Two linguistic approaches are a good starting point for language change. These are the **diachronic** approach – the study of the history and evolution of a language – and the **synchronic** approach – the study of language at a particular point in time.

Ferdinand de Saussure, a French linguist and semiologist of the early 20th century, became interested in synchronic change and looking at language in general, rather than his earlier preoccupation with diachronic change and looking at languages in history. He saw change occurring because of the way that language is continually being rearranged and reinterpreted by people. Taking the semiotic approach to linguistics, he saw language as a structured series of signs with meanings: one side of the sign he called the signifier, and the meanings and mental associations drawn from it the signified.

For example, the signifier 'cat' is made up from three verbal signifiers /c/, /a/, /t/. The signified are all the associations with the signifier. So for 'cat' these might be as follows:

Signifier	Signified
	furry, purring, independent, cunning, hunter, playful, etc.

All words have signifiers, or connotations. Moving from a tangible creature such as a cat, what associations would you have for the adjective 'wicked'? In 21st-century youth sociolect this might connote that something is really cool, good, excellent. But to an 18th-century audience they would have thought evil, bad, sinful, lacking in morals, mean, nasty and so on.

Thinking points

1   What can studying contemporary language tell us about how people's attitudes have changed, for example in using taboo language or dropping sounds from the ends of words as in 'goin''?

2   Do you think words can change their signified aspects and alter their meanings? For example what slang words have changed their meanings apart from 'wicked'?

Within Unit 3 you have the opportunity to consider both approaches. Your attention is concentrated on texts from the Late Modern English period, which most agree is a period of more settled forms of English – for reasons you will encounter later. However, it is impossible to look at texts from the 18th century without feeling that the language used, the formality and the writers' styles differ greatly from our own. Even looking at early 20th-century writing, or hearing old sound recordings, shows a society with distinctive attitudes towards what it was to be polite, how to speak about different social groups and, to our ears, curious lexical choices.

Analysing and examining similar types of texts from across 300 years of the Late Modern English period (as in the recipes on pages 86–87) will help you look at diachronic change; seeing how English has changed lexically, grammatically and graphologically should encourage an interest in discovering the reasons for the change.

Looking at different contemporary texts and data will reveal how language is used by English speakers and writers synchronically in a variety of ways.

Fig. 1 *Language is constantly being rearranged and reinterpreted by the people who use it*

Changes in context, lexis and semantics

In this topic you will:

- discover how the English language has changed in key linguistic areas

- learn new terms to describe lexical and semantic change

- apply new terminology for linguistic features to Late Modern English texts

- link some of the causes of change to features in texts

- consider the impact of different forces on English and reasons for language change.

Key terms

Lexicon: the vocabulary of a language.

Starter activity

To start you thinking about language change, try some of the following tasks introducing you to the history of English, key contextual factors and changing language features over time.

- Go to BBC Ages of English Timeline www.bbc.co.uk/history/british/launch_tl_ages_english.shtml. Feed back three interesting facts that you learned.

- Watch 'The History of English in 10 Minutes' available in 10 brief parts, available at www.youtube.com/. Make brief notes as you watch. Discuss key facts that you can remember for each time period.

- Ask older family members for slang or colloquial words that they used when they were younger. You could give them categories such as relationships, fashion and music to help them. Share these to see if similar or different words are used depending on the age of family members.

Understanding language change

As you study the individual linguistic areas of language change, you might reflect on some of the wider issues of why English, or any language, changes. This topic introduces concepts and terms that you may have touched on in AS, for example, when you looked at how words have been introduced to English – or changed their meaning – because of technology. Although understanding the **lexicon** is important, so too is an understanding of changes to word order, the written presentation of letters and texts and the structuring and ordering of ideas. The sounds of English have also altered and you can engage with some debates surrounding these, too.

You should, as ever, apply a range of linguistic methods to analysing texts. Key areas of change are in the:

- English lexicon as words enter and leave the language or change meanings

- syntax between earlier and later forms of English

- phonology of spoken English and its representation in written texts

- graphology (including typography and orthography): how texts are arranged on a page, font styles and their punctuation and spelling

- discourse structure and the organisation of texts.

As you go through the linguistic areas, don't lose sight of what you should be aiming for with all the texts you encounter; bring your understanding of the separate ideas about lexical, grammatical, phonological and graphological change together effectively and systematically along with an understanding of changing audiences, writers' intentions and the conventions of the genre they are working in.

Changing contexts, changing words and meanings

Throughout your English Language study you are encouraged to reflect on the social contexts of language use and now you have the opportunity to expand this to include historical perspectives. Simply identifying the linguistic features of texts is never enough; an overview of the effect of key factors on language change will increase your linguistic understanding as you can explain features, for example of lexis and grammar, by linking them to how people used them at a particular time.

Why does any language change over time? Of course, it's all to do with people as they:

- invent things and need words to describe them
- change attitudes because of changes in society, or are influenced by others such as politicians or the media
- travel to, move to, trade with or invade other countries.

Research point

Linguists and historians have divided English into key dates and periods as a way to chart the main developments. Changes happened gradually and modern English has evolved over centuries. These divisions suggest that significant changes occurred between certain dates, enough to justify a change of name. Some disagree over the exact transition dates, especially from Middle English to Early Modern English.

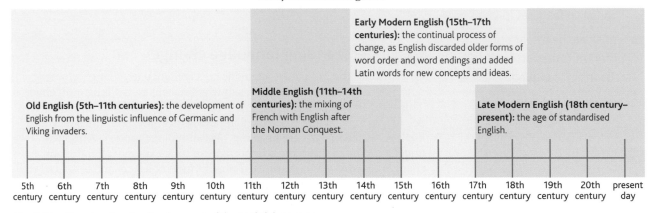

Early Modern English (15th–17th centuries): the continual process of change, as English discarded older forms of word order and word endings and added Latin words for new concepts and ideas.

Middle English (11th–14th centuries): the mixing of French with English after the Norman Conquest.

Old English (5th–11th centuries): the development of English from the linguistic influence of Germanic and Viking invaders.

Late Modern English (18th century–present): the age of standardised English.

5th century · 6th century · 7th century · 8th century · 9th century · 10th century · 11th century · 12th century · 13th century · 14th century · 15th century · 16th century · 17th century · 18th century · 19th century · 20th century · present day

Fig. 2 *Timeline showing the development of the English language*

Thinking points

Using the brief outline of English shown in Figure 2, think about the influences that can make a language change.

Migration, travel, the British Empire and globalisation

People have always moved to different parts of the world, taking their language and culture with them. Some of an introduced language is absorbed into the local one or, in the case of the British Empire, the introduced language (in this case English) can become dominant in the colonised countries – especially as the language of power and government. Countries such as India still use English as the language of administration.

English has also borrowed extensively lexically to accommodate new foods and cultural experiences. We borrowed words like 'curry' and 'tea' for new foods and drink, making our own versions of these words. Travel has meant that we observe other languages and we order 'tapas' when in Spain, a 'cappuccino' or 'espresso' in Italy and a 'pain au chocolat' in France.

Globalisation in the latter part of the 20th century further developed English into a world language, not least because of the impact of technology and American English. Shopping, for example, has become a global business, with designer names and clothing brands from all countries recognisable around the world; think about English global brands like Marks and Spencer and how they are synonymous with ideas about Englishness.

Wars or invasions

The Norman Conquest and the Germanic tribes who invaded over a thousand years ago had a strong impact on how English developed – grammatically, phonologically and lexically. We now have a lexically rich language containing many synonyms because of the people who invaded; using Old English we can 'ask', from the French influences post-1066, we can 'question'. And, although the UK hasn't been invaded for a long time, the language of warfare has affected the words we use. We wouldn't have words like 'collateral damage', 'surgical strikes' and talk of an enemy being 'neutralised' without the modern lexicon of war.

Fig. 3 *The language of warfare has affected the words we use*

The language of science and technology

In the 18th and 19th centuries there were many scientific advances and so neologisms were needed to name the latest of these. Because of the academic prestige of Latin and Greek, many of the new words were formed using these languages, for example 'biology', 'chloroform', 'centigrade' and 'claustrophobia'.

Sometimes we recycle words and use words with higher status – such as Latin or Greek words – for scientific and medical inventions: BSE (Bovine Spongiform Encephalopathy) sounds so much more serious than its colloquial counterpart used by the media ('mad cow disease').

Trade, working practices and new inventions

Throughout history people's occupations and technological developments have changed English. New words are needed to name inventions and to describe what you can do with them. 'Dishwasher' seems a logical choice for the object it names, as does the Macintosh coat for the man who invented it. But what about 'internet'? This seems more metaphorical, showing that names arise in different ways. Even our surnames have links to occupations and past working practices (think of Butcher, Baker, Cooper and Fletcher).

Social, ideological and cultural changes

Changes in attitudes often result in language alterations. When looking at older texts you can see that people held different views about certain social groups. As views have changed about the acceptability of some language use, so English lexis has accommodated them. We discriminate less against certain groups within society in our language use and are **politically correct** when talking about ethnicity, gender or sexuality.

On a less serious note, interests in fashion and culture have been consistent and, as tastes change, so does language. We don't wear 'winklepickers' or 'pantaloons' any more, but might wear 'dolly shoes' and 'thongs'. Next year, we'll need new words! But it's not just about lexis: cultural change also affects the way we sound, the registers we use and our grammatical choices.

The media

The growth of the media and the ways they reach us – print, television, internet, mobile phones – has influenced language. Arguably, a more casual, colloquial and speech-like register has evolved as media styles have become less formal.

Key terms

Political correctness: words or phrases used to replace those that are deemed offensive.

Fig. 4 *Some new words are created by the media to describe contemporary society, for example, WAG*

■ **Further reading**

David Crystal's *The Cambridge Encyclopedia of The English Language* offers more detail about language change, the history of English and its current status and use. Read Part II to support this section as it focuses on lexical and semantic change.

Crystal, D. *The Cambridge Encyclopedia of The English Language*, CUP, 1995

New lexis is often introduced via the media to describe contemporary society, and perhaps persuading us to a point of view. Think of the acronym 'WAG' (used for the wives and girlfriends of footballers) and headlines such as the colloquial 'Gotcha' (used to display patriotic feelings during the Falklands War of the 1980s). This journalese-style language of hyperbole and abbreviation expresses the language of the popular press, but earlier newspapers were also less than reverential to people in society.

However, the modern media are often highly interactive. We can select the channels we watch, when we want to, and blogs allow individuals to report events and opinions from wherever they live. Social networking sites have made personal communication possible between large numbers of people who have never met. 'Facebook' and 'Myspace' are new words created to name these sites and what they do. 'Face' and 'book' as two separate morphemes have been joined together to suggest the idea of an internet book of faces. This is interesting as it changes ideas of what books are (printed texts), linking this with the modern obsession for images rather than words. 'Myspace' puts emphasis on the individual, conveying with the possessive pronoun ('my') the sense of ownership over something that is 'virtual' and abstract when linked to the internet ('space').

Exploring lexical change

So how do we create new words for the English lexicon?

1 We borrow them from other languages, either to fill a gap in our own language or to allow us another word for the same object/idea.
2 We adapt existing words (using morphology) – either a lazy or efficient way to make a new word.
3 We create completely new ones when we don't have anything that will do – probably the least common way.

Neologism describes the creation of a new word or expression, but the term 'coinage' is also often used to describe a completely new word.

Certainly, the early invasions of Anglo-Saxons and Vikings from the 5th century onwards brought new words from Germany and Scandinavia, and the Norman invasion of 1066 brought French words. These words mixed together, along with Latin words from religious sources and educated readers, and English developed into today's language. Our rich lexical history is illustrated by these words.

Table 1 *English synonyms*

Old English/Germanic origin	French/Latin
come	arrive
ask	enquire/request
buy	purchase
motherly/fatherly	maternal/paternal
forbid	refuse/prohibit
pull out	extract

Adapted from http://en.wikipedia.org/wiki/List_of_Germanic_and_Latinate_equivalents

We have many synonyms at our disposal, precisely because of these varied influences, and we can use these in different modes (speech and writing) and contexts (with various audiences) and to create different registers (for example, in legal discourse). In some situations, particular words are more appropriate – perhaps to demonstrate knowledge and understanding. For example, a Latinate word could impress in a university interview, but a more colloquial word would be a better choice when speaking to friends. Using distinctive registers allows you to converge with, or diverge from, your audience as you wish, perhaps to gain either **overt** or **covert prestige**.

◪ 💡 Where do new words come from?

New words can be created in various ways (Table 2).

Table 2 *Ways in which new words can be created*

Term	Definition	Example
Borrowing/ loan word	The introduction of a word from one language to another; these can be anglicised or remain similar to the original in spelling and pronunciation	Anglicised: chocolate (from French, chocolat) Non-anglicised: pundit (from Hindi, meaning a learned person or a source of opinion) now a popular media term for a political commentator or sports expert
Eponym	The name of a person after whom something is named	Sandwich, Braille
Proprietary names	The name given to a product by one organisation becomes the commonly used name for the same product	Tampax, Hoover, Kleenex

Classroom activity 1

In the following passage, borrowings, or loan words, have been underlined.

■ Suggest the countries you think the words have come from. (You can either use your own knowledge, travel experiences or knowledge of other languages to deduce where these might be from or, if you want to match them up more accurately, choose from these options: Spain or South America, the Arctic region, India, Norway, France, Holland, Canada, Greece, North America and Arabic-speaking countries of the Middle East.) What contextual factors (e.g. the rise of the British Empire) caused English to acquire them?

■ Group the words into semantic fields. For example, clothes, food and activities. What does this tell us about words that the English language borrowed rather than created?

Should I wear a <u>poncho</u>, an <u>anorak</u> or my favourite <u>parka</u> when I went out on the <u>ski</u> slope? I packed some clothing and <u>chocolate</u> in my <u>knapsack</u>. My enjoyment of <u>tobogganing</u> was curtailed after I <u>kamikazed</u> into the <u>igloo</u> which was obstructing my path. The <u>anonymous</u> owner was absent but his <u>tattooed</u> neighbour suggested a <u>pow-wow</u>. Fearing he was a <u>cannibal</u> or an <u>assassin</u>, I fled. I <u>trekked</u> back to my hotel and as <u>zero</u> hour approached, I decided some food would cheer me up greatly. What should I choose? If it had been breakfast I would have chosen <u>marmalade</u> and <u>coffee</u>, but it was evening and my mouth watered for <u>sushi</u>, <u>tortilla</u>, <u>moussaka</u> or a <u>shish kebab</u>. Strangely I also fancied a cup of <u>tea</u> and some <u>sherbert</u>. I changed into my <u>dungarees</u> and went to where the <u>barbecue</u> was being held. Next holiday I will go on <u>safari</u> or <u>kayak</u> down a river, or go on a <u>cruise</u>. I thought about lying on a <u>hammock</u> in the sun, although I don't like <u>mosquitoes</u>. After eating I changed into my <u>pyjamas</u> and strummed on my <u>guitar</u>.

Source for the words used: *David Crystal*, The Cambridge Encyclopedia of the English Language, *2003*

Fig. 5 *The English language contains many words borrowed from other languages*

How do you research word origins? *The Oxford English Dictionary* (OED) is one of the foremost and most authoritative sources of English words, and is updated regularly. You may be able to access it free from your local library, or your school or college may have a subscription: www.oed.com. Alternatively, etymological dictionaries provide information about words' origins, allowing you to research spelling, pronunciation, origin and changes in meaning.

Here's an extract for the adjective 'nice' from the OED online. Over the centuries this word has changed from meaning 'foolish, silly' to 'pleasing' and this extract demonstrates a now archaic use of the word. Not only can you see written evidence of the word's usage from Middle to Late Modern English, but also see the changes to English syntax, orthography and spelling.

nice, adj. and adv.

3. a. Precise or particular in matters of reputation or conduct; scrupulous, punctilious. Now rare.

c1387-95 CHAUCER Canterbury Tales Prol. 398 Ful many a draughte of wyn hadde he drawe Fro Burdeuxward whil that the chapman sleep; Of nyce conscience took he no keep. *c1450* (1410) J. WALTON tr. Boethius De Consol. Philos. (Linc. Cathedral 103) 98 Nyce men..Ye seken..To enbelesch youre excellent nature! *a1542* T. WYATT in R. Tottel Songes & Sonettes (1557) f. 48v, He the fole of conscience was so nice: That he no gaine would haue for all his paine. ƚ1573 H. CHEKE tr. F. Negri Freewyl II. iii. 81 He vnaduisedly strooke the young man, and because he is altogether scrupulous and nice, he imagineth that he can not be free from irregularitie. *1693* T. SOUTHERNE Maids Last Prayer IV. i. 35 You shall promise me, for you are so nice in points of Honour. *1703* Clarendon's Hist. Rebellion II. VII. 187 So difficult a thing it is to play an after-Game of Reputation, in that nice and jealous profession. *1709* SWIFT Project Advancem. Relig. 11 Women of tainted Reputations find the same Countenance..with those of the nicest Virtue. *1785* W. COWPER Task III. 85 Men too were nice in honor in those days, And judg'd offenders well. *1826* B. DISRAELI Vivian Grey II. v, I am not very nice myself about these matters. *1843* E. MIALL in Nonconformist 3 227 The Duke of Wellington said..'Men who have nice notions about religion have no business to be soldiers.' *1887* S. BARING-GOULD Red Spider I. xvii. 288, I should get it back again.., and not be too nice about the means. *1938* P. G. WODEHOUSE Code of Woosters xii. 261 Bertram Wooster in his dealings with the opposite sex invariably shows himself a man of the nicest chivalry. *1948* P. G. WODEHOUSE Spring Fever xiii. 127 Obtain possession of it by strong-arm tactics. Up against this dark and subtle butler, we cannot afford to be too nice in our methods.

www.oed.com

Extension activity 1

Using etymological dictionaries you could try the following.

- Look up words from certain semantic fields: for example, food, clothing or music. Find out where these words came from, when they were first used and whether their usage has changed.
- Select one word (for example, nice) to see how it has changed in meaning. Do this once you have studied semantic change (see page 83).

Looking ahead

You can use traditional dictionaries to complete the extension activity or you could search for online dictionaries. Any well-known search engine will produce results, but be careful that these are from credible sources. Checking who has produced the websites will teach you to be a critical researcher, which is important in essays or dissertations that you will write in further education where your assessment depends on the relevance, quality and depth of your research. A credible source is the *Oxford English Dictionary* (see www.oed.com; local libraries often pay for access to this subscription site). Its more advanced searches and sophisticated database will help you to refine your searches and develop valuable research skills.

New words can be created by abbreviating in various ways (Table 3).

Table 3 *Abbreviating words*

Term	Definition	Example
Acronym	A lexicalised word made up from the initial letters of a phrase (sounded as a word)	RADAR
Initialism	A word made from initial letters, each being pronounced	CD
Clipping	A new word produced by shortening an existing one	Edit (from editor)

Acronyms and initialisms often come from medical, military or technological fields where speed in communication can be important, or when creating an inclusive jargon forms a social identity for those in the in-group and excludes others. Look at these examples to demonstrate how abbreviations are formed in these fields:

■ DNA (**D**eoxyribo**n**ucleic **A**cid)
■ BSE (**B**ovine **S**pongiform **E**ncephalopathy)
■ RADAR (**Ra**dio **D**etection **A**nd **R**anging)
■ SWAT (**S**pecial **W**eapons **A**nd **T**actics)
■ LASER (**L**ight **A**mplification by **S**timulated **E**mission of **R**adiation)
■ CD (**C**ompact **D**isk)
■ DOS (**D**isk **O**perating **S**ystem)
■ WWW (**W**orld **W**ide **W**eb)
■ SCUBA (**S**elf-**C**ontained **U**nderwater **B**reathing **A**pparatus).

However, not all acronyms are for serious purposes. A recent example, WAG, was a media coinage, putting footballers' wives and girlfriends into a group. David Crystal sees the popularity of abbreviating words as our liking of 'linguistic economy' and the WAG acronym worked well in tabloid coverage for this reason. Space constraints and technological limitations are other motivations; text-messaging acronyms and initialisms usefully convey messages without wasting characters and reduce words so that complete messages can be seen on screen. Prior to SMS (Short Message Service, or text messaging), personal ads used abbreviations for financial, as well as linguistic, economy – WLTM (would like to meet), GSOH (good sense of humour) and NS (non-smoking) are all recognisable initialisms from 'lonely hearts' columns.

Making new words from old ones and adding to existing words are types of derivational morphological change (Table 4).

Study tip

The ability to analyse examples of lexical and semantic change in the exam data will help you to combine all of the AOs in your responses. Discussing the process of language change is a key concept (AO2) and your exemplification along with its word class is a linguistic feature (AO1). If you can also suggest a contextual reason for its use, for example a change in technology, then this is the third AO combined with your analysis. Also, a methodical approach is important, so group your ideas about lexical or semantic change together in your essay.

Table 4 *Reusing words*

Term	Definition	Example
Affixation – usually in the form of:	The addition of bound morphemes to an existing word	Affixes are sometimes linked to contemporary tastes
Prefixes	The addition of a bound morpheme to the beginning of a root word	Examples of prefixes: mega/uber
Suffixes	The addition of a bound morpheme to the end of a root word	Recent suffixes: (radical)ising
Conversion	A word changes its word class without adding a suffix	Text (noun and verb)
Compound	The combining of separate words to create a new word, sometimes using a hyphen to link them	Size zero Man flu Carbon footprint
Back formation	The removal of an imagined affix from an existing word	Editor became edit
Blend	Two words fusing to make a new one	Smog (smoke + fog)

Affixing and compounding are the most common ways of changing words. Lexical change is often driven by the current context. At the moment, environmental change is a key debate and so needs a host of new words; as well as 'carbon footprint' we have 'carbon offsetting' and 'carbon neutral', showing how collocations form around buzzwords like 'carbon'. Celebrity culture has also produced lexical change: the compound 'size zero' identifies the ultimate body shape and the blend 'celebutantes' describes aspiring young celebrity 'wannabes' encouraged by reality TV shows.

Blackadder, the 1980s television comedy, set one of its episodes in the 1700s, satirising Dr Samuel Johnson's *Dictionary of the English Language* by using lexical change to generate humour. In this scene Blackadder mocks Dr Johnson's achievement and the possibility of recording every word in the English lexicon. How do the writers use affixing to create the made-up words?

■ **Link**

You will encounter Dr Johnson's impact on English language standardisation in the topic Why does language change? (see page 116).

Fig. 6 *'Oh, I'm sorry, sir. I'm anaspeptic, phrasmotic, even compunctious to have caused you such periconbobulations.'*

Johnson:	Here it is, sire. (*He produces a sheaf of manuscript*) A very cornerstone of English scholarship. This book contains every word in our beloved language.
Blackadder:	Every single one, sir?
Johnson:	Every single one, sir.
Blackadder:	In that case, sir, I hope you will not object if I also offer the Doctor my most enthusiastic contrafibularatories.
Johnson:	What, sir?
Blackadder:	Contrafibularatories, sir. It is a common word down our way.

Johnson takes a pencil from behind his ear. He is furious.

Johnson:	Damn!

He starts writing in the dictionary.

Blackadder:	Oh, I'm sorry, sir. I'm anaspeptic, phrasmotic, even compunctious to have caused you such periconbobulations.

R. Curtis, B. Elton, J. Lloyd and ***R. Atkinson***, Blackadder: The Whole Damn Dynasty, *1998*

Blackadder parodies the coining of new words to antagonise Dr Johnson. Mainly adjectives ('anaspeptic', 'phrasmotic', 'compunctious'), they use recognisable affixes – as do the nouns ('contrafibularatories', 'periconbobulations'). Also being mocked might be the 18th-century desire to use Latin and Greek affixes ('contra-', '-otic') to show intellectual status and an elevated register.

Although humorous, this extract demonstrates some of the ways words enter English. But, of course, as words enter English, so other words stop being used and become archaic or **obsolete**. Later examples from Dr Johnson's famous dictionary show how fashionable and topical words from one period don't always stand the test of time. Table 5 lists some previously popular colloquial/slang expressions for a foolish person from the 19th and 20th centuries. How many are familiar to you? Would you use them today?

■ Key terms

Obsolete: no longer having any use.

Table 5 *Change in colloquialisms*

Era of first usage	Word	Origin
1850s/1860s	thick	Schoolchildren's slang
1870s/1880s	twerp	Possibly originated from a surname
	chump	Derived from its earlier meaning – a lump of wood
1900s/1920s	Dumb Dora	Combining a girl's name with an alliterative collocation
	nitwit	An ironically rhymed link between a 'nit' (the egg of a louse) and 'wit'

1930s/1940s	bird-brain	Alliterative compound linking a bird and intelligence
	twit	Derived from the verb meaning 'to taunt'
	clot	Earlier meaning 'lump'
1950s/1960s	barmpot	Northern English dialect (a pot storing yeast)
	pea-brain	Back-formation from pea-brained (metaphorical connections)
	Herbert/Wally/Charlie	Using male names to symbolise connotations of stupidity

Blends, as another way of making new words, retain some of the meanings of the original words and so link two meanings to create a neologism. However, individual morphemes are not used to create the new word, but salient parts of words are merged to create the new noun.

Classroom activity 2

Copy and complete the table below. Which words are being blended? What semantic connections exist between the component words and the newly created ones?

Blend	Blended words	Blend	Blended words
motel		skort	
brunch		Oxbridge	
Wikipedia		labradoodle	
docusoap		boxercise	
guesstimate		netiquette	
Chunnel		confuzzle	

Extension activity 2

Return to the list in Table 5 when you have learned the semantic change terminology (see Table 6). Identify how the words in Table 5 changed from their original meaning, and suggest why they gained their new connotations.

💡 Exploring semantic change

In addition to creating new words, language users are prone to recycling words and changing their meaning. Semantic change, or **drift**, can occur:

- gradually, over time, as old meanings become forgotten
- in response to a new context for a particular word, for example technology
- as current slang where a particular social group takes ownership of an existing word and changes it to suit.

Key terms

Drift: a process of linguistic change over a period of time.

Table 6 *The process of semantic change*

Term	Definition	Example	Change in meaning
amelioration	a word takes on a different, more positive, meaning than it had previously, thereby gaining status	pretty	sly: attractive
		priest	old man: church leader
pejoration	a word takes on a different, more negative meaning than it had previously, so losing status	notorious	widely known: infamous
		idiot	private citizen: someone being stupid
		cunning	learned: deceitful
weakening	a word loses the strength of its original meaning	soon and presently	immediately: in a short while

narrowing (or specialisation)	a word becomes more specific in its meaning	meat	any food: flesh of an animal
		wife	any woman: married woman
broadening (or generalisation)	a word keeps its original meaning but acquires others	place	a broad street: an area

Fig. 7 *Words are often recycled and their meanings changed*

Semantic shifts occur when words expand and contract and then settle for meanings very different to the original. To illustrate this, the word 'pants' originated from the French *pantalon* and referred to men's trousers. In British English, its meaning has shifted to mean underwear (presumably as a shortening of 'underpants', or 'undertrousers'). American English still uses 'pants' to mean 'trousers', showing that this semantic change did not occur in the USA.

More recently semantic change has occurred because of political correctness (PC), which seeks to redress some of the linguistic bias that featured in your AS study of power and gender. PC alternatives for the following two phrases remove gender bias or judgements based on physical ability or appearance: man-made (artificial); maiden name (birth name).

Other types of semantic change can also relate to less concrete changes in interpretations of words and look for new meanings and associations to be made from existing words, often combined in more abstract ways.

Table 7 *Metaphorical changes*

Type	Definition	Example	Description
Metaphor	A word acquires new meanings because it is used metaphorically	bug	An insect or crawling creature, or to annoy, or a fault in a system
Euphemism	A way of describing something unpleasant in a more pleasant manner	down-sizing	Making workers redundant
		passed away	Died
		surgical strikes	Bombing people in a war
Idiom	A speech form, or an expression, that can't be understood literally from the meanings of the individual parts	pull your socks up	Try harder
		bull in a china shop	Clumsy

Key terms

Euphemism: inoffensive word or phrase used to suggest something less pleasant.

Idiom: a speech form or an expression of a given language that is peculiar to itself grammatically or cannot be understood from the individual meanings of its elements.

Classroom activity 3

Copy and complete the table below, identifying the type of semantic change represented by the words given. Use etymological dictionaries to help you.

Word	Semantic change	Word	Semantic change
doctor		web	
gay		mouse	
virus		a domestic	
guts		friendly fire	
punk		hoodie	
vulgar		starve	

Key lexical changes across Late Modern English

Table 8 *Influences on word creation*

Century	Some neologisms	Some influences
18th	sandwich vaccination torpedo mob	Science and medicine Classical languages (Latin and Greek) Attitudes to class and social roles
19th	biology chloroform claustrophobia	Industrialisation and new inventions Latin and Greek Science and medicine British Empire Travel
20th/21st	genocide laser McWorld doodle-bugs chavs pukka	Technology (especially IT) Globalisation World wars American English Consumerism and leisure time Social attitudes – gender, ethnicity, sexuality Youth sociolects and non-standard forms Ability to record speech

💡 🔍 Exploring words and contexts together

Linking contextual influences to language change explains many coinages or changes in semantics. Looking at these recent words brings together some of the new terminology you have acquired in this topic with the reasons for their introduction or semantic shifts.

Table 9 *Words and their contexts*

Word	Meaning	Contextual influence
phishing	You might recognise this word from its internet usage as meaning obtaining personal and banking details fraudulently through emails and fake websites. It's a metaphorical extension relating the activity of fishing to the hope of catching, or baiting, an unsuspecting victim. Orthographically, the 'ph' instead of 'f' uses a contemporary slang-style spelling, differentiating it from the original word.	Neologism resulting from technology.
metrosexual	Here two morphemes are joined by affixing 'metro', probably an abbreviation of 'metropolitan' meaning 'city', as a prefix to 'sexual'. This media term describes a new type of urban man interested in shopping and appearance, embodied in well-known personalities such as David Beckham. For retail and fashion industries this stereotyping offered marketing potential, also providing a catchy word for journalists.	You can see the influence of the media, fashion and society here.
blog	Another term resulting from technological developments, blending 'web' and 'log' and then clipping the word. Similar to a diary, it is posted publicly on the internet.	In addition to technology influencing language change, this word highlights how people's desire for social networking in a virtual, rather than real, world has changed language.
bootylicious	A term of praise meaning sexually attractive (and usually directed at women), that derives from rap music and blends 'delicious' and 'booty', US slang for buttocks. Interesting, too, how the noun 'booty' has extended metaphorically and broadened from its origin; it was associated with goods or property seized by pirates or in wars and 'booty' was a valuable prize, usually for men.	American musical and cultural impact on English is demonstrated with this word.

💡 **Extension activity 3**

Use the online *Oxford English Dictionary* (www.oed.com) to find words that:

- have originated in different centuries (e.g. searching the 19th century might produce scientific words)
- have been introduced from different languages (e.g. searching the 18th century might show a Latin influence)
- started being used in particular time periods (e.g. by selecting 1914–18 you could search the effects on English of a war).

From these, identify what your research shows about the influence of contextual factors.

Study tip

Learning the new lexical and semantic terminology for language change will help you precisely and effectively explain the key features of texts, helping you meet the main assessment objectives (AO1 and AO2).

Exploring lexical and semantic change through Late Modern English

As applying linguistic methods systematically is an important skill being tested, looking for changes to words and meanings is crucial. Identifying such features can be invaluable for assessments focusing on diachronic change, so here are three recipes for further investigation.

- Hannah Glasse, *The Art of Cookery made Plain and Easy* (1747)
- Charles Elme Francatelli, *A Plain Cookery Book for the Working Classes* (1852)
- Ainsley Harriott, *Meals in Minutes* (1998)

Classroom activity 4

Read the three recipe texts carefully, jotting down all the words from the recipes that you think show examples of lexical change (neologisms, compounds, borrowings, for example) or illustrate semantic change (broadening, narrowing, etc.).

Write up your findings before you read the text on page 87. Then compare your findings with the those in the text. Were you as precise in your use of linguistic terms? Did you make links between the language used and the contextual reasons for it?

To make a Currey *the* India Way.

TAKE two Fowls or Rabbit, cut them into fmall Pieces, and three or four fmall Onions, peeled and cut very fmall, thirty Pepper Corns, and a large Spoonful or Rice, brown fome Coriander Seeds over the Fire in a clean Shovel, and beat them to Powder, take a Tea Spoonful of Salt, and mix all well together with the Meat, put all together into a Sauce-pan or Stew-pan, with a Pint of Water, let it ftew foftly till the Meat is enough, then put in a Piece of Frefh Butter, about as big as a large Walnut, fhake it well together, and when it is fmooth and of a fine Thickness difh it up, and fend it to Table. If the Sauce be too thick, add a little more Water before it is done, and more Salt if it wants it. You are to obferve the Sauce muft be pretty thick.

Hannah Glasse, The Art of Cookery made Plain and Easy, *1747*

No. 3 Economical Pot Liquor Soup.

A thrifty housewife will not require that I should tell her to save the liquor in which the beef has been boiled; I will therefore take it for granted that the next day she carefully moves the grease, which will have become set firm on the top of the broth, into her fat pot, and keeps it to make a pie-crust, or to fry potatoes, or any remains of vegetables, onions, or fish. The liquor must be tasted, and if it it found to be too salt, some water must be added to lessen its saltness, and render it palatable. The pot containing the liquor must then be placed on the fire to boil, and when the scum rises to the surface it should be removed with a spoon. While the broth is boiling, put as many piled-up table-spoonfuls of oat-meal as you have pints of liquor into a basin; mix this with cold water into a smooth liquid batter, and then stir it into the boiling soup; season with some pepper and a good pinch of allspice, and continue stirring the soup with a stick or spoon on the fire for about twenty minutes; you will then be able to serve out a plentiful and nourishing meal to a large family at a cost of not more than the price of the oatmeal.

Charles Elme Francatelli, A Plain Cookery Book for the Working Classes, *1852*

wan kai thai-style red curry

Thai-style curries are very 'in' at the moment. We all seem to love the combination of exotic spices with that creamy coconut taste. And to think you can have all this in about 15 minutes – it's well worth trying. The curry paste I use is available in most large supermarkets.

Serves 4 PREPARATION: 5 MINS | COOKING TIME: 15 MINS

1 tablespoon sunflower oil
1 onion, thinly sliced
2 tomatoes, roughly diced
400 g (14 oz) can coconut milk
1 tablespoon Thai red curry paste
500 g (1 lb 2 oz) cubed, skinned white fish such as cod, haddock or coley
juice of 1/2 lemon
1 tablespoon soy sauce
a handful of fresh basil or coriander leaves
salt and pepper
cooked rice and steamed sugar-snap peas or mangetout, to serve

Heat the sunflower oil in a large, non-stick pan and cook the onion over a high heat for 4–5 minutes until beginning to brown. Add the tomatoes and cook for 1 minute then stir in the coconut milk and curry paste. Bring to a gentle simmer and add the fish; cook gently for 4–5 minutes until the fish is just tender.

Stir in the lemon juice, soy sauce and fresh herbs and season to taste. Spoon the rice into serving bowls and gently ladle over the fish curry; serve with sugar-snap peas or mangetout.

NUTRITION NOTES PER SERVING:

calories 172 | protein 23.3g | carbohydrate 9.3 g | fat 4.9 g | saturated fat 0.62 g | fibre 1.7 g | added sugar none | salt 1.47 g

Ainsley Harriott, Meals in Minutes, *BBC Worldwide, 1998*

Although you can recognise many words that are specific to cookery, evidently some semantic change has occurred. Some narrowing has taken place – 'fowls' now refers only to chickens or game birds, but previously meant all birds, and has become archaic; 'liquor' has now narrowed to mean alcohol by most, although as chefs still use it in this way the term could be considered more specialist. The noun 'shovel' has narrowed to be primarily used to refer to a garden, rather than a kitchen, implement. The **archaism** ('broth') might still be used dialectally but would be likely to be simply termed 'soup' by most nowadays. Most interestingly, the noun 'scum' has broadened. For chefs it can still be used in the cooking sense to describe the unpleasant matter that rises to the surface of liquid, but its slang use has transferred this to refer to people despised by others in society. Look, too, at the use of 'in', a colloquial term used to describe something popular, presumably an abbreviation of the phrase 'in fashion'.

Lexically some compounds ('Tea spoonful', 'sauce-pan', 'Stew-pan') have become single words; this process is still evident in the 1852 compounds ('table-spoonfuls') but by 1998 the new hyphenated compound is 'non-stick', showing the influence of technological development. Also in the 20th century the way that we shop has affected the lexis with the noun 'supermarket' created to describe the place we go to buy our ingredients. (Incidentally, the linguist Steven Pinker describes the affix 'super' as being 'promiscuous', as it can be attached to any word class.) Scientific neologisms ('nutrition' etc.) are more evident in the latest recipe, as are the number of borrowings, especially from East Asian countries. And what about the word 'currey' itself? Hannah Glasse's recipe is the first recorded for it in England, so it must have been a fresh, anglicised borrowing.

Adjectives in 1852 are used differently. Today we might find something too salty, rather than 'too salt' and 'saltiness' would be used rather than 'saltness'. The 'y' is a common manner of creating an adjective but so too is the suffix 'ness' – perhaps the 'i' was added for phonological effect! The title, too, uses the proper noun 'India' as an adjective.

Key terms

Archaism: an old word or phrase no longer in general spoken or written use.

Fig. 8 *Cookery is an example of one area where a great deal of lexical change has occurred over the years*

Study tip

Evaluating the influence of contextual factors on spoken and written texts is an important assessment objective (AO3). Learning these key contexts and applying them to data throughout your study will ensure that you remember them.

Further reading

The online *Oxford English Dictionary* has some good resources and worksheets to support you in researching individual words and to enable you to search the online version effectively. These are available at http://public.oed.com/resources/for-students-and-teachers/a-level/. For example, you can look at the summary of the word 'naughty', revise word formations and also read what the OED thinks about the purposes of a dictionary, which introduces ideas that you will encounter later in this module about attitudes to language change in Late Modern English.

Extension activity 5

The OED 'What's new' page (http://public.oed.com/whats-new/) provides links to their quarterly updates on new words added to the online dictionary. It offers word lists and articles both about these new additions and how dictionaries chart changing word usage.

Make a list of some of the new words and identify the type of lexical and semantic change processes they exemplify. For example, are they a blend or has the word changed its meaning, either negatively (pejoration) or positively (amelioration)? Give a contextual reason for the change such as changes in society's attitudes or because of a new invention.

Extension activity 4

A good way to compare similar texts from different time periods is to reflect on the genre conventions used and assess whether these have changed. Make a list of the genre conventions you would expect to see in a recipe.

Look again at the three curry recipes and ask yourself the following questions.

- Has the instructional genre and purpose remained the same? If so, have the linguistic features usually associated with instructional writing stayed the same? If not, in what ways have they changed? Break these features into language methods (grammar, lexis/semantics, discourse and graphology) and explore similarities and differences between the recipes.
- Has the audience remained the same? If not, how have the users of recipe books changed over time and how has this affected their presentation? Is there evidence that social and cultural attitudes towards cooking having changed?
- Have science and technology affected the recipes in either the methods used or the ingredients?
- Have travel and globalisation had an impact?

Science and technology

In 1747 measurements are imprecise, where cooking is until 'the meat is enough'. In 1852 the indicated time period ('twenty minutes') suggests either a greater awareness of time or an ability to measure it, and by 1998 timings and nutritional information are precise. Both the older texts show the limited technology available: in 1747 the seeds are browned 'over the Fire in a clean Shovel', whereas in 1852 the soup is stirred 'with a stick or a spoon on the fire'. By the 20th century, cooking implements have advanced to being 'non-stick'. Layout, too, has been affected by advances with computerised printing, where fonts can be varied for the various sections of the modern recipe, becoming part of the discourse structure as well as a graphological device.

Social and cultural attitudes

1747's 'Send it to table' imagines that a servant creates the dish, demonstrating a class-based and hierarchical society, whereas in 1852 the economical soup is being produced by women for their own families. Both chefs use the same adjective ('plain'), understanding the type of cooking that will appeal to their audience – one perhaps because the 'currey' is more exotic than the audience is used to and the other for economic reasons. Today we seem to want more exotic dishes ('wan kai thai-style curry'), which are considered fashionable ('in'), to serve for smaller numbers ('serves 4'). The detailed instruction for the modern audience also suggests either inexperienced or leisure-time cooks, who cook for pleasure rather than necessity. Even the purposes of the recipes have been affected by culture, with Harriott representing the modern TV/celebrity chef who is marketing his book – see the persuasive introduction, an added feature to the typical discourse structure of an instructional recipe. However, both Glasse and Francatelli were 'celebrities' and well-known in their own time.

Travel and globalisation

Clearly the ingredients have become more varied as people have travelled more and it has become easier to import them. But, even in 1747, this was happening with coriander used to flavour the dish – an influence of the emerging British Empire and colonisation of India. Other ingredients, such as the rabbits, show that people were still sourcing food locally.

Changes in written style

Fig. 9 *Technological advancements, such as mobile phones and text messages, help to shape language change*

Starter activity

Begin by thinking about any spelling rules you can remember being taught (for example, 'i' before 'e', except after 'c') and spelling rules that you deliberately break in your written communication. What rules do you give yourself for using 'correct' or non-standard spellings? Debate the following.

- Does spelling matter?
- What makes spelling complicated?

Exploring orthographical, punctuation and text design change

Although there was a big drive in the 18th century to prescribe all aspects of written language use, spelling had already gone through some standardisation from Old English onwards. Caxton's introduction of the printing press to England in the 15th century had a huge influence on standardisation: spelling could be codified because the technology allowed it. With more people having access to the written word, rules became sensible to enable clearer communication.

English spellings have taken centuries to establish. Today it is recognised that some people find accurate spelling difficult. Some spellings have to be memorised because of irregularities (such as homophones) and rules learned for common patterns such as doubling consonants (sit/sitting). Our spelling heritage reflects old pronunciations, and some rules and oddities have, like grammar and lexis, resulted from the influences of other languages on the evolution of English.

In the 21st century, technology has caused spelling changes, showing that language, despite efforts to retain elements of it in a fixed form, constantly changes. Think how you spell words differently when you text, rather than in other forms of writing, and you can see that even when you know what is 'correct', you choose to flout conventions for linguistic economy or speed, or just because it's easier!

Classroom activity 5

Look at the three texts on page 90. The first is an extract from John Gabriel Stedman's *Narrative of a Five Years Expedition Against the Revolted Negroes of Surinam* which also provides an interesting anti-slavery story. The second is from Dorothy Wordsworth's private journal; she was the sister of the famous poet, William Wordsworth. The third is a series of comments posted by a Facebook member in response to photos her friends have posted.

- What features of the orthography/spelling seem non-standard?
- Can you identify the 'rules' being used by the writers for their orthographical/spelling choices?

During the ſtay in this place the companies frequently walked on ſhore, and I accompanied them in their excurſions; but the pleaſure I had flattered myself with, from exchanging the confinement of a ſhip for the liberty of ranging over a delicious country, was damped by the first object which preſented itself after my landing. This was a young female ſlave, whoſe only covering was a rag tied round her loins, which, like her ſkin, was lacerated in ſeveral places by the ſtroke of the whip. The crime which had been committed by this miſerable victim of tyranny, was the non-performance of a talk to which ſhe was apparantly unequal, for which ſhe was ſentenced to receive two hundred laſhes, and to drag, during ſome months, a chain ſeveral yards in length, one end of which was locked round her ancle, and to the other was affixed a weight of at leaſt a hundred pounds. Strongly affected with this ſhocking circumſtance, I took a draft of the unhappy ſufferer, and retained a dreadful idea of the inhumanity of the planters towards theſe miſerable ſubjects to their power.

John Gabriel Stedman, Narrative of a Five Years Expedition Against the Revolted Negroes of Surinam, *1796*

"...I sate with W[illiam] in the orchard all the morning and made my shoes. In the afternoon from excessive heat I was ill in the headach and toothach and went to bed – I was refreshed with washing myself after I got up, but it was too hot to walk till near dark, and then I sate upon the wall finishing my shoes." (26/7/1800)

"I made pies and stuff the pike – baked a loaf. Headach after dinner – I lay down. A letter from Wm rouzed me, desiring us to go Keswick. After writing to Wm we walked as far as Mr Simpson's and ate black cherries. A Heavenly warm evening with scattered clouds upon the hills. There was a vernal greenness upon the grass from the rains of the morning and afternoon. Peas for dinner." (3/8/1800)

Dorothy Wordsworth, private journal, 1800

haha we planned 2 wear as little as poss :P lol

Thanks lol i dont think i am!!! x

I nooo i havent even seen you round school recently lol

Am good lol you?

Omg we look different now lol x

Lovin the hat haha x

gawjess : P x

I no!! it looks soooooooo cool!!!!! (:

www.antimoon.com

Research points

According to Dr Mark Sebba, a central issue with English spelling is that it has a many-to-one or many-to-many relationship between letters (or letter combinations) and sounds, unlike a phonemic orthographic model that has a one-to-one relationship. He suggests that this is typical of a standardised language with a long written history, where changes to sounds have affected pronunciations and where loan words have come into the language unchanged. He exemplifies this with the sound /u:/ as this can be represented orthographically as <o> (to), <oe> (shoe), <ue> (blue), <oo> (too), <ew> (flew) and <ou> (group).

Fig. 10 *Ghoti = fish*

What are the reasons for orthographical change?

Why has spelling changed? For four main reasons: phonological, technological, standardisation and due to the influence of other languages.

Phonological

As the sounds of English changed, so the written word needed to accommodate this. For example, our modern 'silent e' rule evolved from old inflectional endings where sounds were pronounced to show the word's function; it now marks long vowels. In Middle English the terminal -e was a key feature, often used at the end of words where we would now omit it ('roote', 'soote'). This -e may have been linked to Middle English pronunciation, but died out in Early Modern English as people became unsure whether to write it as it was no longer sounded.

Other sounds that became silent, although still in the written word, are the /mb/ of 'thumb' and the /l/ in words such as 'walk'. However, not all words that end 'lk' follow this, e.g. 'milk' and 'sulk'. Further Middle English developments were the use of double consonants to show that the vowel before this was short, as in 'dinner' compared to 'diner'.

Taking the sound /h/ for example, it is interesting to show how spelling can influence pronunciation. Comparing the pronunciation of 'hour' and 'hotel' demonstrates that in 'hour', the /h/ is silent despite its spelling and in 'hotel' it is sounded. In words like 'knee' and 'gnaw' consonant clusters became reduced to the /n/ but the spelling stayed the same. Sometimes spellings have been simplified with words like 'physick' losing its final -k, but there does not seem a consistency as other words have retained their -ck ending despite the sound just being a /k/. Other simplifications have occurred in words with established consonant clusters like 'ct', such as 'practical'. Eighteenth-century printing conventions would have presented the 'ct' with a **ligature**, and although this has since been dropped the letters have been retained.

Technological

Printing practices in the 1800s shaped the presentation of letters, especially the long 's'. The long 's' was left over from Old English and continued in use into Late Modern English. It was used initially (at the beginning) and medially (in the middle), but the short 's' was always used at the end of words. The long 's' was used until 1800, when it was replaced by the short 's'. As it didn't have a phonological function, the phoneme did not need a different grapheme and, because of printing practices when pages (and letters) had to be individually set, it was

Fig. 11 *Ligatures*

■ **Key terms**

Ligature: the linking of two graphemes, once common practice in printing but now becoming less common.

deemed unnecessary. Throughout Late Modern English technological advances have driven graphological opportunities so now we can choose to use non-standard forms depending on the medium (e.g. text messaging), the audience (e.g. friends) and the function (interactional); or, as in advertising, non-standard choices can send a message about the product ('Beanz Meanz Heinz', 'milk's gotta lotta bottle', 'finger lickin' good'). Earlier than this Caxton's printing press in the 15th century encouraged spelling standardisation because it facilitated mass printing. But in the Early Modern English period (1450–1700), individual printers established their own conventions and styles – as did writers – so uniformity was not deemed important at first. Printers wanted to fit words neatly on a line, so they began to drop letters such as the terminal –e. At other times they added letters because they got paid by the number of letters. You can see another resonance with text messaging: writers want words to fit neatly on a screen, or change spellings to keep within the required number of characters.

Standardisation

During Late Modern English, spelling was further standardised and codified in dictionaries and spelling books. Before this, spelling had been determined by individual choices, rather than by commonly agreed rules.

Some of the earliest standardisation was with French after the Norman invasion of the 11th century. French scribes began to include their own spelling patterns, replacing earlier versions from Old English. For example, 'qu' replaced 'cw' in words like 'queen', and the 'c' with the /s/ sound as in 'deceive' replaced the harder /k/.

During the Renaissance of the 15th and 16th centuries, scholars wanted to model English spelling on the classical patterns of Ancient Greek and Latin. So, over time, the letter 'h' was added to words such as 'throne' and 'b' was added to words such as 'debt'. Words such as 'rhyme' were altered from 'rime' for the same reason. Other words such as 'receipt' and 'parliament' were also changed. You might notice that for many of these the spelling does not match the pronunciation, although for some it has changed the way we say the words.

Influences from other languages

Borrowings from other languages can affect spelling, as you saw when exploring loan words on page 79. Often one way to guess the etymology of a word is to look at its spelling, especially if it is a **non-anglicised loan word** (as opposed to an **anglicised loan word**). From looking at the spellings of words such as 'spaghetti' and 'yacht' it is clear that these are not originally from English. Patterns of borrowings can be seen from clues such as affixes, silent letters and final consonants. The influence of French and Latin is evident in prefixes like 'pre', 'pro', 'con' and suffixes such as '-ion' and '-ity'. Silent letters from Greek spelling can be seen in 'psychology' and 'pneumonia' and even Germanic influences from Old English perhaps live on in spellings with consonants like '-dge' and '-tch'.

Changing punctuation

Punctuation has both grammatical and rhetorical functions. It separates clause elements, and gives weight and emphasis to points we wish to make. Like other linguistic aspects it also has gone through notable changes and developments.

A process of expansion in the number of punctuation symbols occurred as the written mode became more important but it has simplified again, with a more informal, sparser writing style being popular in recent years. Most punctuation marks have a long history. Caxton used the period (.) and the colon (:). He also used the oblique stroke (/) – called the virgule – a punctuation symbol we now call the 'slash' and use in our technological communications; it was replaced by the comma during the 16th century.

However, not all punctuation was used as we use it now, even if the symbols look familiar. In texts from early in the Late Modern period:

- commas are more liberally used to link long, extended clauses and full stops are not always where we would expect them

- colons and semicolons are common features to separate clauses, thus creating more sentence complexity

- apostrophes extended to signifying the possessive and to representing missing letters. Apostrophes were also used commonly to signify a missing vowel when it did not signify a sound, as in 'work'd', but this practice has not continued into Present-day English. This was particularly the case in literary text where it affected metre

- speech marks began to be used to differentiate between speech and writing

- contractions occur in various ways. Still popular at the beginning of the Late Modern English period was the use of **proclitic contractions** such as ''tis'. In the 18th century there was a gradual shift to **enclitic contractions** such as 'it's'. (Poets typically used contractions such as 'ow'st'; however, some of these might be for the poetic metre, as the contractions alter syllable length.)

- another common typographical, rather than punctuation, feature used is the ampersand (&), which had originated as a ligature of 'E' and 't' and combined in the abbreviation of the Latin term et cetera as &c.

> ■ Key terms
>
> **Proclitic contraction:** where a separate word becomes part of the word following it.
>
> **Enclitic contraction:** where a separate word becomes part of the word preceding it.

Nowadays we use punctuation differently when using discrete forms of communication. When texting, which has more of a speech-style, you may find that you use punctuation only to mark prosodic features, but use them in non-standard, multiple forms (!!!) and at the end of sentences (.) but not in contractions (dont) and with limited capitalising of first words in sentences or for names (meet at james house l8er). However, in your academic essays you apply standard forms to create the right effects.

■ Research point

Lynne Truss's 2003 book *Eats, Shoots and Leaves* provided a humorous but cautionary reflection on the state of English punctuation. Here is one of her anecdotes to persuade readers of the importance of using punctuation correctly.

> A panda walks into a café. He orders a sandwich, eats it, then draws a gun and fires two shots in the air.
>
> 'Why?' asks the confused waiter, as the panda makes towards the exit. The panda produces a badly punctuated wildlife manual and tosses it over his shoulder.
>
> 'I'm a panda,' he says at the door. 'Look it up.'
>
> The waiter turns to the relevant entry and, sure enough, finds an explanation.
>
> 'Panda. Large black-and-white bear-like mammal, native to China. Eats, shoots and leaves.'

Lynne Truss, Eats, Shoots and Leaves, 2003

She also credits some of the current misunderstanding of punctuation rules to the fact that before the 19th century it was customary to put an apostrophe before the plural inflection on foreign, borrowed words ending with a vowel, such as 'banana'.

Thinking points

1 What does this joke suggest about the important function of punctuation?

2 Why can other forms of punctuation, for example the apostrophe, cause the same confusion?

Changing capitalisation

By Late Modern English capital letters had begun to be capitalised according to the rules we follow today – mainly because 18th-century grammarians felt that a system was needed. Previously, in Early Modern English, capital letters were used, as now, at the beginning of every sentence and every proper name. They were also used rhetorically for personified and abstract nouns; indeed, writers capitalised any noun that they considered important. However, you may still see some of these practices in texts from the early 18th century. To show how capitals were used, here is a 1676 text about a herbal remedy, St John's Wort, from *The English Phyſitian Enlarged* by Nicholas Culpeper.

> Government and Vertues. It is under the Coeleſtial Sign Leo and under the Dominion of the Sun. It hath power to open Obſtructions, to diſſolve Swellings, to cloſe up the lips of Wounds,and to ſtrengthen the parts that are weak and feeble. The Decoction of the Herb and Flowers,but of the Seed eſpecially in Wine, being drunk, or the Seed made in a Powder,and drunk with the Juyce of Knot-graſs, helpeth all manner of Spitting and Vomiting of Blood,be it by any Vein broken inwardly by Bruiſes, Falls or however. The ſame helpeth thoſe that are Bitten or Stung by any venomous Creature: and is good for thoſe that are troubled with the Stone in the Kidnies : or that cannot make Water; and being applyed, provoketh Womens Courſes. Two drams of the Seed of St. John's-wort made into Powder,and drunk in a little Broth,doth gently expel Choler or congealed Blood in the Stomach : The seed is much commended being drunk for forty dayes together,to help the Sciatica, the Falling-ſickneſs and the Palſie.

Nicholas Culpeper, The English Phyſitian Enlarged, *1676*

Q. What is the meaning of the word faculty, *when applied to learning?*

A. As the word *faculty*, ſubjectively conſider'd, imports the capacity or genius of a man; ſo objectively conſider'd, it ſignifies the ſeveral arts and ſciences; as *Theology, Law, Phyſick, Philo-ſophy,* &c.

Q. Whence is the word parliament derive'd?

A. **The word is of** *French* **original, and is deriv'd from the word** *parlement,* **which ſignifies diſcourſ -ing, conferring, or converſing with. And this is again deriv'd** *à parler la mente,* **to ſpeak ones mind; becauſe in conferences we declare our ſentiments.**

The British Apollo, or, Curious Amusements for the Ingenious, Google Books (www.books.google.co.uk)

These were two questions posed by readers in an early 18th-century magazine called *The British Apollo, or Curious Amusements for the Ingenious* and subtitled: 'To Which are Added the Most Material Occurrences Foreign and Domestick'. Readers were invited to ask any question and, while some were more typical of modern problem pages and were relationship based, these showed readers' interest in the English language. They are also good examples of the typical orthographical, typographical and punctuation features that you may encounter in 18th-century texts.

Extension activity 6

In the 21st century advertising often deliberately breaks orthographical, punctuation and spelling rules for effect. Collect examples of recent adverts from magazines. You could also see whether this has been a recent phenomenon by looking at older 20th-century adverts on websites such as www.vintageadbrowser.com.

Table 10 *Applying language methods and data analysis*

Language method	Individual feature	Analysis/comment
Orthography	Long ſ	The long ſ appears at the start and in the middle of words and is clearly still used in printed texts.
	Physick Philosophy	Spellings of words ('Physick') show an older form with the -ck ending still used. Words have been created from the Greek and use a ph- rather than an f ('philosophy').
	Parliament/parlement/a parler la mente	Discussion of 'parliament' is interesting, showing both the non-anglicised French spelling and that adopted in Early Modern English. The origin of the noun is also given, suggesting that it was a blending of a phrase that had a literal meaning and was then used to present the purpose of a parliament.
Typography	Italics	Used for borrowed words ('French') and to separate the question from the answer.
	Ligatures ('ct'/'&c')	Common ligatures of the time period are used.
Punctuation	Capital letters	There are already some practices that we recognise, such as the use of capitals at the beginning of sentences, but not on all nouns, so perhaps this was already beginning to change, although this is only one example and generalisations should be avoided.
	Apostrophes (consider'd, ones mind)	Apostrophes are used for the silent vowel in the -ed verb endings. However, the possessive form 'ones' is not marked with an apostrophe as it usually is in modern English.
	Semicolons, colons, full stops and question marks	A range of punctuation is evident, mainly for syntactical clarity in separating subordinate clauses with commas and semicolons.
Layout	Q&A discourse structure	The layout is helpful to show the reader's question and the writer's response on behalf of the newspaper. Each is indented for visual clarity.

Changing layout and text design

Of course, the visual appearance of texts has always been important to readers, and the ability to lay out a text has changed with technology. Early manuscripts were handwritten but the visual appearance of a text was also important, with colour and pictorial images used to bring the text to life. Printed fonts developed, and mass production replaced the laborious handwritten process for major works. Graphic design has evolved through Late Modern English, really expanding with computer technology and the ability to reproduce photographic images. Graphic symbols now have a semantic function, with this field of study defined as typography.

Fig. 12 *Using emoticons is one way of connoting our feelings in the texts that we create*

■ **Key terms**

Emoticons: the online means of showing facial expressions and gestures.

■ **Classroom activity 7**

Investigate punctuation, orthographical and spelling changes by comparing the following three texts.

How is punctuation used differently in each text? How do these add to the writers' intended effects on the audience and their message, as well as to grammatical complexity? What has changed orthographically? Can you suggest why these changes have occurred? Creating a table like Table 10 is a useful way to see visual comparisons from which you can analyse the changes in features systematically.

■ **Classroom activity 6**

Look at the same words in different fonts. What are the connotations of each font and how does it affect the message contained in the text?

Graphology is important

Graphology is important

Graphology is important

Graphology is important

Graphological features of 18th-century texts included the use of italics for stress, but today, we have great graphological freedom with the ability to adapt word-processed texts easily for a specific audience and purpose. Advertisers use this to influence us, but we also play with the meanings of texts we create. This is evident in text messages, blogs and entries on social networking sites, where we manipulate graphological features for a particular effect. Smileys :-) and other **emoticons** connote our feelings. Underlining suggests how strongly we feel about something and colours can be decoded for our moods. Internet texts have also changed the way texts are read, no longer in the linear form of printed books but in a non-linear manner as we focus on areas of text that visually appeal to us or scan texts for the content we seek.

Here I ſlepped on ſhore, with my officers, to wait on Captain Orzinga, the commander, and delivered three of my ſick men into his hoſpital; where I beheld ſuch a ſpectacle of miſery and wretchedneſs as baffles all imagination; this place having been formerly called *Devil's Harwar*, on account of its intolerable unhealthineſs—a name by which alone I ſhall again disſtinguiſh it, as much more ſuitable than that of Slans Welveren, which ſignifies the welfare of the nation.

Here I ſaw a few of the wounded wretches, who had eſcaped from the engagement in which Lieutenant Lepper, with ſo many men, had been killed; and none of them told me the particulars of his own miraculous eſcape: " I was ſhot, Sir," ſaid he, 'with a muſquet-bullet in " my breaſt; and to refit or eſcape being impoſſible, as " the only means left me to ſave my life I threw myself " down among the mortally wounded, and the dead, " without moving hand or foot. Here in the evening " the rebel chief, ſurveying his conqueſt, ordered one of " his captains to begin inſtantly to cut off the heads of " the ſlain, in order to carry them home to the village, " as trophies of their victory: this captain, having al- " ready chopped off that of Lieutenant Lepper, and one " or two more, ſaid to his friend, *Sonde go ſleeby, caba* " *mekewe liby den tara dogo tay tamara;* The fun iſ juſt "going to ſleep, we muſt leave thoſe other dogs till to- "morrow.

Vol.   I.   T

John Gabriel Stedman, Narrative of a Five Years Expedition Against the Revolted Negroes of Surinam, *1796*

Key features you may have noticed about the grammar are as follows.

■ **Negation**: constructing a negative in the 18th century is unlike the modern use of **dummy auxiliary** verb 'do'. Examples here are 'no very uncommon occurrence', 'I know not', 'for windows we have none', 'Italians seem to me to have no feeling of cold'.

■ **Syntax**: in this text the syntax differs from modern usage, for example with 'certain it is' the complement comes before the main subject and verb and in 'continues still' the adverb comes after the verb.

■ **Pronouns**: Piozzi's choice of 'one a little' employs a pronoun that we now view as archaic and representing a Received Pronunciation (RP)-type accent.

■ **Prepositions**: choices seem odd, such as 'at London' instead of in London.

■ **Contractions**: here the lack of contractions throughout the text seems noteworthy, for example 'while I am starving' would be more likely to be presented today using a contraction. This could connote a more formal style or a change in practice in later Modern English to adopt more conversational tones in writing.

Research points

The auxiliary 'do' is characterised in Present-day English by the acronym 'nice'. Joan Beal in her chapter on syntactic change in Later Modern English from *English in Modern Times* gives examples of these.

■ Use in **n**egative sentences, e.g. She did not eat the bread.

■ **I**nversion of auxiliary and subject in interrogative sentences, e.g. Did she eat the bread?

■ **C**ode usage, avoiding repetition of a lexical verb, e.g. She ate the bread and so did he.

■ **E**mphatic usage, e.g. She did eat the bread!

Thinking points

Why do you think poets favoured the auxiliary 'do' when writing verse?

Looking at this extract, you can see that the punctuation enhances the complexity of the text for a modern audience. The majority of the sentences are compound or complex and the extract shows the fashionable style of the time in its multi-clause sentences with colons and semicolons joining runs of connected sentences.

The Late Modern English period also contains some important changes in grammatical usage. Literary texts from the 18th and 19th centuries demonstrate stylistic differences from 20th-century literature. Grammatically, sentences were likely to be longer, with embedded clauses and phrases, but these have become simpler. Using more subordinate clauses, influenced by Latin, became a fashionable way to make discourse more elaborate and to display one's learning. This style continued well into Late Modern English but has perhaps reversed now with many writers adopting a simpler style.

Key terms

Dummy auxiliary: the verb 'do' which is used to form questions and negatives or to add emphasis in a statement.

Study tip

Being confident with grammatical analysis is important at this level, showing that you are more confident in your linguistic knowledge. You revised this in Section A Language acquisition, so you should be able to identify word classes accurately. The important application to language change is to see how the syntax (word order) might have changed from Late Modern English to Present-day English.

On the next pages you will see that some grammatical features have changed quite significantly over the Late Modern English period. And, just as some become more widely used, others that you may see in older texts have declined in usage during Late Modern English. These include:

■ **Key terms**

Subjunctive: a grammatical mood.

Fig. 14 *Subjunctive phrases*

- the **subjunctive**, where the conditional *if* still appears regularly but other forms have declined. In the present tense, 'be' forms the subjunctive and 'were' is in the past tense. To illustrate this use, Mary Astell, a feminist writer of the early 18th century, writes in *Some Reflections Upon Marriage*, 'But if Marriage be such a blessed State, how comes it, may you say, that there are so few happy Marriages?' In the past tense, a phrase like 'if I were you' demonstrates that we still use the subjunctive in this way

- passive voice, formed by the auxiliary verb 'be' and the past tense – as in 'The report was handed to me'. The passive was more commonly used in early Late Modern English but has now become associated with legal registers and as a grammatical feature that obscures rather than adds clarity because it omits the agent, the doer of the action

- modal verbs like 'shall' to mark the future in the first person have declined, perhaps as some of the rules governing when to use certain forms have been simplified

- of-genitive – for example, 'the bonnet of the car' – would probably be replaced today with 'the car's bonnet' as a more economical style of noun phrase

- wh-relative clause – 'which' has been replaced by 'that', either reflecting spoken language use and colloquialisation or because grammar checkers and word processors often reject 'which' as inaccurate

- third-person pronoun with 'he' acting as gender neutral, perhaps a result of the feminist movements of the 1960s and 1970s and their efforts to make language equal

- pronoun – 'whom' is disappearing as the inflected form of the object pronoun and is being replaced by 'who', possibly because of its association with a more formal style or a lack of awareness of its specific grammatical function.

Link

More about the influences of Latin on the 18th-century standardisation of English and the more modern desire for informalisation can be found in the topic Why does language change? (page 116).

Classroom activity 8

David Crystal in *The Cambridge Encyclopedia of the English Language* uses examples from Jane Austen's *Emma* to illustrate some characteristic grammatical qualities of the 18th and early 19th centuries. Match the right grammatical feature in Table 11 with Crystal's examples.

Table 11 *Jane Austen and 19th-century grammar*

Example from Austen	Grammatical feature
He told me in our journey … She was small of her age	Irregular verbs
She say you to the day? She doubted not …	Tense usage
It is a nothing of a part … To be taken into the account …	Contracted forms
Fanny shrunk back and much was ate …	Prepositions

I am so glad we are got acquainted. So you are come at last!	Articles
The properest manner … The richest of the two …	Auxiliary verbs
Will not it be a good plan? It would quite shock you … would not it?	Adverbs
I stood for a moment, felling dreadfully. It is really very well for a novel.	Comparative/superlative adjectives

Adapted from **David Crystal**, The Cambridge Encyclopedia of the English Language, *CUP, 2003*

Some features of modern grammatical change are being affected by speech practices as the boundaries blur again between the spoken and written mode:

- be + -ing construction of verbs, known as the progressive aspect, has increased over the Late Modern English period – for example, 'I'm preparing dinner'
- phrasal verbs are being formed – for example, talk with, show up, clean out
- semi-modal verbs are more popular – for example, need to, have got to
- verb inflections are being regularised – for example, 'learnt' to 'learned'
- irregular verbs are still altering – for example, 'I've wrote it down for you'
- new auxiliary-like verbs, using 'get' and 'want' in a verb phrase
- comparative and superlative adjectives are formed by using 'more' and 'most' rather than using suffixes – for example, 'er' and 'est'
- adverbs are being replaced by adjectives – for example, 'You've done great!'
- the s-genitive is broadening to use with non-human nouns – for example, 'the car's bonnet'
- omission of the definite article – for example, 'world-famous singer Beyoncé'
- relative clauses using 'that' or having zero-relativisation are increasing – for example, 'the man that I saw yesterday' or 'the man I saw yesterday'
- pronouns are changing, perhaps for reasons of increasing gender equality – for example, 'they' (for a singular) or coordinated 'he/she'.

Further reading

Much of the list of features that are declining in usage in Present-day English given here has come from Christian Mair and Geoffrey Leech's 2006 study of corpora and their summary of the recent findings of other linguists. To read the complete chapter on Current Changes in English syntax, go to www.lancs. ac.uk/fass/doc_library/linguistics/ leechg/mai_and_leech_2006.pdf.

Geoffrey Leech's *A Glossary of English Grammar* is also a very helpful reference book that explains grammatical terms in a clear and accessible manner.

Leech, G. *A Glossary of English Grammar*, Edinburgh University Press Ltd, 2007

Research points

William Labov explains significant shifts in language use as occurring in two distinct ways. The first he calls 'change from below', which is 'unconscious' and possibly from a lower social class. The opposite is 'change from above', a 'conscious' or deliberate change that is introduced by the dominant social class or speech communities that have prestige and status.

Labov published his conclusions in his 1994 book, *Principles of linguistic change, Internal factors*. Most of his research was on speakers in American cities, but it can be used to support other

■ Looking ahead

Many modern linguists draw conclusions about what has already changed, and what is still changing in language use, by using studies of corpora, a body of naturally occurring data and consisting of thousands or even millions of words found in different texts that make a database and can be searched by date, text type or mode. This, therefore, combines a computational-based process, providing quantitative data from a representative sample from which to draw conclusions, with more traditional qualitative discourse analysis. At higher-educational level, making your own research methodologies that are suitable for the topic and data and use a variety of approaches, including primary data, is a significant research skill. You could also use corpora as a basis for your language investigation.

aspects of language change in its broader ideas about trends in the way that language changes.

He theorises that the change from below begins with a local pattern, associated with a particular social group and then its usage becomes more widespread and used by new groups. If it replaces the old form, that old form is seen as archaic and an irregularity. Some generalised findings are that:

■ most advanced changes are found among younger speakers
■ most advanced speakers belong to groups with the greatest local prestige
■ women are generally more advanced than men as far as new and vigorous changes are concerned.

Thinking points

1 How can you account for women changing language more?

2 Why do you think young people have such an impact on language change?

3 What local prestige groups could you suggest are affecting language change now?

The Rules of Civility

in every corner; but you muſt inſlantly withdraw, and attend his coming in the Anti-Chamber.

If he be indiſpos'd, and in Bed, you muſt go away without ſeeing him, unleſs he ſends for you in: and if you be admitted, your Viſit muſt be ſhort; for ſick people are uneaſie, and ſubjeċt to the Operation of their Phyſick: You muſt likewiſe remember to ſpeak ſoftly, and oblige him to anſwer as little as poſſible.

Above all, you muſt have a care of ſitting down upon the Bed, eſpecially if it be a Woman; for that is univerſally indecent, and favours of Clowniſh Familiarity, unleſs they be much below you, or perſons with whom you are more than ordinarily intimate.

If he be reading, writing, or ſtudying, you muſt by no means diſturb him; but expeċt till he be at leiſure, before you accoſt him.

If he deſires you to ſit down, you may do it, tho' with ſome Heſitation and Reluċtance, which will be a great inſtance of your reſpeċt; and be ſure to place your ſelf at the lower end, which is always next the door where you enter'd, as the upper end is always where his Lordſhip is pleas'd to diſpoſe himſelf.

You muſt, when you ſit down, obſerve to take a worſe Seat than his Lordſhip: a *Chair with Arms* is the beſt; a *back Chair* is the next; and a *Stool* the worſt of the three. When you ſit down, you muſt not place your ſelf cheek-by-jole by his Lordſhip, but remove your Chair ſomething before him, that he may take notice of your Attention; for ſitting ſideways towards him is more reſpeċtful than to place your ſelf full in his face.

> You muʃt not put on your Hat, unleʃs his Lordʃhip commands it: You muʃt enter with your Gloves on; and when you are placed, ʃit quietly upon your Seat, not clapping your Leg upon your Knee, nor playing with your Hat, Gloves, &c. nor picking your Noʃe, or ʃcratching, &c.
>
> You muʃt forbear hawking or ʃpitting as much as you can; and when you are not able to hold, if you obʃerve it neat and kept cleanly, you muʃt turn your back,

Antoine De Courtin, *The Rules of Civility; Or, The Maxims of Genteel Behaviour*, Gale ECCO, 2010 (translated from French into English in 1703)

Classroom activity 9

Look at the extract from *The Rules of Civility; Or, The Maxims of Genteel Behaviour*, published in 1703. This was an advice guide, published to help people behave respectfully towards those of a higher social class.

■ Where is the subjunctive used in the text? How many times can you see it in this extract and with what purpose?

■ Which pronoun forms are used? Are there any that are now archaic?

■ What verb forms are used?

■ What other linguistic features (orthographic, typographic, punctuation and lexical/semantic) are interesting from a change perspective?

◉ Key grammatical changes across Late Modern English

Table 12 *Late Modern English: grammatical changes*

Century	Practices	Some influences
18th	Formal style with complex sentences, multiple subordination and embedded clauses	Standardisation Hierarchical and formal society with emphasis on conventions and rules Writing valued as separate from speech
19th	Grammatical formality still evident, although sentences less complex than in 18th century	Continuing standardisation Changes in class attitudes Beginnings of universal education Dialectal voices represented in literature (for example, Dickens)
20th/21st	Simpler syntax and coordination, including minor and simple sentences, more popular in media/advertising Non-standard spelling and punctuation used in text/email forms	Worldwide and American English Technology Social levelling and equality Oral language/forms affecting writing styles Growing informality Growth of entertainment and leisure industries

Currently, persuasive media such as advertising use pronouns as synthetic personalisation, creating a pseudo-relationship with their audience. Think also about how political speakers use pronouns to play on their audience's feelings and make direct appeals – 'we' as including the audience in their opinion or to take responsibility and 'you' to appeal to the audience directly. However, despite the fact that we only have one second person pronoun, subtle distinctions can be made between the authorial tone and voice.

■ Link

Synthetic personalisation is covered in greater detail in the Language and power topic of the AS book.

■ Research point

Norman Fairclough, a contemporary linguist, coined the term 'synthetic personalisation' to describe how advertisers use direct address to create a sense of a personal and individual relationship with an intended audience. This persuasive device often results in a more conversational text and so seems more appealing to the intended audience as it pretends a close, friendly relationship with them.

Thinking points

1 Why do you think Fairclough calls it 'synthetic'?

2 What other persuasive texts use this kind of personalisation to appeal to their audiences?

■ Language change and gender

You can use your knowledge of gender concepts to explore language change data. However, over the 300-plus years that Late Modern English covers there have been many social changes for women, from the first rise of a campaign for women's rights in the late 18th century to the 20th century, which saw the feminist movements achieve votes for women and social and workplace equality. So, gender may be a contextual factor that is important to explore in change data but, if you are applying specific theories and ideas about male and female language use, it can be a significant AO2 concept.

Key areas that may be interesting to explore in both historic and contemporary texts are:

- representation of men and women through lexis/discourse/pragmatics
- stereotyping of male and female behaviours and characteristics
- expression of ideas that reinforce the deficit/dominance and difference approaches
- examples of writers (or speakers) 'performing' their gender
- lexical and semantic fields that may be associated with a particular gender.

One recent grammatical change that applies to gender is the shift from the previously gender-neutral pronoun use to either the plural pronoun 'they' used in the singular form or the combining of he/she. These have occurred as a response to social perceptions of equality and contrast with the 'he' used as a norm and convention in 18th-century writing. Other historic gendered language features are:

- generic man – for example, mankind
- male first – for example, 'Mr and Mrs Jones would like to invite you'
- titles indicating women's marital status – for example, Miss/Mrs
- occupational suffixes indicating gender – for example, waitress/actress
- marked terms that suggest the 'correct' gender for occupations – for example, lady doctor and male nurse

- different connotations of supposedly equivalent terms – for example, spinster and bachelor
- metaphors that both represent and stereotype male and female qualities – for example, the personification of nature as a woman.

Further recent linguistic solutions have been offered to counteract some of the biases indicated above. In the 1960s and 1970s some suggested 'Ms' as another abbreviation of the term 'mistress', but this lacked any indication of whether the person was married. Gender-neutral job titles have also evolved and suffixes tend to be omitted. Furthermore, some more pejorative terms for women have been reclaimed (i.e. employed by the group they were initially used to attack) and are used to express female solidarity, although not all commentators would view these taboo terms as positive.

Fig. 15 *Gender differences*

Research point

In the early 20th century, Edward Sapir and Benjamin Lee Whorf formulated their hypothesis about language with two elements to their theory:

- linguistic relativity – that cultures see the world in different ways and use language to encode this difference
- linguistic determinism – the way we perceive the world influences not only our language but the way we think.

Link

More gender issues and theories are contained in the Language and gender topic of the AS book. Use these sections to revise the key ideas about dominance, difference and deficit approaches.

Thinking points

The Sapir-Whorf hypothesis argues that our world view is determined by the structures of language.

1. How can this be applied to these earlier uses of language in Late Modern English?

2. How is a changing view of women reflected in the structures of English today?

Classroom activity 10

Compare the following three extracts from magazines from consecutive decades of the 20th century. The first is an article from a 1950s magazine. The second is a 1960s magazine article. The third is a 1970s problem page from *Jackie*. Not only do these provide an opportunity to look at specific linguistic features, they also offer scope to focus again on one of your key social contexts: gender.

- What lexical and semantic features are used to represent and stereotype women?
- How far have these features changed in the three extracts?
- Which pronoun forms are used and how do they add to the authorial voice?
- What changing contextual factors can you find evidence for between the 1950s and 1970s?

It's a joy to think about summer dresses, isn't it? Lovely to greet those first sunny days with a brand new frock.

I think we can all manage at lease one new dress this summer, even with close budgeting . . . so here is a selection of the latest styles from which to choose. I have chosen these dresses for their variety of design, for their reasonable price, for their obvious wearability, and because they are washable. There's someting for every occasion, so I feel sure you'll find one which is just right for you.

They will give you a clear picture of the new season's styles, and help you to get ready now for sunny days ahead.

Let's see what they have in common, so that we can recognize fashion trends for the new season. Lines generally are slender, but there is comfortable fullness in the skirts; sleeves are very short and abbreviated; waists are well-defined, with stiffened or inset belts; skirts are a little shorter than last year.

There's a good choice of fabrics — ranging from fine taffeta and rayon jersey, to hard wearing gingham and cotton spun.

If you are looking for something for best, there's 'Norma', in non-creasing silky rayon jersey. The midriff fits smoothly, and the bodice is gathered into a high, drawstring neckline, forming brief cap sleeves. This is a pretty style for the girl with a good figure, and excellent, too, for her friend with a smallish bust, as the gentle gathers successfully conceal any deficiency in measurements. The bold flower print comes in a wide variety of colours, on a white ground.

Smart enough for a wedding, or for a summer dancing date, is 'Susannah', in finely striped taffeta. Row upon row of honeycomb hand-smocking at the waist-line gives an expensive-looking touch to the swirling skirt. A draped collar turns back from the squared neckline, and matching buttons trim the bodice. Colours are green or tan and white.

For the perfect holiday dress, I choose 'Malibu' in an attractive leafy print. The low neckline is edged with an elasticized ruffle, to be worn on or off the shoulders. There are big patch pockets on the gathered skirt.

For the teens and twenties, there is 'Louisiana'—the ever-popular gingham, in this year's large duster check. The full skirt has shirred pockets placed squarely on the hips, the high neckline is trimmed with a saucy frill, and puff sleeves complete the picture.

As I said before, all these dresses can be washed and ironed in an evening—an important point to remember, and they are coming into the shops now. Write to me if you would like further details.

'*Summer Preview*', 1950s magazine article

I could go on and on—like I always do—about pretty things in a girl's bedroom. How about dolls? I know you can't use them, but little traditionally-dressed dolls are so pretty to scatter in odd spots. And how about pretty chocolate boxes for stockings and hankies?

And candlesticks are not just for lighting romantic, cosy tête-á-tête meals. They also look gorgeous on either side of a mantlepiece.

Oh, and just before we finish off our little chat—well, my chat—let's get really personal. We all use hair rollers—don't try to deny it—it does no good! And, let's face it, these rollers are about the most unfeminine things you can use. Someone once said that they were like a rocket base on top of a woman's head—and that about sums it up!

'*Beauty is Where Beauty is*', 1960s magazine article, *1965*

DEAR CATHY & CLAIRE – I'm 14 and badly want to go to college when I leave school. Art is my best subject and my art teacher encourages me a lot, so I'd like to have a career to do with that.

The trouble is, my parents are dead against it. They say I have to leave school next year and get a job to help out at home. I just can't get through to them that this is something really important to me and that I could do well if I have the correct training.

We're not that badly off, although there are three younger than me and the thought of a dreary office job or working in a factory repels me. Please tell me what to do for the best as we keep having rows about it and it's making me very unhappy.

When somebody has an obvious talent for something and is getting forced into something they don't want to do, it's very frustrating. The fact that you're encouraged at school means you can make something of yourself in that line of work, and we think it's a crying shame to see talent being wasted.

We sympathise, but we think you should also look at it from your parents' point of view. Their reasons are obviously financial – and the fact that you don't think so is probably due to your mother's good management!

We suggest that you ask your art teacher to have a talk with your parents and let them know that your chance of success in this field is very real. If they decide to let you stay on, they will be giving up a lot for you, and we hope you appreciate it, and do your bit to help, too. A Saturday job, for instance, would provide you with your own pocket money and keep you in tights and all the little extras that you take for granted, but which raise the bill for your parents that little bit higher.

Find out from your careers officer at school about grants for further education – we're pretty sure you'd qualify. And don't be afraid to give up a few things. It's all in the cause of Art! Good luck!

The Cathy and Claire page, Best of Jackie magazine, *Prion Books, 2005*

As you analyse these texts you might also want to reflect on how gender is represented. The magazine excerpts are of particular interest because they cover three decades of the 20th century; however, finding texts from the two earlier centuries of the Late Modern English period aimed at advising men or women will reveal important changes in attitudes.

Table 13 *Key features of gender representation in the three magazines*

Era	Linguistic features
1950s	■ Lexical choices ('lovely') seem typical for women, along with the tag question ('isn't it?').
	■ Much focus is placed on practicality ('wearability', 'washable') with pragmatic implications for women's domestic roles ('can be washed and ironed in an evening').
	■ It is assumed that women understand specific terms for clothing design ('abbreviated', 'inset belts') and for material ('taffeta').
	■ Judgemental comments are made about physical shape ('a deficiency in measurements').
	■ The graphology and descriptions of the dresses connote appropriate ways to behave and focus on the right stance.
	■ References to styles ('low neckline', 'short skirts' and 'saucy frill') hint at changes in styles to come.
	■ There are named dresses for different ages – suggesting ideas about suitability or a lack of individuality.
	Contexts: post-war Britain, recovering from war but beginning of decades of consumerism. Women in domestic roles, but technological advances (such as the washing machine) helping release women from the kitchen.
1960s	■ Lexical repetition of the adjectives 'pretty' and 'gorgeous' supports ideas about women's use of 'empty adjectives'. Baby talk-type lexis ('hankies') reinforces the impression of women in a less powerful position.
	■ References to talking ('our little chat' and 'I could go on and on like I always do') reinforce notions of women using an 'inferior', or deficit, language style.
	■ Words ('romantic', 'tête-à-tête', 'candlelight') emphasise girls' interest in love rather than serious topics, adding to the pragmatics of femininity and feminine behaviours running throughout the text; the pre-modification used for dolls ('traditionally-dressed') connotes the desire for conformity and overt prestige. The comparison of rollers ('a rocket base') suggests an undesirable look, with 'rocket' having more masculine connotations.
	Contexts: more liberation and opportunities for women emerging. The decade of the mini-skirt!

1970s	■ The problem-page topic is career opportunities, although the options for the girl are initially limited because of her parents' attitudes ('a dreary office job' or 'factory'), creating an implied sense of difference from boys' aspirations.
	■ Sense of different socialisation with the verbs ('appreciate', 'help'), which imply how the girl should behave if she is allowed to continue at school.
	■ Domestic finances are still linked to the female role ('mother's good management') and even the suggestion of a Saturday job seems to be to contribute only to frivolous female items ('to buy tights').

Contexts: educational attainment for girls improving and more career opportunities.

Study tip

Aim to develop a systematic approach to analysis. Planning and annotating texts for different features (lexis, grammar, orthography, etc.) will help you group your ideas together.

Extension activity 8

Look at past language-change examination data or older texts online and find 18th-century texts that present men and women. A good online text to explore the presentation of women would be *The lady's companion: or An infallible guide to the fair sex* (1745) (http://archive.org/stream/ladyscompaniono00ladygoog#page/n9/mode/2up). Another 18th-century text in which you can explore the presentation of men is *The Spectator* (1711), a daily publication aiming to offer its readers interesting topics to discuss with friends (www.bl.uk/learning/timeline/large126933.html). Analyse these separately, or compare them, and look at the manner in which they represent gender, stereotypes and aspects of suggested gender performance through the language choices.

Language change and power

Manners and politeness were very important in 18th-century society and continued to be so into the 19th century and beyond. This was a reflection of an English society that was very hierarchical and class based. Politeness was a dominant social tool, used by those with higher social status to exclude those they considered were not of 'good breeding' and background, and to maintain their own positions of wealth and status. As you will also see when looking at attitudes to language change below, politeness is also connected to ideas about 'proper' and 'improper' uses of language.

One way that power is linguistically encoded is through titles and terms of address. While these might be used by many in society, like Mr and Mrs, honorifics show social rank and hereditary status, left over from an English power and class system centred on an aristocracy.

Extension activity 9

Parliament is a good place to see that some archaic language practices are still being used. Listen to a parliamentary debate or visit the Hansard website for a transcript of daily events in parliament and note the titles used. Research why some MPs are only 'honourable friends' and others are 'Right honourables'.

Link

Revise power concepts by reading the Language and power topic of the AS book. Reflect on the ways that these could be applied to language change.

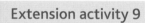

Research points

Penelope Brown and Stephen C. Levinson's politeness model centres on notions of 'face', with a desire to be approved seen as 'positive' face and a desire not to be impeded in acting in a particular way as 'negative' face. Within this, they identify strategies that speakers use. One thing that they have focused on in their elaboration of their model is that address terms can be used as politeness markers, specifically that:

■ intimate address terms act as markers of social closeness and show positive politeness

■ honorifics as markers of deference to others is a feature of negative politeness.

Thinking points

1 Why do honorifics and address terms matter in British culture?

2 What other language features are important in showing politeness?

In addition to address terms, you might see writers use other politeness strategies and, although their theory really concerned speech, you could explore these in your analysis of language change texts. Table 14 shows further positive and negative politeness strategies.

Table 14 *Politeness strategies*

Positive politeness strategy	Negative politeness strategy
Claim common ground	Use indirect speech acts
Notice, attend to the hearer's wants, needs, goods	Question/hedge
Exaggerate interest, approval, sympathy	Be pessimistic
Use in-group identity markers (address forms, jargon, slang, in-group dialect)	Give deference
Seek agreement (choosing safe topics, repetition)	Minimise the imposition
Avoid disagreement (agree, white lies, offering hedging opinions)	Apologise (admit wrong, indicate reluctance, give reasons, beg forgiveness)
Gossip, small talk, joke	
Convey cooperation	
Assert speaker's knowledge of hearer's wants	
Offer, promise, be optimistic, include both speaker and hearer in activity, give reasons, assume reciprocation	
Give gifts	

Here is a letter, originally handwritten, sent in 1788 to the Steward of a local landowning family in Cheshire. The Steward's role was to manage the landowner's financial affairs and duties as a landlord, handling both business and personal requests for assistance on the part of the large estate.

> Dr Sr
>
> Upon Perusing part of a Letter of yours sent to Mr Grimshaw, I find it is your wish that I write to Mr Legh concerning the small quantity of Timber I had from Haydock, for the use of the intended Parler at the end of my House – But as I cannot think of troubleing him with a Petition so trifling in its nature, I have given up my Intention of Building, & the Timber shall be returnd in the state I receiv'd it – I did not apprehend at the time I apply'd for a little Timber, for the above purpose, that it wd. have been a greater Crime in me, then an other, to have been accommodated with it; but I find I was mistaken, and as the whole human race are liable to errors, I hope this will not be an unpardonable one in me – It is not my wish to secret any part of my Conduct in this business; nor that of my friends; therefore shall give you a brief account of it – I apply'd to Mr Rigbey for a little Oak Timber, for the aforesaid purpose, to accommodate my friends. he said he was sorry to deny my request, but it was much wanted at the Coalpits, and he thought it could not give offence, if I made use of a little Dale, as a substitute – Thus Sr have I given you a faithfull account of this mighty business, which I should have made you acquainted with the last time I had the pleasure of seeing you but it slip'd my memory – And I cannot help observing, that this alarm came with the worst Grace from Shaw Alanson, of any man in the neighbourhood – You will pray be so obliging to inform your Dairy Maid her mother is very bad indeed; but she is proper care taken of – she has Eliz Croft to attend her –
>
> I am Dr. Sr.
>
> Yrs Sincerely
>
> E Ackers

Letters written to Richard Orford, a steward of Peter Legh the Younger at Lyme Hall, Cheshire. Collection held in the John Rylands Library, University of Manchester

Classroom activity 11

■ What language features demonstrate positive and/or negative politeness?

■ What power relationships are shown in the letter?

■ What other language features suggest that this is an 18th-century text?

Language change and technology

Hearing people use words like 'hashtag' on Twitter as a means of referencing a key word or phrase in speech shows instantly that technology has had one of the largest impacts on language change in recent years. Our language use is both shaped by the mediums we use to communicate and we shape it according to which medium we use. This can be illustrated with the Twitter example: not only do the character restrictions shape how you construct your comment, they also give you the freedom to be creative in your language choices.

In the same way, writers in earlier centuries were affected by their communication mediums. Printing allowed for mass production, wider audiences and led to the growth of different genres. The novel was an 18th-century phenomenon and success story as the growing middle class who were able to read provided a larger audience. In the 21st century electronic devices such as e-readers have revolutionised and revitalised the novel, providing instant access to books and offering options to readers to customise these by changing font sizes. Other early production methods, such as handwriting texts, were laborious but meant that letters and notes were fashioned personally, with errors and changing thought processes evident. There was no facility to spell check and edit. So, each age has its technology and fashions it to suit.

Further reading

David Crystal's *Internet Linguistics: A student's guide* uses up-to-date examples and is an engaging read for exploring the internet's effects on today's language.

Crystal, D. *Internet Linguistics: A student's guide*, Routledge, 2011

Study tip

Like gender, technology can be a contextual factor (AO3) as well as a conceptual point (AO2). The distinction is how you include it in your response. If you analyse the impact that changing technology has on the production or reception of the data, then this is AO3. When you begin discussing either the affordances of the medium or referring to Crystal, you are engaging with the concepts and issues (AO2) surrounding the use of technology.

Research points

In *Internet Linguistics, A student's guide*, David Crystal defines a language variety as containing distinct language features, ones that correspond to your application of language methods over your study of English Language. The written varieties are a useful starting point for analysing technological texts, because each medium is distinct:

■ graphic features (typography, page design, spacing, illustrations, colour)
■ graphological features (italics, bold, spelling, punctuation)
■ grammatical features (sentence structure, word order)
■ lexical features (word choices)
■ discourse features (structure and progression of ideas).

Thinking points

1. Can different technological mediums be regarded as different varieties of English?

2. What would you add to this list for spoken varieties of English?

Extension activity 10

Make a list of different mediums of current technological communication forms (e.g. Tumblr, Twitter, Facebook, webpages, etc.). Using Crystal's list, identify the distinctive features for each one.

For each, consider the different audiences and purposes. Do you think these influence the language features that the sites require?

A key general concept to apply with technology is that of the affordances – the possibilities – that the specific technology allows. Some particular modern ICT affordances suggested by Conole and Dyke in 'What are the affordances of information and communication technologies?' (2004) are accessibility, speed of change, diversity, communication, collaboration, reflection, multimodality, surveillance and immediacy. Some affordances can also have constraints attached. Conole and Dyke exemplify this with the immediacy of accessing up-to-date information as an affordance, but the constraints of this speed could be issues about the quality of the information, the credibility of sources and the lack of critical thought that may have been given to the information offered. Likewise, if you look at texts from earlier in Late Modern English, you might see differences because of the technology available at the time and the constraints often resulting from the print-based or handwritten formats.

Sampling some of the ways we use the internet today (as communicators for social purposes, as consumers to buy, as researchers to find out information, as contributors in reviews and blogs, etc.) will highlight the effect technology has had on us. However, technology has also changed genre and language use throughout history and it is possible to make sensible observations about language change from looking at the affordances offered by changing printing practices and advances in communication, for example the impact of the telegraph and the use of Morse code in the mid-19th century.

Although it is impossible to exemplify all technological mediums and issues given the variety of data you could encounter in the exam, the First World War soldier's handwritten letter from 1916 explores some of the ways that technology can affect communication.

■ Link

A good source of revision for technology (such as electronic items) is to revisit the Language and technology topic in the AS book, which focuses on contemporary use, examples and issues.

You also consider the contextual impact of technology when looking at recipes (pages 86–87).

■ Classroom activity 12

Read this extract from a letter written by a soldier during the First World War. The complete letter is 16 pages long, beginning on 29 June and ending abruptly on 3 July after he tells his family of his positive feelings about the next phase of the advance.

- How does the communication medium of a letter affect its structure?
- In what way does the handwritten nature of the letter affect the content and discourse structure?
- What contextual factors are important here? How do these affect the language he uses?

Thurs: June 29th. Sent letter off yesterday. Hope it reaches home – hear that letters possibly held up – certainly only green envelopes & field p.c.s getting through. Boys were to have gone over parapet this morning but last night orders came out for 48 hours delay owing to wet & bad conditions of trenches & roads. Impossible to follow up with artillery – roads so bad. We had received orders to 'stand to' all night but now cancelled for couple of days. Having quiet day.

June 30th – Resting much as possible in case of emergencies. Dinner time happened to say to Amy it was my birthday, 5 minutes afterwards small parcel handed to me containing lovely silver-plated cigarette case & note with birthday wishes from Billie – don't know how he managed to get such a splendid present just handy unless he knew & asked despatch rider to get one at Amiens.

Private letter written by John William Mayer

Changes in speech style

In this topic you will:

- explore changing attitudes to spoken English in Late Modern English

- analyse linguistically changing representation of speech styles in Late Modern English

- understand the ways in which spoken English has changed.

Starter activity

Listen to phonological variation in the Sounds Familiar? learning section of The British Library website (www.bl.uk/english). This will introduce you to regional variation, the changing sound of English, and it offers case studies and activities. Start thinking about the sounds of English and debate some of these questions.

- Is there English that sounds 'proper'? Can you think of speakers who speak in this way?

- Why do people either dislike or prefer some English accents? What are your preferences and why?

- What is affecting the way we pronounce words today in English? Is it the internet or American that influences pronunciation perhaps?

Key terms

Omission: the leaving out of a phoneme in a group of phonemes clustered together.

Assimilation: the influence exercised by one sound upon the articulation of another, so that the sounds become more alike.

Exploring phonological change and changing speech styles

During Late Modern English the spoken mode has risen in status and value and is another form that shows how language has changed. However, as the development of recording technology has only been relatively recent, the sounds of English before the mid-19th century have to be worked out from written clues. That the sound of English has changed considerably is not in dispute, but why it has is more hotly debated.

First, what about the phonological aspects of your own spoken language? Do you say 'hanging' or 'angin'? 'Football' or 'foo'ball'? 'Handkerchief' or 'hankerchief'? These examples highlight the main ways in which spoken language changes.

- **Omission**: Where sounds disappear from words. Often this involves the clipping of the final consonant. In the example of the slang word 'hanging' (suggesting something is not very nice!) the omission can be at the beginning as well as the end. Also, we tend not to pronounce the medial 'g', preferring to say 'hanin'.

- **Assimilation**: The pronunciation of one phoneme is affected by an adjacent phoneme: 'don't you' is usually pronounced 'dohnchu' in natural speech.

Jean Aitchison, in *Language Change: Progress or Decay*, cites this as a natural tendency occurring within all languages. So why have speech styles changed? The main reasons for phonological change are the following.

- **Ease of articulation**: As you saw above, we often make spoken words and phrases easier to say. We also abbreviate words. You don't often refer to your 'mobile telephone', instead probably preferring to call it your 'mobile' or your 'phone'. Some people would view changing phonology as a sign of laziness rather than an inevitable process. The big phonological changes of previous centuries, such as the Great Vowel Shift of 1400–1600 where the sounds of the vowels changed (for example, 'sight' would have been pronounced with the 'ee' sound in modern 'meet'), occurred across all English society as the language evolved from its mixed heritage and made the spoken language more like today's oral form.

- **Social prestige and changes in society**: People move around more and, along with mass communication, the result is less regional variation. The impact of radio and television has grown over recent decades and the **informalisation** of these media has affected the spoken language. Also, some people's desire to create cultural identity has caused more sociolectal variations and a move against 'correct' speech.

Even in the 20th century, speech styles changed. In the early days of radio, BBC presenters used **Received Pronunciation (RP)**, the prestige accent associated with the upper classes. Clearly there has been a significant change: now the regional diversity of presenters is celebrated and you can list a host of television personalities from all parts of Britain. Even the Queen has apparently adapted her speech. A report in the scientific journal *Nature* in 2000 cited a study that noted how her accent had changed between the

1950s and the 1980s. Analysis of her vowel sounds showed that whereas her pronunciation of 'had' used to almost rhyme with 'bed', it is now closer to 'bad'. The study concluded that the blurring of accents was occurring throughout the media, with a downwards convergence towards the language styles of younger people, rather than for any geographical reason.

■ Research point

Convergence is part of Howard Giles' accommodation theory, which centres on pragmatics and how speakers adjust their speech behaviours to accommodate others, showing their need for approval.

However, **divergence** is the opposite. When people diverge from others, it may be to make their accent stronger or to adopt exaggerated speech behaviours in order to distance themselves from other speakers – or to reinforce their different identity.

Convergence and divergence can be upwards (towards RP) or downwards (to a regional or sociolectal variation).

Thinking points

1. Why do you think the Queen might be downwardly converging?

2. If it is happening, what could the general trend towards downwards convergence in society suggest?

3. In what situations might you want to converge or diverge from others?

The term 'Estuary English' was coined in the 1980s by David Rosewarne in his *Times Educational Supplement* articles, and described the effect of London accents spreading through counties adjoining them along the Thames. Estuary English – a mixing of 'ordinary' London and south-eastern accents with RP – is seen by some as RP's possible successor as the Standard English pronunciation. It conforms to Standard English grammatically and lexically, but has distinct phonology. Another feature that distinguishes it from being just another regional variation is that, like RP, speakers from all regions use it. Some of its key features are:

- glottal stops ('foo'ball', 'Ga'wick')
- 'l' vocalisation, where the 'w' sound replaces 'l' ('foo'baw')
- yod coalescence, another common feature of Estuary English, where the 'y' sound (as in 'yod') is changed because of the preceding consonant ('fortune' used to be pronounced 'fortyoon' and is now pronounced 'forchoon').

What may be happening is the desire to accommodate other people's speech styles and dialect levelling, where the distinctions between different accents and dialects are becoming less apparent.

■ Research point

Norman Fairclough, the linguist responsible for synthetic personalisation (see page 104), believes that this is part of what he terms conversationalisation. He believes that there have been 'shifting boundaries between written and spoken discourse practices, and a rising prestige and status for spoken language'. Many linguists see this informalisation and personalisation of language in today's language use and credit spoken language with driving changes in the written mode.

■ Key terms

Informalisation: the way in which language is becoming increasingly informal in all areas of society.

Received pronunciation (RP): the prestige form of English pronunciation, sometimes considered as the 'accent' of Standard English.

Divergence: when a person's speech patterns become more individualised and less like those of the other person in a conversation.

■ Further reading

Joan Beal's *English in Modern Times 1700–1945* gives a historical perspective on the changing sounds of English and attitudes to these that is relevant to your study of Late Modern English. Read Chapter 7, Defining the standard of pronunciation: pronouncing dictionaries and the rise of RP. As well as her detailed linguistic summary of changes, Beal sees the links between phonological change, the ideologies behind these and changes in society.

Beal, J. *English in Modern Times 1700–1945*, Arnold, 2004

Thinking points

1. What types of written communication might provide evidence for these 'shifting boundaries'?

2. Do you think that these linguists are right in their view that language is more informal now? How would you support this?

However, regional accents are often judged against people's attitudes and feelings about them. Dennis Freeborn, in *Varieties of English*, summarises them into three views.

1   **The incorrectness view**: All accents are incorrect compared to Standard English and the accent of RP. Freeborn refutes this, citing evidence that accent's popularity originates in fashion and convention; RP became the standard because it had social prestige, rather than being more correct than any other variety.

2   **The ugliness view**: Some accents don't sound nice. This seems to be linked to stereotypes and negative social connotations, especially as the least-liked accents seem to be found in poorer, urban areas.

3   **The impreciseness view**: Some accents are described as 'lazy' and 'sloppy', such as Estuary English, where sounds are omitted or changed. Freeborn offers the glottal stop as an argument that some sound changes are logical and governed by linguistic views.

Dialectal representations of speech (**eye dialect**) have developed in prose throughout Late Modern English. Writers have experimented with realistic 'voices' for characters, including famous writers like Charles Dickens who, in the 19th century, created distinctive, idiolectal voices for his characters. These showed not only their social status and class, but also gave them individuality. The extract below, from *Great Expectations* (1860), depicts a young boy's meeting with an escaped convict.

> After darkly looking at his leg and me several times, he came closer to my tombstone, took me by both arms, and tilted me back as far as he could hold me; so that his eyes looked most powerfully down into mine, and mine looked most helplessly up into his.
>
> 'Now lookee here,' he said, 'the question being whether you're to be let to live. You know what a file is?'
>
> 'Yes, sir.'
>
> 'And you know what wittles is?'
>
> 'Yes, sir.'
>
> After each question he tilted me over a little more, so as to give me a greater sense of helplessness and danger.
>
> 'You get me a file.' He tilted me again. 'And you get me wittles.' He tilted me again. 'You bring 'em both to me.' He tilted me again. 'Or I'll have your heart and liver out.' He tilted me again.
>
> I was dreadfully frightened, and so giddy that I clung to him with both hands, and said, 'If you would kindly please to let me keep upright, sir, perhaps I shouldn't be sick, and perhaps I could attend more.'

www.bibliomania.com

The two versions of the same story on page 115 (together with Table 15), one from 1956 and the other from 2002, illustrate changing speech styles, as well as representing changing contexts.

'The Four Marys' from
Bunty, **D.C. Thomson**,
1956

'The Four Marys' from
Bunty, **D.C. Thomson**,
2002

Table 15 *Comparing the two versions of 'The Four Marys'*

1956	2002	Comment
Oh, what darlings! We have three dogs at home already. I'm afraid my mother wouldn't be too keen …	Aw, look at those puppies! They're so cute! But we've three dogs at home …	Interjections (oh, aw) represent a changing phonology. Lexical choices represent the age of the young girls ('darlings', 'cute'); 'cute' implies an American influence. Both words seem 'typical' of female language, according to some gender theorists (e.g. Lakoff). Negative politeness ('I'm afraid') is a feature of 1956 compared with the more direct and non-standard style of the recent text ('But …').
I want one of those puppies you have on display, my man.	My name's Smythe-Bennett. I wish to purchase one of these puppies.	The 1956 mother's choice of vocative ('my man') connotes class attitudes, along with her imperative tone ('I want'). This contrasts with the more equal, and polite, tone of her introduction and verb choice in 2002 ('my name's', 'I wish').
Which one do you want, Mrs Fishwick?	Lovely, aren't they? Which one do you want?	So too has the man's address to the mother changed. Instead of using her title ('Mrs Fishwick') in a respectful manner he simply says 'Which one do you want?', again suggesting a more equal relationship in the service encounter between customers and service providers.
Oh, it doesn't matter … It's just a fad on Hubert's part. He'll probably soon tire of it.	It doesn't really matter. Tom will soon tire of it.	Note the alteration to the boy's name. An unfashionable name now, 'Hubert' was probably chosen to represent a stereotypically spoilt boy and this would have been understood by the 1950s audience. In 2002 the choice is 'Tom', a popular name with no particular connotations.

Why does language change?

In this topic you will:

■ consider some contemporary and historical attitudes to language change

■ discover the process of standardisation and evaluate its impact

■ describe the difference between descriptive and prescriptive attitudes.

Key terms

Prescriptivism: an attitude to language use that makes judgements about what is right and wrong and holds language up to an ideal standard that should be maintained.

Fig. 16 *Dictionaries are one reason why spelling is more rule-bound than it used to be*

Starter activity

The title of the topic poses the question, 'Why does language change?' Before studying this further, reflect on your learning about the topic so far. Can you suggest five reasons for change? Share your list with others if you can. How many separate reasons for changes can you think of?

The focus, so far, has been on changes to specific linguistic features of English, and some of the reasons for these. However, the changing attitudes of language users themselves are also interesting. It is important to consider how, and why, we arrived at the Standard English used now, and to think about people's views about the varieties of English we can use. Throughout your study you will encounter diverse attitudes to the ways in which language changes, and you should become accustomed to interpreting these, not only for the ideas expressed but also for their impact on English over time and the historic contexts in which they were expressed.

Exploring language standardisation

You cannot look at texts from all language periods without seeing that a process of standardisation has occurred. As you become familiar with Late Modern English texts (your main study focus) you can see the transitions in style and usage from 1700 to the present day. Language has been standardised in all the key linguistic areas.

■ **Lexis and semantics**: Dictionaries have attempted to 'fix' the meanings of words, or reflect semantic changes.

■ **Grammar**: Printing and **prescriptivism** have fixed some syntactical rules, captured in grammar books.

■ **Spelling**: Dictionaries, spell-checkers and the teaching of spelling rules make spelling more 'correct' and rule-bound than it used to be.

■ **Graphology**: Printing has allowed for more uniformity, and even cursive handwriting styles are taught to children in school.

You might suggest that recent technological developments have affected language standardisation, with people making more idiolectal choices over things like text spelling. But does this simply create another standardisation opportunity?

Perhaps it is worth starting by posing some questions, allowing you to reflect on the reasons for standardisation.

■ Why standardise a language?

■ Who is responsible for standardising language?

■ How is language standardised?

The first one is the easiest to answer. Your response might be that standardisation is essential so that speakers and writers of a language can communicate with one another effectively, and their messages can be understood. Standardisation also places value on a particular dialect of a language, giving it prestige and a national identity. The second and third questions are linked: standardisation has a long history; it happened gradually as the result of some key factors.

- Printing allowed conventions of spelling and punctuation to evolve and, as many argue, gave southern dialects supremacy in creating Standard English

- People's desire to stabilise, fix and codify the language became stronger and resulted in grammar books and dictionaries that recorded rules for written English.

So you can see that standardisation was driven by people for social and political reasons and supported through technological advances that made it possible to codify language and create rules. However, standardisation is very much caught up with attitudes and values, such as those of prescriptivism that you considered in the last section, and notions of what is 'correct' and 'poor' English usage. Good practices are reinforced through teaching and educational standards, agreed by government bodies. Much political and media rhetoric is heard concerning raising literacy standards and maintaining English grammatical rules. Even your assessment objectives embody ideas about the way you should be writing. The wording of AO1 demonstrates the emphasis placed on your written English.

'Select and apply a range of linguistic methods, to communicate relevant knowledge using appropriate terminology and coherent, accurate written expression'.

For some people, standardisation itself is not a problem, but the notion of 'fixing' the language to rules from the past – specifically the 18th century in grammatical terms – is more difficult to justify. And the biggest challenge to English comes from the nature of language as a dynamic force that constantly evolves and changes because speakers use it differently.

Emerging standardisation

The drive for standardisation had been a gradual process over centuries, enabled by printing technology and the establishing of a particular dialect (Standard English) for printed texts and assisted by the crucial changes to English grammar, lexis, punctuation and phonology occurring in Early Modern English and during the **Renaissance**.

But it was in the 18th century, at the start of Late Modern English, that standardisation was more firmly established. The grammarians of the 18th century left a more lasting effect on English, and their work has resulted in many of the 'rules' you apply when you use written Standard English; famous examples are not using double negatives and not ending a sentence with a preposition.

In 1755 Dr Samuel Johnson recorded and described the words in use at the time in the first major dictionary. The rise of traditional grammar in the 18th century was the result of all the pressures to make language conform and to set down rules, driven by grammarians. Bishop Robert Lowth's *Short Introduction to English Grammar* (1762) and Lindley Murray's *English Grammar* (1794) contributed to trying to order and 'fix' the English language into a prestigious and standard form. Part of this prestige involved the revering of Latin and incorporating some of its rules into English. The spoken language and the language used by ordinary people was judged inferior by 18th-century standards, linking ideals about English usage to class attitudes.

■ **Key terms**

Renaissance: from the French for rebirth, it refers to a cultural movement in European history from middle of the 14th to the 17th century which looked back to the classical age for its inspiration.

Fig. 17 *Although not the first to compile a dictionary, Dr Johnson's was the most ambitious and started a trend for dictionaries*

Jonathan Swift, another respected writer of this period, disliked the new colloquial language and phrases which included such fashionable features of pronunciation as the clipped and contracted words used particularly by poets (Drudg'd, Disturb'd, Rebuk't, Fledg'd). Here extracts from his 1711 letter to an influential MP entitled 'A Proposal for Correcting, Improving and Ascertaining the English Tongue' set the tone for 18th-century attitudes to making English a pure and standard form. Following this is an extract from the Preface to Johnson's 1755 dictionary.

A neat way to summarise this standardisation process is to use Einar Haugen's four-stage model of language development. The last two stages are directly relevant to your study of language change from 1700.

Table 16 *Einar Haugen's four-stage model of language development*

Stages of development	How this occurred
Selection	London-based variety selected, based on Midlands dialect. London was the centre of power and had the largest population. Caxton's 15th-century printing press was also London based.
Elaboration	In the 14th century English began to take over from French as the language used in state affairs.
Codification	Dictionaries codify lexis/semantics and grammars codify the rules of English in the 18th century.
Implementation	Printing implemented Standard English, and respected writers like Swift and Johnson used their authority to assert what they believed was 'correct' and 'proper' English. The Education Act 1870 promoted the teaching of Standard English and this has continued to the present with such policies as the National Curriculum.

■ Further reading

If you are interested in understanding more about some modern views of standardisation, read Kerswill and Culpeper's chapter in Part 2 of *English Language: Description, Variation and Context*. Other chapters in the same section cover changes in specific linguistic methods, such as phonology and grammar, and also give relevant and up-to-date views about historical and contemporary language change.

Culpeper, J., Katamba, F., McEnery, T., Kerswill, P. and Wodak, R. *English Language: Description, Variation and Context*, Palgrave, 2009

■ Classroom activity 14

As you read these extracts, check words that seem archaic to you in the *OED*, or another etymological dictionary. What are Swift's main criticisms in this extract? How does this differ from Johnson's feelings about his ability to 'fix' language, especially words?

■ Research point

Many linguists disagree with the view that Standard English developed as a continuous process from Anglo-Saxon origins to now. Indeed, Crystal calls it 'the standard story', implying that this is a narrative and fictional representation of English language history. Kerswill and Culpeper discuss two theoretical approaches to looking at the history of English in a more complex manner:

■ sociolinguistic – acknowledging variations by social group, gender, region and ethnicity

■ critical – measuring variations against power relationships and ideologies of the time.

They argue that one of the most dominant ideologies is the standard ideology, viewing Standard English as correct as, and better than, other forms of English.

Thinking points

1 From your study of English standardisation, how far do you agree that it is continuous?

2 What evidence could you offer for the idea that power and ideologies have affected English during the period of Late Modern English?

My LORD; I do here in the Name of all the Learned and Polite Persons of the Nation, complain to your LORDSHIP, as *First Minister*, that our Language is extremely imperfect; that its daily Improvements are by no means in proportion to its daily Corruptions; and the Pretenders to polish and refine it, have chiefly multiplied Abuses and Absurdities; and, that in many Instances, it offends against every Part of Grammar. But lest Your Lordship should think my Censure to be too severe, I shall take leave to be more particular.

Several young Men at the Universities, terribly possed with the fear of Pedantry, run into a worse Extream, and think all Politeness to consist in reading the daily Trash sent down to them from hence: This they call *knowing the World*, and reading *Men and Manners*. Thus furnished they come up to Town, reckon all their Errors for Accomplishments, borrow the newest Sett of Phrases, and if they take a Pen into their Hands, all the odd Words they have picked up in a Coffee-House, or a Gaming Ordinary, are produced as Flowers of Style; and the Orthography refined to the utmost. To this we owe those monstrous Productions, which under the Names of *Trips, Spies, Amusements*, and other conceited Appellations, have over-run us for some Years past. To this we owe that strange Race of Wits, who tell us, they Write to the *Humour of the Age*: And I wish I could say, these quaint Fopperies were wholly absent from graver Subjects. In short, I would undertake to shew Your Lᴏʀᴅꜱʜɪᴘ several Pieces, where the Beauties of this kind are so prominent, that with all your Skill in Languages, you could never be able either to read or understand them.

Jonathan Swift, 'A Proposal for Correcting, Improving and Ascertaining the English Tongue', 1711

That it [the Dictionary] will immediately become popular I have not promised to myself; a few wild blunders, and risible absurdities, from which no work of such multiplicity was ever free, may for a time furnish folly with laughter, and harden ignorance in contempt; but useful diligence will at last prevail, and there can never be wanting some who distinguish desert; who will consider that no dictionary of a living tongue ever can be perfect, since while it is hastening to publication, some words are budding, and some falling away; that a whole life cannot be spent upon syntax and etymology, and that even a whole life would not be sufficient; that he, whose design includes whatever language can express, must often speak of what he does not understand; that a writer will sometimes be hurried by eagerness to the end, and sometimes faint with weariness under a task, which Scaliger compares to the labors of the anvil and the mine; that what is obvious is not always known, and what is known is not always present; that sudden fits of inadvertency will surprize vigilance, slight avocations will seduce attention, and casual eclipses of the mind will darken learning; and that the writer shall often in vain trace his memory at the moment of need, for that which yesterday he knew with intuitive readiness, and which will come uncalled into his thoughts to-morrow.

Dr Samuel Johnson, from the preface to A Dictionary of the English Language, 1755

Johnson's *A Dictionary of the English Language* offered definitions of about 40,000 words. Although earlier dictionaries had existed, this was the most ambitious, starting the trend for dictionaries that culminated in the *Oxford English Dictionary* in the 19th century. These examples from Johnson's dictionary show how words come into fashionable usage, then sometimes fade away: 'blatherskite' (nonsense); 'fleer' (a mocking word or look); 'gulosity' (greediness); 'kickshaw' (something ridiculous) and 'tonguepad' (a great talker). These could all now be classed as obsolete, rather than archaic.

The 19th century simply built on the standardisation process, and mass education and literacy programmes reinforced the 'ideal' standards in written English. Indeed the focus for centuries of standardisation has been on written English, creating a distance and difference between this mode and spoken English.

The seemingly constant conflict between some people's desire for stability and purity in language use and the reality of the world we live in is exemplified in this cartoon strip.

Lynn Johnston, 'For better or for worse' cartoon strip, 22 April 2007

Some major dictionaries and grammar books that have played an important part in standardisation include the following.

- **1755**: Dr Johnson, *A Dictionary of the English Language*
- **1762**: Robert Lowth, *Short Introduction to English Grammar*
- **1794**: Lindley Murray, *English Grammar*
- **1884**: First '**fascicle**' of the *OED* (*Oxford English Dictionary*)
- **1926**: Henry W. Fowler, *Modern English Usage*

What attitudes affect standard and non-standard language use?

Having had the opportunity to study the history of standardisation and some 18th-century attitudes towards English usage, it is important to consider how attitudes to standardisation and the changing nature of English have developed. A good starting point is to look at your own use of English. What do you think affects your use of English?

What you considered important is possibly much concerned with your identity – where you come from and the social groups you belong to – and part of this is linked to standard and non-standard forms or your views of prestige. Language choices we use in our speech and writing reveal much about us as individuals and as members of wider cultural or social groups.

💡 Exploring prescriptive or descriptive attitudes

This activity assessed what you knew about rules. Now think about how you felt about the differences. Do you think the version is right, or that it doesn't matter as the non-standard English versions are perfectly understandable? Do you think it's important to write correctly or do you think it is fine to adapt your language according to the context or medium of communication – for example, if you are speaking or texting as opposed to writing a formally assessed essay for your English Language A Level? Ask yourself which of the statements in Figure 18 best describes how you feel about language.

Fig. 18 *Prescriptive versus descriptive attitudes*

If you agreed with the statements in the boy's point, then you are taking a prescriptive view, believing that high standards should be maintained. This point of view places value on the purity of language and that there is both 'good' and 'bad' language. Prescriptivism is about looking at the past and seeing current English usage as showing declining standards. Judgements are made about regional dialect and sociolectal forms, such as slang, as being inferior to the main dialect of written English, Standard English.

Agreeing with the girl's point shows that you take a descriptive view of language, believing that change is inevitable and necessary, and should be embraced instead of resisted. Variation in English, whether regional or social, is valued and judgements are not made on the basis of best or worst. Different forms of language are legitimised as providing variation, rather than being inferior. **Descriptivism** gives spoken English the same status as written forms.

Descriptivism is a more recent approach, resulting possibly from English as a global language and from linguists' research into how language is actually used. There are English speakers all over the world and the different varieties add to the lexicon and repertoire of grammatical structures.

Research point

Jean Aitchison, in her 1996 Reith Lectures (The Language Web), posed the question 'Is our language in decay?' She used a series of metaphors to suggest people's worries and fears about language change.

- **Damp-spoon syndrome**: Language changes because people are lazy, like leaving a damp spoon in the sugar bowl, which is vulgar and in bad taste. This view presupposes that one type of language is inferior to another.

💡 Classroom activity 15

Before finding out linguists' views, reflect on your own. Read the following sentences, then rewrite them in Standard English. Some of the changes are grammatical, others are lexical. Think about your responses to both forms. When would it be more, or less, acceptable to use one form rather than the other?

- I didn't do nothing wrong.
- Who are you going out with?
- Can you borrow me this pen?
- You was right, wasn't you?
- That was sick.
- r u goin 2 james house l8er.
- Den im goin 2 da cinemas.

Key terms

Descriptivism: an attitude to language use that seeks to describe it without making value judgements.

■ **Crumbling castle view**: Language is like a beautiful castle that must be preserved. However, language has never been at a pinnacle and a rigid system is not always better than a changing one.

■ **Infectious disease assumption**: Bad/poor language is caught like a disease from those around us and we should fight it; but people pick up language changes because they want to, perhaps in order to fit in with certain social groups.

Thinking points

1 What aspects of language do some people find inferior?

2 In what ways do people try to preserve language?

3 Do you think we can 'catch' language use from others?

Extension activity 12

Thinking about these debates and people's fears over language change, evaluate these points.

■ How do the debates of previous centuries compare with arguments put forward today about language change?

■ In Johnson's preface to his dictionary he said that no lexicographer 'shall imagine that his dictionary can embalm his language, and secure it from corruption and decay'. To what extent do you think he was right? What evidence would you give to support your viewpoint?

■ Although we follow many rules today, what evidence is there that grammar hasn't been completely fixed?

Key terms

Colloquialisation: where writing uses language more typically seen in spoken registers.

Economisation: where certain written genres (e.g. newspaper reporting) have resulted in compressed styles of writing in order to communicate information efficiently and sparingly.

■ Exploring language debates

The view that English is in decline and not being used properly isn't new. Here are some historical opinions that could be compared with the views being expressed by some of today's writers.

■ In the 18th century, the age of prescriptivism, many writers proposed that an Academy of English be set up to establish the rules of English usage, although this never happened. The main fears were: the speed of change, the lack of official control over change, and writers' disregard for grammar and spelling.

■ In the 20th and 21st centuries there seems to have been a greater informalisation, as fewer distinctions are made between the spoken and written mode, and non-standard forms of English (such as dialects or text language) are valued. Debates have centred on society's attitudes towards language used about specific groups, hence the notion of using politically correct English. Other altered attitudes are to the use of taboo language, as you only have to contrast television programmes of the 1950s with the language allowed on television now. The 20th century marked the popularity of the descriptivist attitude to language change among linguists, although other influential members of society (the government and the media) often offer prescriptivist ones.

Placing these feelings in an earlier context, in Early Modern English, some people in the 16th century were upset that writers and scholars borrowed words from Latin, Greek and other European languages to name inventions and ideas. Others saw this as a criticism of English vocabulary, calling the new words 'inkhorn' terms (presumably because they were associated with scholars). Earlier, in the 14th century, many worried that English was changing because of the French influence (brought over as the language of the ruling classes when the Normans invaded in 1066), fearing that English would disappear as a distinctive language.

Research point

As well as informalisation, other terms are used to explain recent changes. According to Biber these are:

■ **colloquialisation**
■ **economisation**.

Thinking points

1 What examples of colloquialisation could you give?

2 What other communication mediums offer evidence for economisation?

💡 Key changes in attitudes across Late Modern English

We can compare the opening pages of the three textbooks below (written between 1750 and 1996) to show how much attitudes to grammar have changed: Ann Fisher, *A Practical New Grammar with exercises of bad English* (1750); John Ash, *Grammatical Institutes, or an Easy Introduction to Dr. Lowth's English Grammar* (1760); David Crystal, *Rediscover Grammar* (1996). Consider the following.

■ What are the writers' attitudes towards English?

■ How does each text reveal its descriptive or prescriptive attitude in its language?

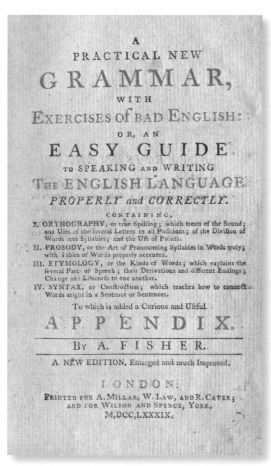

Ann Fisher, A Practical New Grammar with Exercises of Bad
English, *1750*

THE Importance of an *English Education* is now pretty well underſtood; and it is generally acknowledged, that not only for Ladies, but for young Gentlemen deſigned merely for Trade, an intimate Acquaintance with the Properties and Beauties of the *Engliſh* Tongue would be a very deſirable and neceſſary Attainment; far preferable to a Smattering of the learned Languages.

John Ash, Grammatical Institutes or, An Easy Introduction to Dr. Lowth's English Grammar, *1760*

What is grammar?

Grammar is the business of taking a language to pieces, to see how it works. Its study has fascinated people for over 2,000 years – since the time of the Ancient Greeks. But in recent years, grammar has come to be unpopular. People have become uncertain about its value, and many schools have ceased to teach it, or they teach it very selectively.

Currently, the topic is controversial. Some argue strongly that the teaching of 'old-style' grammar (along with multiplication tables) would be a solution to the supposed problems of deteriorating standards in modern education. Others, remembering with dread their first close encounter with grammatical study, argue equally strongly that to reintroduce grammar in its old form would be a disaster.

The aim of this book is to explain what English grammar is about, so that people can make up their minds on the matter. My own view is that the study of grammar is something that **everyone** can find fascinating, fruitful, and even entertaining. It taps the same instincts for thinking about language that are used when people play Scrabble, complete a crossword, or fill in gaps in sentences, as they do in TV game shows like *Blankety Blank*. But grammar, compared with these activities, turns out to be rather more useful, socially and educationally.

David Crystal, Rediscover Grammar, *Longman, 1996*

Ann Fisher's use of the pre-modifier 'bad' for English in the title of her book immediately sets the tone for the text and announces it as a prescriptive standpoint. She emphasises that it is a guide to speaking and writing 'properly' and 'correctly', both adverbs describing the appropriate manner of communication with 'properly' repeated to describe the right stresses ('accent') to be placed on spoken words. To us the phrasing seems odd, showing that some aspects of style, grammar and lexis have changed since 1780 ('connect words aright'), but 'right' links with the adjective 'true' applied to spelling and the notion of correct language that runs through the opening of her textbook.

Interestingly, Ash's text reveals much about 18th-century gender and class attitudes to language study; note that both 'Ladies' and 'young Gentlemen designed merely for trade' are singled out as benefiting from this book about practical English. The pragmatic assumption is the value placed on 'the learned languages' (Latin and Greek) for higher-class men. The phrase 'intimate acquaintance' makes the learning of English sound highly personal and easier to acquire for the types of people studying this than 'a smattering' of Latin. This text, from this extract, does not put forward explicitly the prescriptive view, but it is suggested in the nouns ('properties', 'beauties').

Crystal is defensive of grammar study, using negative words ('unpopular' and 'uncertain', 'old-style grammar') to describe people's attitudes to studying it, suggesting that for many English seems to have lost its 'value'. This is a post-prescriptive point of view stressing that people's fear and dislike of grammar ('dread', 'disaster') may be rooted in their educational experiences of being taught it. This formal teaching was exactly what the 18th and 19th centuries wanted to achieve in order to 'prescribe' the teaching of 'proper' grammar. In the 19th century these teaching methods were enshrined in school practices. Crystal discusses people's enjoyment of words and word-games and uses adverbs ('socially', 'educationally') that could be compared with some of the benefits that Fisher and Ash saw. Arguably, Crystal does not take a descriptive attitude himself here but talks about other people's responses to grammar. However, by acknowledging their feelings rather than imposing his solution seems to be a descriptivist stance.

🔽 Changing attitudes and changing contexts

As you study language change and texts from different eras and sources, you can see how attitudes have changed with regard to your key social contexts of power, gender and technology. For example, issues of political correctness might be evident in contemporary texts discussing gender, for example using 'birth name' instead of 'maiden name' so as not to judge a woman by her sexual status. With power along with other key changes you might see different formality levels used by writers and speakers to suggest a changed relationship with their audience. Good examples would be to compare political speeches from 1700 to the present, to see differences between politicians' rhetoric; or to look at the language of advertising for the tone used to address their target audiences.

Taking the technological context and recent ICT developments as a particular focus, you will be aware that texting and instant messaging have polarised views lately, reviving the prescriptivist and descriptivist debates. In an article in the *Daily Mail*, 'I h8 txt msgs: How text messaging is wrecking our language' (September 2007), John Humphrys (a respected broadcaster on *Today*, a Radio 4 current-affairs programme) aired his views about text-speak, and his disappointment with the OED for taking hyphens out of words because they think people don't have time to use them.

> It is the relentless onward march of the texters, the SMS (Short Message Service) vandals who are doing to our language what Genghis Khan did to his neighbours eight hundred years ago.
>
> They are destroying it: pillaging our punctuation; savaging our sentences; raping our vocabulary. And they must be stopped.

Classroom activity 16

Read the extract from Humphrys' article and focus on the following two aspects.

1 What evidence is there that he is taking a prescriptivist approach? Support your points by identifying specific features of his language choices that suggest this, for example the semantic field of violence.

2 Analyse the language in the article for features of lexical/ semantic and orthographical change, for example the noun 'vandal' is interesting to look at for its etymology and its semantic change.

This, I grant you, is a tall order. The texters have many more arrows in their quiver than we who defend the old way.

Ridicule is one of them. 'What! You don't text? What century are you living in then, granddad? Need me to sharpen your quill pen for you?'

You know the sort of thing; those of us who have survived for years without a mobile phone have to put up with it all the time. My old friend Amanda Platell, who graces these pages on Saturdays, has an answerphone message that says the caller may leave a message but she'd prefer a text. One feels so inadequate.

(Or should that have been ansafone? Of course it should. There are fewer letters in that hideous word and think how much time I could have saved typing it.)

The texters also have economy on their side. It costs almost nothing to send a text message compared with a voice message. That's perfectly true. I must also concede that some voice messages can be profoundly irritating.

My own outgoing message asks callers to be very brief – ideally just name and number – but that doesn't stop some callers burbling on for ten minutes and always, always ending by saying: 'Ooh – sorry I went on so long!'

But can that be any more irritating than those absurd little smiley faces with which texters litter their messages? It is 25 years since the emoticon (that's the posh word) was born.

It started with the smiley face and the gloomy face and now there are 16 pages of them in the texters' A–Z.

It has now reached the stage where my computer will not allow me to type the colon, dash and bracket without automatically turning it into a picture of a smiling face. Aargh!

John Humphrys, 'I h8 txt msgs: How text messaging is wrecking our language', Daily Mail, *24 September 2007*

Study tip

Don't assume that all Unit 3 texts are genre-based. Some may be articles like this one, which exemplify different points of view, asking you to evaluate attitudes towards language change and link to ideas discussed throughout your study of language change.

■ Extension activity 13

Reflect on your own experiences of studying English Language. Do you think that this course offers a descriptive or prescriptive view? Base your evaluation on a consideration of:

■ the topics covered in the different modules

■ the discussions you have had in class around some of the topics

■ the assessment objectives and what aspects of language study they reward.

■ Research point

David Crystal, in *Rediscover Grammar*, sees what he calls a tridialectal future for us, an extension of bidialectism, where people use their national standard and a regional dialect. He says that we move comfortably between three dialects in various situations:

■ at home we will use the dialect of the region from which we come

■ travelling around Britain, for work or pleasure, we will use Standard English

■ travelling around the world we will use World Standard English.

Thinking points

1 On what variety of English do you think World Standard English will be based?

2 Can you evidence this tridialectism from your own experiences?

Examination preparation and practice

In this topic you will:

- understand what you will be asked to do in the examination

- learn how you will be assessed in the examination

- use student responses and feedback to improve your performance.

Study tip

As the texts are all data-based, don't be tempted into essay-like responses detailing the historical background of language change. Remember to work with the data in front of you.

Assessment

As part of the $2\frac{1}{2}$ hour examination you will spend half of the time allowed on Section A Language acquisition and half the time allowed on Section B Language change. You need to answer one question from each section.

You will have the choice of two questions for Section B Language change. There are a variety of data types that you can expect to see. These include:

- written and spoken data

- comparisons of similar genre texts from different dates within Late Modern English – testing your knowledge of diachronic change

- extracts from dictionaries

- articles about language change.

All questions are data-based, meaning that you will have facsimiles of written material produced from 1700 onwards.

Assessment objectives

AO1: Select and apply a range of linguistic methods, to communicate relevant knowledge using appropriate terminology and coherent, accurate written expression (7.5%)

AO1 is worth up to 24 marks. You are credited at the highest level if you are systematic in your approach to the data in front of you. Read the question carefully, note the main parts of it and annotate the exam paper before you start writing. Focus particularly on identifying relevant linguistic features, using the linguistic methods that are familiar from your English Language study (grammar, phonology, etc.). Make sure you write clearly and accurately in the exam, as this shows that you are able to use English yourself effectively.

AO2: Demonstrate critical understanding of a range of concepts and issues relating to the construction and analysis of meanings in spoken and written language, using knowledge of linguistic approaches (5%)

This is worth 16 marks. It is testing what you know about the theories and concepts you have studied in English language, from both AS and A2. Aim to be selective in your choice of theories and theorists to discuss. Unlike language acquisition, there are fewer specific theorists to learn for language change, and your discussion will be more on the ideas and attitudes to language change in Late Modern English. Make sure you have some understanding of what had happened to English by the dates of the texts you have to analyse as this will inform your comments.

AO3: Analyse and evaluate the influence of contextual factors on the production and reception of spoken and written language, showing knowledge of the key constituents of language (2.5%)

This is worth 8 marks. Read both the question and the data carefully, noting down the significant features of context you can see. Such information could include the historical period, the social and political attitudes of the times, and the ways people lived and accessed the types of text you have in front of you to interpret. All the factors that you have looked at that affect language change (technology, travel, fashion, etc.) could be relevant to link to your interpretation of features within the data. So consider how the context affects the language used and don't make a discussion of context separate from your analysis of the data.

◤ Practising for the exam

In this section you have the opportunity to practise the types of question that you might meet in the Unit 3 examination. Practising small tasks, as you have done throughout the topics, has been important to ensure your understanding of all the different linguistic areas and methods you can use in your analysis. However, practising extended writing tasks is the most useful thing you can do, as it tests your ability to look in detail at data, and assesses your ability to apply what you know about language change.

Write your answer to the question below, keeping the assessment objectives and mark scheme in mind. Check your answer against the sample response that follows and read the comments, matching these to the mark scheme extracts provided. Add these to your own ideas to see what a comprehensive answer could have included. Evaluate your own answer to decide what you could have done differently.

Preparing wisely

Knowing the topic thoroughly will be the biggest help to you, giving you confidence when you face the previously unseen data. You know what revision methods work best for you, but remember the assessment objectives and their weightings when you are revising, and in the examination when you are constructing your answer.

Practice question

Q3) **Texts E** and **F** are letters written home by soldiers on active service. **Text E** is from a word-processed version of a handwritten letter sent during the Crimean War in 1854. **Text F** is an email written during the Iraq War in 2003.

Referring to both texts in detail and to relevant ideas from language study, explore how language has changed over time.

AQA January 2005

Text E

Camp before Sebastopol

Nov 20 1854

Dear father,

i only received your kind letter and newspaper for wich i am extremely thankful i was glad to find that you was all in the enjoyment of good health as thank god it leaves me att present When I wrote To you last i stated that i had orders to proceed to the siege of sebastopol we landed on the crimea on the 14th of sept and marched for our scene of operations that night without any tents and the only covering we had was a single blanket in addition to our great coats and to make matters worse there was a fal of heavy rain the very first night of our bivuoaking wich Though a bit of a Damper in the most of us however we proceed joyful on our way elated with the hopes of meeting the Russians – We had turned out severall nights the pickets having been alarmed with the Cossacks that lurks in the neighbourhood of our camp

We have had a very severe Storm on Tuesday last it blewe down nearly every tent in the encampment leaving them in pieces if such weather was continuing it would kill the most of us i hear that we lost 20 vessels and one of them called the Prince containing all the warm clothing for the army also 200 000 in [unclear] it is a serious los to the whole of us as we are nearly naked John Macklin of the Royal artillery was taken to hospital from this and i hear since he is dead i have only received 2. of the papers and 3 letters that you have sent and i wish you would be kind enough to send me a newspaper occasionally and a copy of this to sisters and brother as i have no time to write To them we are now before sebastopol and god knows when we will take it and there is a talk of our remaining Here for the winter if so it will kill half of us please to give my kind love To all relations and accept the same of me from your affectionate Son J Honey

Directions
   Private J Honey
   10 Com R S & Miners
   British army Crimea
   Before Sebastopol

P.S. please to give this piece of [unclear] to Miss Clark She is a much loved cousin

The Military Museum of Devon and Dorset

Text F

HOLA PEOPLE!

BEEN MEGA REDDERS 2DAY FIRST HOT SUNNY DAY FOR 2 WEEKS, HAS JUST BEEN OVERCAST + WINDY AND THE ODD MEGA HONKING SANDSTORM WHERE U CAN SEE (?), UR TENT TRIES TO BLO DOWN AND EVERYTHING INSIDE + OUTSIDE OF TENT FILLS UP WITH SAND.

APART FROM SAND IN EVERY ORIFICE AM DOING FINE AND STILL PLAYING THE WAITING GAME, BUT ON STANDBY ALL THE TIME AND COULD BE GOING OFF WHENEVER, WHEREVER SO WE HAVE TO 'STAY BENDY' AS WE KEEP GETTING TOLD. GOT SKY TV ON CAMP SO KEEP TRACK OF WHATS GOING WITH THINGS [personal information omitted]

SAY HELLO TO MY MILLIONS OF FANS WHO KEEP PHONING UP! AND TRY NOT TO WORRY TO MUCH, HAVE A DRINK FOR ME INSTEAD (DID HAVE BEER BUT NOW DRY DUE TO OBVIOUS REASONS)

LOADS OF LOVE [personal information omitted]

Georgina Foss

Data response exercise 1

Before you read the student answer, plan your own answer.

1 Annotate the data.

2 Make a list of linguistic features that you think are interesting to analyse for language change (elliptical constructions, capitalisation, etc.).

3 Identify concepts that you think are important to explain these changes (lexical change processes, descriptive attitudes, technology, etc.).

4 Note significant contextual factors (audience, purpose, writers, historical events, etc.).

5 Share these with others in your group. Do you have the same features, concepts and contexts or can you add more by sharing?

6 Either write a practice paragraph or a complete answer.

7 Read the student answer and compare it to your own. Read the comments and assess your own response (or that of another student). What suggestions would you make to improve your response?

Student answer

With this response the student has chosen to approach the data through contextual factors (AO3), but linking the main point about the effect of technology to a quotation from the texts shows close reading of the actual data.

The approach to the question remains comparative, a helpful approach in these types of data sets, allowing the response to be systematic in style and based on applying linguistic methods (AO1).

Some of the contextual factors (AO3) are perhaps a little speculative, but they seem valid and sensible interpretations in light of the data.

AO3 is strength of this response but, as it is the least weighted assessment objective, more of these contextual factors could be linked to explicit features of the data in order to show AO1 knowledge.

The obvious change that has occurred between the two texts is the use of technology in the email. This makes communication much quicker and easier for the soldier in 2003, as it is less time-consuming and does not require typical letter conventions, such as the sender's address and date found in the later texts is automatically inserted in an email. Also it is evidently more efficient as J Honey says in his letter 'I have only received 2 of the papers and 3 letters that you have sent', implying the postal service was less reliable than a guaranteed email. However the soldier in Text F also comments on the parcel being left in the rain and so clearly this is still relevant to soldiers today despite the 150 year difference.

The register of the handwritten letter is much more formal as he addresses it to 'father' showing a respectful relationship and also it is interesting that Text F addresses the email to 'people', whereas in 1854 this would not be typical of a letter, to address it to several people. Text F also uses 'hola', which is unusual as it is a Spanish borrowing, but shows that the soldier is trying to be lighthearted and upbeat with his email.

The content of Text E is very informative, describing all the current status of the army, and the weather and problems they had encountered. This is possibly due to the fact that this sort of news was unavailable at the time, whereas now the army can be monitored on the news online etc. It could also be that the soldier in E is writing to his father and so would be expected to share this information whereas in Text F the solider writes to a collective audience and thinks they do not necessarily need to know this information, preferring to reassure them that he is fine by making jokes (sand in every orifice) to keeping an informal and upbeat tone to show that he is happy and not scared to be at war. However in Text E the solider expresses his worries at his ill-health and does not try to reassure his father, which shows that this was not expected of a relationship between father and son in 1854.

Both use non-standard language but for different reasons. There are mistakes from the soldier in E with his verb formations, such as 'you all was' and with the relative pronoun 'Cossacks that lurk'. There is also non-standard punctuation with a lack of commas and full-stops, despite being well after standardisation. I think this is because this letter preceded mass literacy and education and it is highly possible that this soldier was not taught in a school for long. However in Text F the soldier uses non-standard spellings such as 'ur' and '2day' and graphological features such as the + sign, heavily influenced by technology. These are a form of spelling using homophones and numeric substitutions used to save time and characters within the message. The soldiers here would have limited time to write their emails because others probably need access to the computer too. Even the choice of capitals for the whole text indicates that it might have been competed in a hurry.

Text E still has evidence of Early Modern English, with older syntax such as 'on Tuesday last' and the spelling of 'blewe' with the terminal –e, 'att' with a now obsolete double consonant and 'wich' without the 'h'. As standardisation was a long, continuing process it's possible these words and rules were still becoming standardised.

Both texts contain army jargon and field specific lexis. Text E uses 'siege', 'bivouacking' and 'encampment', although Text F uses less: 'standby', 'bendy', perhaps because it is possible for the audience of F to see what's happening on television and the writer needs to be less explicit. Text F is much more colloquial and informal. The way Text F is written represents speech in its spontaneous and colloquial style, shown in the exclamatory sentences and the humorous comments 'say hello to my millions of fans', possibly to reassure his reader using his typical idiolectal style. His imperatives at the end 'say', 'try', and 'have' all seem to have pragmatic meanings for his readers to keep positive for him. Indeed, this text seems more interactional, a result of the immediacy of email contact as compared to a letter sent from Russia to Britain in wartime in the 19th century. The 1854 soldier describes his situation in a more matter-of-fact tone and does not try to euphemise his thoughts, such as 'if so it will kill half of us', although uses politeness features such as modal verbs 'I wish you would' also indicating respect for his father.

> This paragraph takes the response back to a more detailed application of a range of linguistic methods (AO1), with non-standard English, grammatical, punctuation and spelling choices grouped together effectively. AO3 is again evident with connections made with specific features, showing the ability to select 'judicious examples' (AO2). An understanding of language concepts and issues underpins this whole section.

> Sensible and well-observed points here showing AO2 strengths. An understanding of language change as an ongoing process shows good understanding of the changes to English over time. Generalised historical observations are avoided in favour of close focus on specific details of syntax and spelling.

> Again the clustering of exemplified linguistic features shows the ability to evaluate the data and combine the demands of the assessment objective to maximise the data; this also suggests that the student has used their time helpfully to plan their response.

Comment

This answer's strength lies in its contextual awareness, interpreting the context thoughtfully in the light of the data (AO3). There is a range of linguistic methods (AO1) – including lexis, grammar, orthography – and the written expression is fluent. Some awareness of language concepts (AO2), especially in relation to language change (using relevant terminology such as register, idiolect, mode), suggests a clear understanding of the areas studied. This is a strong, engaged response given the time constraints of an exam.

There is, of course, more that could be said about the texts and this is an opportunity for you to select other features of the two letters that could be discussed.

■ Further reading

Aitchison, J. *Language Change: Progress or Decay?*, CUP, 1991

Beard, Adrian *Language Change*, Routledge, 2004

Bragg, M. *The Adventure of English*, Sceptre, 2004

Crystal, D. *The Cambridge Encyclopaedia of the English Language*, CUP, 1995

Elmes, S. *The Routes of English*, BBC Books, 2000

Freeborn, D. *Varieties of English*, Macmillan, 1991

Games, A. *Balderdash & Piffle*, BBC Books, 2006

Assessment objectives:

- **AO1** Select and apply a range of linguistic methods, to communicate relevant knowledge using appropriate terminology and coherent, accurate written expression (5 per cent of the A Level mark).

- **AO2** Demonstrate critical understanding of a range of concepts and issues related to the construction and analysis of meanings in spoken and written language, using knowledge of linguistic approaches (5 per cent of the A Level mark).

- **AO3** Analyse and evaluate the influence of contextual factors on the production and reception of spoken and written language, showing knowledge of the key constituents of language (2.5 per cent of the A Level mark).

- **AO4** Demonstrate expertise and creativity in the use of English in a range of different contexts informed by linguistic study (7.5 per cent of the A Level mark).

Key terms

Synoptic: bringing together a full range of skills and viewpoints.

Investigating language is a fundamental process to the study of the English language and this coursework unit is your opportunity to immerse yourself in a particular language topic, carry out your own linguistic research, and reflect upon your findings. Although you have engaged with the research of other linguists in your study, and will have carried out some data-gathering and data-analysis activities in your work so far, this unit will probably be the first time you undertake a language project that is quite as independent, structured and academic in its approach. You might find the skills you use in your investigation are more like those used in the fieldwork of a social science subject whereas your media text will allow you to thoroughly explore the detail, background and context of a language issue.

This unit is designed to be **synoptic**, which means that it draws upon all of the skills and material that you have encountered so far in the course. The coursework is assessed in the form of two pieces that you will produce, which are linked by the topic you have investigated: a language investigation and a media text.

Section A Language investigation

The language investigation is where your coursework unit begins in earnest, and forms its major part. With the guidance of your supervisor (likely to be your class teacher), you will be able to choose any topic that will lead to a fruitful focus on language. You might find there is a particular topic you would like to pursue that you have covered in the course so far – for example, gender, power and technology, and the language of particular genres from AS, or child language acquisition and language change from A2. However, your choice does not have to come from these areas, and you may want to explore an area of particular interest to you – for example language variation in accent and dialect, or language and conversational interaction.

Once you have chosen your topic, this section will help you to navigate your way through the process of investigation. This includes learning how to: read around your chosen subject; collect, present and analyse data; and discuss your findings, placing them within the wider debate of the subject.

Section B Media text

The media text is the smaller section of the Investigating language coursework, both in size and in terms of how many marks it is worth. It shares some ground with the AS coursework you have done, in that you will write for a specific audience, purpose and context – for example, a newspaper editorial or magazine article – all for a non-specialist audience this time, unlike the more technical investigation write-up. Having explored a particular topic in your investigation, the primary purpose of the media text is to inform your intended audience in more detail about a related aspect of language study.

A Language investigation

Introduction

In this section you will:

- learn what makes a successful investigation focus
- consider the stages involved in an investigation
- acquire some of the terminology relevant to investigating language.

Key terms

Data: examples of any kind of language in use collected, sourced, or presented for analysis.

Reliable: used to refer to data that is an accurate reflection of real language use.

Empirical: work that comes from observation and experience, rather than pure theory.

Objective: an unbiased, factual view of a subject.

Subjective: a view of a subject that includes personal opinion.

Hypothesis: a statement of theory to be tested by research and data analysis.

Methodology: the design of an investigation and the stages it goes through.

Qualitative: data analysis that focuses on individual instances of language use and analyses them closely and in context.

Quantitative: data analysis that summarises findings in larger sets of data and presents statistical findings.

The investigation you are embarking on is about trying to find out new things about language by using a clear and open process that others can understand and learn from. In a sense, this involves finding out some sort of 'truth' about how language works – so be prepared to work with what your **data** throws up, even if it isn't quite what you were expecting (assuming it is **reliable**).

Your investigation can be on any topic whatsoever, so long as it is focused on language – in fact, it is important that you choose something that motivates you and that you have a personal interest in. However, it is vital to remember that your investigation should take an **empirical** approach, grounded in data, and lead to **objective** conclusions, rather than **subjective** opinions – so you must avoid allowing any preconceived ideas to prejudice what you can find out about a topic you know well.

In all, your final investigation should be up to 2,500 words in length (which doesn't include your data or appendices). Because the investigation is a more scientific piece of work, it should go through a series of particular stages, and be presented in a way that deals with each of them deliberately. These stages are as follows.

- **Introduction**: This allows you to discuss the topic you have chosen, including your reasons for choosing it, and any links to existing research. You can also present a **hypothesis** here, or an overall research question, to help shape your overall aims and specify what aspects of language you will analyse.
- **Methodology**: A description of the process you went through from beginning to end in your investigation, including a reflection on any issues that you encountered.
- **Analysis**: This is the most important part of your investigation, involving a systematic analysis of your data using linguistic terminology, which can be a blend of **qualitative** and **quantitative** approaches. You should also include details about the contextual factors involved in your data.
- **Conclusion and evaluation**: Here you will interpret the analysis of your data and present your conclusions in relation to the hypothesis you set out. You will also have the opportunity to make points about the overall successes and challenges involved in your investigation in the evaluation, and give ideas for further study.
- **Bibliography and references**: Details of any sources you used to help you: books, websites or articles.
- **Appendices and data**: This is where you will include the data that you collected, as well as copies of any other material needed to fully understand your investigation (e.g. a copy of a consent letter you sent, or a questionnaire you used).

Make sure that you include all of the named parts of the investigation detailed here, and that they are clearly labelled in your final draft: these are sections specifically set out by the examination board.

Focusing your investigation

In this topic you will:

- consider the variety of possible subjects for your investigation

- revisit some ideas from Units 1, 2 and 3

- explore some additional areas of language use

- begin making a shortlist of possibilities for your investigation

- think about possible questions and hypotheses to base your work on

- understand the importance of secondary sources and the danger of plagiarism.

Key terms

Primary data: spoken or written data collected by a researcher.

Corpus: a large, text-based collection of data, usually stored electronically so that it can be quickly analysed and searched.

Ethically sound: this refers to the methods of gathering data and conducting an investigation that make sure it won't mislead or offend anyone.

Link

There is more information about data collection in the 'Methodology: collecting your data' topic on pages 150–152.

Starter activity

Have a 'language chat' with someone and find out the things that you really care about in the speech and writing around you. Try asking each other questions like 'Who do you know that speaks really distinctively?', or 'What was the most striking thing you read online recently?' and get into the detail of what it was about these things that interested you: it might well contain the seed of something you want to take on further and investigate.

Possible subjects

The range of possible areas of language use you can investigate is virtually limitless; the only restrictions on the subject of your investigation are that it must have a clear language focus, and be based on the collection and analysis of 'real' **primary data**. This usually means gathering or accessing specific, real examples of language in use. These may be print-based sources and/or the recording and transcribing of speech, or even accessing a collection of 'raw' data already in existence, known as a language **corpus**.

Before you start to settle upon potential investigation topics, take on board the following three additional guiding principles that will help steer you towards a successful idea:

- **The investigation must be of manageable scope:** With only 2,500 words available for your academic analysis and report, you will have to limit yourself to a specific area of enquiry, and a limited quantity of data. It is impossible, for example, to carry out a comprehensive survey of the writing produced by a class of 30 primary school children.

- **It must be practical:** This means the material you wish to collect needs to be reasonably accessible. The project must also be realistic in terms of the time and resources available to you – tackling lots of heavily detailed transcription, for example, might prove too much.

- **It must be ethically sound:** It is not usually acceptable to base your investigation on the study of material that would be considered offensive, or to use unethical methods of data collection.

- **Find a meaningful context:** Think about what you would really like to find out about the English language through your investigation: it shouldn't just be an empty exercise. Also, choose something that has a place in the real world of language use and users, rather than just something entirely abstract.

This still leaves a potentially vast range of possibilities, and you might well ask 'where do I start?' This topic will encourage you to begin to create a shortlist of your own potential choice of topics.

Building on existing units

One approach is to revisit some of the topics you have already studied, and to use the work you carried out for the AS units and in Unit 3 as a starting point for Unit 4. As you do so, it is useful to frame a number of questions arising from a particular topic, any one of which could become the basis of an investigation.

Unit 1: Categorising texts

Unit 1 equipped you with a strong foundation in the form of the range and depth of linguistic concepts and terminology it introduced and applied to texts – your investigation should make purposeful use of a linguistic register throughout, so use your notes and glossary work from last year to help you establish this.

In addition, Unit 1 was based around the analysis of a range of different texts and genres, and work with existing research was begun in the form of the topics of gender, power and technology.

Text varieties

The Text varieties section of Unit 1 foregrounded the importance of audience, purpose and context (these can be considered a part of the **social variables** that will affect the data you work with) in shaping particular texts, and the range of textual varieties available across spoken, written and mixed modes.

You will be analysing closely some form of spoken or written data in your investigation, and the way that the Unit 1 examination asked you to isolate particular linguistic features translates well into the need to identify particular **linguistic variables** in your investigation.

In general, the most successful investigations of this type are based on a question or an issue which can be explored by comparing two or more pieces of data, with a focus on one or two controlled variables at a time. This means comparing like with like: if, for example, you were interested in how the language style of radio presenters on different stations (say Radio 1 and Radio 2) reflected their different target audiences, you would need to record examples of similar programmes from each station (perhaps the morning breakfast show or a phone-in), rather than trying to compare a music programme with the chairing of a political discussion or a celebrity interview.

For example, a question like 'How does the presentation of the news reflect the needs and interests of different audiences?' would need to try and keep all other variables the same by limiting the data to a single medium (print-based, web-based, radio or television) and by comparing the way the same stories are presented on the same day. Television news offers many possibilities: you could compare the language of the children's news programme *Newsround* with the *BBC 1 Six o'clock News* bulletin of the same day, concentrating on the headlines and perhaps two or three of the major news stories they both cover. Or you could compare the language of the main bulletins on the major terrestrial channels – BBC1, ITV1 and Channel 4 – with a focus on one or two news (or sports) items.

Print-based news has traditionally offered many possibilities for study. For example, you could consider how political bias is reflected in the coverage of the same story by papers of contrasting loyalties, comparing, say, the *Daily Telegraph* and *The Guardian*. Or you might consider how news output with a local audience (whether print-based, radio or television) differs from the national media.

Study tip

The examination board is keen to see unique investigations that reflect a student's own interests in language – not least because something a student has shown a personal interest in often turns out to be a more involved, original and sophisticated piece. It is essential to make sure you keep your focus closely on language and aim to meet all the success criteria. Work closely with your supervisor to turn your own ideas into a real, working language investigation.

Key terms

Social variables: the ways in which the context of data differs by social factors like age, gender, ethnicity and social class.

Linguistic variables: specific linguistic features identified as markers for possible variation in an investigation.

Link

For more advice on social variables, see the paragraph on controlling the focus of your variables on page 142.

Fig. 1 *Comparing differing language styles, such as those of DJs, would be a possible language investigation*

Classroom activity 1

Listed below are four further broad questions which might be the starting point for an investigation. Suggest for each of them examples of suitable data that might be collected as the basis of the study.

1   How far does the language of advertising vary according to the gender of the target audience?

Fig. 2 *Newpapers offer many possibilities for study*

Key terms

Secondary data: data that has already been collected by another researcher, which is made use of in a new investigation.

2 How does a 'live' commentary on radio differ from one on television?

3 How do the publishers of popular magazines use language to appeal to readers of different ages?

4 How do teachers vary the language they use according to the class they teach?

Language and social contexts

These core topics from Unit 1 first brought you into contact with another important element of your investigation, in the form of **secondary data**, when examining the research and theories of other linguists. Unit 4 offers you the chance to incorporate secondary data sources by putting a particular linguist's ideas or findings to the test, or bringing in work from others to add depth to your own.

Table 1 suggests a range of issues from your AS work on gender, power and technology, and related questions that you could take further in an investigation:

Table 1 *Possible investigation ideas related to Unit 1*

Gender and language use	How true is it that males use less phatic talk than females?
	How early in their development do gender differences in language start to appear in boys and girls?
Representation of gender in language	How does language represent and construct ideas of masculinity and femininity in magazines?
	How do males and females differ when they describe themselves on dating websites?
Power and conversational discourse	How is status and dominance shown in domestic, social or professional discourse?
	How do people in authority control and manage conversations in formal situations such as meetings?
Power and written texts	How does the language of legal texts convey power and authority?
	In what ways has the language of Christian hymns and songs changed throughout the modern English period?
Power, persuasion and rhetoric	How do politicians use persuasive language to exert influence and achieve impact?
	Which accents do people find more persuasive in telesales marketing?
Language and new technology	Do male and female celebrities 'tweet' differently?
	How similar to or different from 'real' interaction is the 'conversation' in internet chat rooms?
Radio, television and phones	How do phone conversations differ from face-to-face talk?
	Is texting more like speech or writing?

Classroom activity 2

Choose one of the specific questions from Table 1 and suggest the kinds of data you would collect in order to investigate it well. Come up with a point about the way the data would need to be collected, and a point about the sort of data you would need in each case.

Unit 2: Creating texts

The skills and study in Unit 2 will be of considerable use in Section B's media text, but they also provide rich pickings for potential investigations into the language of particular genres of texts. Consider the suggestions in Table 2, arising out of the main purpose areas you studied in Unit 2.

Table 2 *Possible investigation ideas related to Unit 2*

Texts to persuade	How is language used to persuade in radio advertisements?
Texts to inform	What methods are used by the writers of software instruction manuals to present complex information to non-specialist audiences?
Texts to instruct	How is advice and instruction delivered by a teacher in the feedback they write on assessed work?
Texts to entertain	How is the language of a passage in a *Twilight* novel used to shape the production of a film scene?

 Extension activity 1

Look back at some of the texts you studied as part of your original writing coursework for Unit 2, Section A. Make a note of at least one potential area for further investigation. For example, if you studied a number of speeches in preparation for your 'Writing to persuade' piece, you could develop this into a study of political oratory and rhetoric.

Unit 3: Developing language

Unit 3 opens up two very rich areas for language investigation in the form of language acquisition and language change. This area allows for a choice of rich **diachronic** or **synchronic** approaches to your data collection: working with children's speech as a 'snapshot' of their language at that time, or over several stages of their development. Table 3 lists just a few of the possibilities in these areas.

Table 3 *Possible investigation ideas related to Unit 3*

Child speech development	What part does child-directed speech play in the development of early language? What similarities and differences are there in the early language acquisition of twins/siblings? How does the language acquisition of a child with a learning difficulty differ from that of other children?
Child literacy studies	How do early reading books/schemes support and develop early reading? What does a child's reading aloud, and the mistakes they make, reveal about the process of learning to read? What variations are there in the rate at which children acquire early writing skills?
Language change	How has the language and style of news reporting changed during the last 100 years? What linguistic changes have taken place in children's literature over the 19th and 20th centuries? How does teenage slang and colloquial language differ in children's television drama from the 1970s to the 2000s?

 Key terms

Diachronic: relating to language study that looks at language across time, and aims to understand the way it changes.

Synchronic: relating to language study that focuses on studying the context and variation of an instance of language use at one particular time.

Study tip

If you opt to carry out an investigation into one of the Unit 3 areas of language acquisition and language change, you do not need to observe the same restrictions specified for the examination of texts written after 1700, or children's spoken language up to the age of 7.

Longitudinal study: a data-gathering exercise for investigation that takes place over a significant period of time, for example recording the same child's language use over several weeks or months.

Care giver: the term used to refer to the main adult who looks after a child.

Child-directed speech: a distinctive form of language use employed by adults when interacting with young children.

Cockney: a distinctive dialect spoken in the London area.

Scouse: a distinctive dialect spoken in Merseyside.

Accent: the distinctive pronunciation patterns used by a particular group of people.

Dialect: the lexical, semantic and grammatical patterns of language use distinctive to a particular group of people.

Non-standard: language use of any kind that differs from standard grammatical, lexical, semantic, phonological or graphological uses.

As an example, child speech development investigations could take the form of a **longitudinal study** of one or two children, given the time period that may well be available to you. This would involve observing their progress by making several recordings (perhaps at monthly intervals) over a period of around six months, with the children engaged in similar activities. Studying children at any period between the age of approximately 15 and 40 months is likely to reveal tangible and interesting developments. A related focus could be to extend data collection to include the interaction of child and **care giver**, to examine the role of **child-directed speech** and the nature of carer support, once again ensuring that you arrange to record and study similar types of interaction.

■ **Classroom activity 3**

Examine the other topics in Table 3, and for each suggest some specific examples of data you would collect in order to answer them scientifically, in a similar way as decribed for the treatment of child speech development.

Wider investigation topics

Outside of the topics that you have studied so far, there are many other profitable areas of the English language that you might choose to investigate further, including those of accent and dialect variation, World English issues and some other specialist areas, discussed below.

🔍 Accent and dialect

When the word 'accent' is mentioned you may well conjure with ideas of some of the more recognisable speech forms like **Cockney** or **Scouse**, which you can often hear in day-to-day life, or through the media. However, **accent** and **dialect** is potentially a much wider area of investigation than this: not only could you look into variation in the language of people from different parts of the country; you could also include all sorts of sociolect forms: the ways people use language depending on their occupation, race, social class and other social factors.

The terms 'accent' and 'dialect' are often used to differentiate between phonological, pronunciation differences (accent) and wider lexical, semantic and grammatical differences in the language people use (dialect), which will give you an idea of the scope for both range and depth of analysis. Investigations of this kind are usually based around identifying **non-standard** usage of English in a particular accent, dialect or sociolect. They are also usually based on spoken data, although it is possible to find examples of such varieties in written forms too.

Fig. 3 *Child language development provides wide scope for an investigation*

■ **Data response exercise 1**

The following data is a transcript of two young Scouse speakers. Read it closely and:

■ identify any non-standard language features you can see

■ describe each one you find as linguistically as you can

■ consider what sort of investigation this type of data would be part of, and what other data you might need alongside it.

Transcription conventions are given on page v.

A:	'ow do you know I was gonna friggin' tell 'im
B:	I just knows (.)
A:	youse better promise | me |YOU won't tell
B:	| wha'|
B:	I ain't never gonna | tell |(1.0) am I
A:	| you better|

5

Fig. 4 *Different accents, dialects and sociolects often contain non-standard language features*

In addition, investigating accent and dialect can bring you into contact with some lively current research and debate into areas like **Estuary English** (see page 113), and some excellent resources, like the accent recordings archive on the Collect Britain website, and BBC Voices project. It could also be a source of considerable personal interest as you may well have family or friends who have strong accents or dialects of some kind, and who would make ideal subjects for collecting your data.

 Extension activity 2

Undertake some wider reading into accents and dialects to see if it is an area that interests you for investigation. Use the BBC and Collect Britain websites as a starting point.

■ http://sounds.bl.uk/accents-and-dialects
■ www.bbc.co.uk/voices

Language around you activity 1

Make a mind map of the varieties of language use you come into contact with each week, be it from friends, family, colleagues, television, radio, the internet or another source. Use it to identify any potential areas of investigation around you.

🔍 World English

The issue of World English is related to the idea of accent and dialect varieties. Under this umbrella term are the range of different forms of English spoken across the world, from the more obvious examples of the differences between American, British and Australian English, through to **creole** forms that use English in combination with other languages to create new English language hybrids.

Possible investigations in this area might be to compare the language of American, British or Australian English soap operas, newspapers, magazines or websites, focusing on the different pronunciation patterns, lexical items, word meanings and grammatical structures used.

Creole-based forms tend to be a more specialised area, but there is a good deal of rich spoken and written data available, and even literary sources. The linguist Mark Sebba has investigated the language of Caribbean immigrant communities in England, and the phenomena of **London Jamaican** and **code-switching**.

Classroom activity 4

The extract from John Agard's poem 'Listen Mr Oxford don' makes use of Jamaican creole forms as well as Standard English, in poetry, while the conversation between C, L and V is part of Sebba's original London Jamaican research. Identify the standard and non-standard language in both and make notes on potential investigations that you could see arising out of them.

Key terms

Estuary English: a variety of English with its roots in the Thames estuary area, but seen to be spreading to many other parts of the UK.

Creole: a language variety created by contact between one or more language forms and becoming established over several generations of users.

London Jamaican: a distinctive variety of language blending Cockney, Jamaican creole and Standard English forms.

Code-switching: a language skill that enables the user to change between different languages and language varieties while speaking.

139

I ent have no gun
I ent have no knife
but mugging de Queen's English
is the story of my life

I don't need no axe
to split up yu syntax
I don't need no hammer
To mash up yu grammar

John Agard, 'Listen Mr Oxford don', Mangoes and Bullets, *Serpent's Tail, 1997*

C no Laverne (0.1) Laverne you shouldn't take no more pictures like that of me
L no, sorry right you didn't want me to take [tɛk] it over you right 35
   I just had to sneakup
V You see (wha woman wear no)
   <laughter (0.5)>
C what was I ⌈wearin'? that's Nicolette!
V   ⌊* * * * * *   yeh look at her in her 40
   (sexy) jean guy (.) deadly!
? eh heh
C 'n 'er trousers
L hih that's me! (0.6) ⌈Valerie cut me off there bwo::y!
C   ⌊(must be the one in my bathroom) 45
V no I never! It's just my wardrobe that's all
(1.0)

Mark Sebba, London Jamaican, *Longman, 1993*

Key terms

Anti-language: language that is used by a particular group to prevent others from understanding them.

🔍 Specialist areas

There are also many specialist interests that you could look to for inspiration for your investigation. These could be something that you have a particular enthusiasm for and knowledge of yourself, for example in graphic novels, computer programming languages, or the lyrics of particular genres of music, or particular kinds of writing.

Extension activity 3

Use the following webpages to look into two distinctive **anti-languages**, which could be used as a focus for your investigation.

■ Leet (language used by 'hackers' and other online computer groups): www.scribd.com/doc/33022717/Leetspeak-History-internet-and-communications-shorthand-speaking

■ Polari (language used by homosexual men in the 20th century, researched by Paul Baker): www.ling.lancs.ac.uk/staff/paulb/polari/home.htm

💡 Look around you

An alternative way of choosing a subject to investigate is to think of the many language experiences you encounter in your own daily life and which interest you – there is certain to be some original raw material here. From there, it's a question of pursuing some aspect of language use which has attracted your attention or curiosity.

Let's take the case of Mark, who is currently studying English Language. Consider his profile in Table 4, and the examples of potential data and investigations around him.

Take your time to settle on the ideas you would like to follow for your investigation. Use the examples and methods suggested here to explore widely and don't be afraid to keep several different potential projects open, until you settle on the best choice.

Table 4 *Profile of Mark Hudson, an English Language student aged 17*

Details about Mark's life	Potential investigation ideas
Current occupation: Student at a sixth form college.	Interactions between friends at college, singling out a variable of age or gender in particular. Or perhaps an investigation into the official literature of the college and how it communicates with students, or promotes itself in comparison to other, similar institutions. Or a comparison of the internal emails written by students and teachers.
Location: Has lived in Manchester since he was 11. Previously lived in Birmingham.	Perhaps he has relatives in the Midlands – potential for study of regional dialect/accent in their use, or in his local area, or a comparison of the two. Could also use Giles' Communication Accommodation Theory ideas of convergence to test how far Mark's accent shifts towards local speakers, or sticks to his original Manchester accent, when talking.
Subjects studied: English Language, History, Sociology and Maths.	Mark's academic subjects also offer possibilities: apart from the speech styles of his teachers (already suggested) he might look at the ways teachers write their reports, or provide feedback on work, or present information via handouts … or look at the language of the textbooks he is required to read.
Family: Lives with mum (secretary), dad (market-stall holder) and two younger brothers (aged 10 and 13). He has three surviving grandparents and one surviving great-grandmother.	Mark could compare the language use and attitudes of the various generations in his family. This could include an investigation into their accents and dialect use, or their attitudes towards slang.

■ Link

Look back at page 50 to remind yourself about the concept of convergence in speech.

■ Extension activity 4

Read some recent investigations to get an idea of how topics, methodology and data are handled. Your school or college will be likely to have copies of successful pieces of work carried out by former students, or will be able to help you obtain examples provided by AQA.

Classroom activity 5

Copy and complete the table below, which contains details of three further aspects of Mark's life. For each of them, suggest potential data sources and investigation ideas that you can see arising.

Details about Mark's life	Potential investigation ideas
Part-time job: Helps out on his dad's market stall on Saturdays.	
Interests and hobbies: Football – plays for local team in Sunday league and supports Manchester City. Cars – has recently passed test. Music – plays guitar in a band with friends.	
Media habits: Enjoys a variety of music; reads car magazines; contributes to online Manchester City supporters' forum. Favourite programmes: enjoys reality TV shows such as *I'm a Celebrity ...* and *Big Brother*.	

Framing a focus for your investigation

In most examinations you have little control over the questions you have to answer, but for Unit 4, the choice is yours. Once you have some ideas about the kinds of language areas you might like to investigate, you need to define precisely what it is that you are going to look for, and the sort of data you will need.

The best investigations go beyond mere description of the data, and engage in some *issue* or *debate* arising from it. For example, you may decide to test out some of the ideas associated with language and gender you encountered in Unit 1, or explore the controversy about the use of phonics in the teaching of reading.

Controlling the focus of your variables

It is usually only realistic to tackle one or two main social variables in your focus. Social variables are the differences in the backgrounds and characteristics of the participants in your language data. If you are contrasting the language in female Facebook posts and male Facebook posts, your variable is gender. But this means you should be careful to eliminate other variables as far as possible by using males and females of similar ages and from similar social backgrounds. Otherwise, what you find out might reflect those differences more than differences connected to the gender itself.

With this in mind, there are two ways in which you can provide yourself with a sufficiently precise focus for your investigation – by framing it as a hypothesis, or as a question.

Your focus as a hypothesis

Setting up your investigation around a hypothesis creates an investigation that seeks to test one or more assumptions or expectations against the data that you produce. Look at the following example.

■ Female speakers will use more politeness strategies than males in informal mixed gender conversation.

This will guide the structure of your investigation and will be foregrounded in your introduction section as you set out the aims and hypothesis there. An investigation that takes this tack is particularly appropriate for challenging existing research, or for testing a stereotype.

When it comes to structuring your analysis section and concluding your findings, the hypothesis will be an important factor. You might like to consider setting more than one hypothesis, in order to allow you to be more systematic. For example, the hypothesis above could be broken down into the following group of hypotheses that 'unpick' a couple of distinctive features that might be seen to contribute to 'politeness strategies':

■ **H1:** Female speakers will use more positive lexis towards other speakers than males in informal mixed gender conversation.

■ **H2:** Female speakers will use more fluent turn-taking strategies than males in informal mixed gender conversation.

■ **H3:** Female speakers will give more back channel support than males in informal mixed gender conversation.

From this perspective, each hypothesis can be tested individually in the analysis, and the conclusion can bring the findings together to reflect upon the extent to which the 'politeness strategies' hypothesis is true.

Your focus as a question

Sometimes an investigation is less explicitly based on testing a particular theory of language, and more to do with exploring actual language usage. In this case, it would be more appropriate to structure your investigation around a particular question. For example, if you are setting up a comparison:

■ What differences are there in the language used by David Cameron and Ed Miliband to describe the issue of climate change?

As was the case with the hypothesis, you might also want to consider setting more than one question to cover the related areas of enquiry you would like to pursue in your research. For example, this might allow you to break down the linguistic coverage, or to open up a related debate attached to your investigation.

■ **Q1:** What differences are there in the language used by David Cameron and Ed Miliband to describe the issue of climate change?

■ **Q2:** Does the language that David Cameron and Ed Miliband use reflect differing attitudes towards the issue of climate change?

In this case, a particular process to the investigation becomes evident, and helps to structure the analysis and conclusions of the research as a whole.

Figs 5 and 6 *Your investigation could be based on a comparison, for example, the differences in language use between politicians*

Study tip

If you study other subjects in the natural or social sciences, you will be familiar with the more technical aspects of how to put together a methodology. As the investigation is more of a scientific piece of work, you could make purposeful use of some of the research elements you have come across in other subjects, like a null hypothesis or alternative hypothesis.

■ Classroom activity 6

Below are some questions and hypotheses suggested by students as possible starting points for their investigations. Make comments about how well you feel each one would work and rank them from 1 to 3 in terms of which would make the strongest investigation.

1 **Topic**: A comparison of newspaper reports of shipping disasters from the *Titanic* (1916) to *The Herald of Free Enterprise* (1987).
Hypothesis: The reports will reveal lexical, grammatical and graphological evidence of an increasingly informal, populist and visually oriented style of reporting.

2   **Topic**: A study of how members of my family interact in different situations.
    Question: What differences are there in the way members of my family address and talk to each other in different domestic contexts?

3   **Topic**: A comparison of the oratory techniques of Tony Blair and Winston Churchill.
    Question: What linguistic features do the speeches of Tony Blair and Winston Churchill have in common?

💡 🔍 Your investigation proposal

When you begin to settle on a number of specific areas that you could investigate, it is a good idea to write up your thoughts, to look at how viable each **proposal** is, and to submit it to your supervisor for advice. Keep your mind open at this stage and aim to put forward at least three ideas, to give each one the room to grow and allow you to decide which will be the best to pursue into a full investigation.

Your proposal doesn't need to take any particular form (your supervisor may well ask you to use a form or system he or she is used to), but it does need to provide as clear an account as possible of the following aspects.

1   Your link to, or interest in, the investigation area.
2   The sort of data you plan to collect – if you can provide a sample, even better.
3   Where and how you plan to gather your data.
4   The main areas of language and features you aim to work with.
5   The question or hypothesis at the heart of your idea.
6   Details of any related linguistic research or theories.

Look at the following proposal by an A2 student, Maxine. Table 5 shows to what extent she has provided insight into each of these six strands, and it is followed by a sample of the sort of advice a supervisor would give at this stage.

■ **Proposal 1**: I am interested in training to be a primary school teacher as I love getting involved with helping really young kids learn. My mum works in a primary school and I sometimes go in and help her. For my investigation, I would like to find out more about how the creative writing of children in the early years of primary school compares with the later years. I would collect examples of their writing – this could be writing that has already taken place and is in the students' folders, or my mum would be able to help me set up opportunities to produce some new work. The writing would be stories, hopefully of the same subject and would be handwritten. The main frameworks that I would be using would be lexis and grammar, but I would also like to look at some semantic and phonological devices as this is something that the pupils work on developing. Other than expecting the later writing to be better, I'm not sure what my overall aim would be, so I'd really like some advice on that!

Fig. 7 *Your investigation could involve an area you are interested in pursuing a career in, e.g. teaching*

Table 5 *A breakdown of Maxine's investigation proposal*

Investigation criteria	Information given
1. Your link to, or interest in, the investigation area.	She is interested in training to be a primary school teacher and loves getting involved with helping really young kids learn.
2. The sort of data you plan to collect – if you can provide a sample, even better.	She gives examples of handwritten stories, and aims to be able to keep the subject constant to allow better focus on linguistic variables.
3. Where and how you plan to gather your data.	Her mum works in a primary school and can go in to help and get new or existing data, so she should find opportunities to collect data easy to arrange.
4. The main linguistic methods and features you aim to work with.	She is aware that lexis and grammar will be essential, but also has ideas about semantic and phonological devices.
5. The question or hypothesis at the heart of your idea.	She is expecting the later writing to be better and wants to find out how the children develop their writing ability across these age groups.
6. Details of any related linguistic research or theories.	She had not mentioned any at this stage.

Here is an example of the sort of advice a supervisor would give at this stage.

■ This looks like it could work well, Maxine.

- Your strong personal interest and link should help make the project involved and enjoyable.
- It would probably be better to gather new data yourself as you could also **interview** pupils to gain some insight to their writing alongside.
- Written data would be good to work with, and you could take some time to collect a 'good' set before moving forward.
- It would be a good idea to link the investigation to some sort of research background, or even details from the National Curriculum or Literacy Strategy to give it some perspective.
- Begin thinking about more specific language features that you would like to focus on from the frameworks that you mention.

Classroom activity 7

Below are two more proposals submitted by a student, Maxine, for her supervisor to advise on.

1 Read each one and test that it covers each of the six points given on page 144 by making notes (you might like to draw up a basic table to help compare them).

2 Decide on the advice you would give Maxine about each proposal.

■ **Proposal 2:** My favourite topic from AS was the language and gender research we looked at, in particular the Robin Lakoff handout about women using more words for colours. I think this is true, and I would be interested in testing it out with students at college. My idea would

■ Key terms

Interview: an interaction between two or more people for a specific purpose.

Study tip

Don't be afraid to change your investigation design in the early stages, either because you realise it doesn't fit together, or in the light of advice you have received. Making sure your idea works and the data you aim to collect is realistic is essential before you start to move into the more analytical stages later in the project.

be to show males and females a series of colourful pictures and ask them to describe what they see. I would be working with semantics in detail and also lexis.

■ **Proposal 3**: As you know, my family and I are originally from Birmingham before we came to London. I was 8 and my sister was 6 when we moved here and I've noticed that, although I still have traces of a Brummie accent, me and my sister now speak much more like my friends who have lived in London all their lives. My mum and dad both still have really strong Birmingham accents, like my grandparents back in Birmingham, although my grandma says they have changed a bit. I would like to compare my accent with my parents and grandparents to see how it has changed, and if mum and dad's have also changed. I think this relates well to the idea of Estuary English, although I would need to research this more. I would expect to have to analyse phonology in great depth, but I think I would need to look at other areas as well.

Secondary sources

A useful source may introduce you to some of the most interesting or controversial aspect of a given topic, just as Fairclough's ideas about power and Tannen's ideas about language and gender did in Unit 1. You can use it as a point of departure and a basis for comparison with your own study, referring to it in both your investigation report and your media text – perhaps in your introduction, or just in passing as you proceed with your analysis. It will certainly be useful in your conclusion to show that you are aware of the work that other researchers have carried out, and to discuss your findings in relation to these.

Here are some of the main ways that examining existing research can help you with your own investigation.

■ **Useful approaches and terminology:** The kinds of areas of language and terminology used in published research can provide a suitable style model for your own academic analysis.

■ **Methodologies for experimental research:** Some experimental or survey-based research may provide you with a useful model for carrying out your own investigation; look in particular at how the data collection was arranged to ensure it was ethical and valid.

■ **Results or hypothesis to test:** The conclusions and results of earlier research could inform your own hypothesis or focus question. You could decide to test these earlier findings.

Link

Use the Further reading on page 174 for advice on some texts that might provide secondary sources of material for your investigation.

Study tip

If bringing secondary sources into your investigation, make sure you do not plagiarise the work that you use. You should acknowledge the source of anything you refer to.

Extension activity 5

The following ideas and research frameworks about language were all introduced in Unit 1. For each, design an investigation that would test, apply or develop them.

1 Fairclough's three-part method for analysing advertisements in terms of power.

2 Levinson and Brown's application of face theory and other aspects of politeness.

3 Ideas about 'women's language' proposed by Lakoff, Holmes and Coates.

The dangers of plagiarism

The nature and dangers of plagiarism have already been noted as you prepared your Unit 2 coursework. In your investigation and media text, as with your original writing last year, you must distinguish between legitimate research of secondary sources, which you explicitly acknowledge, and intellectual theft, which includes any unacknowledged 'cutting and pasting' and other presentation of such material as if it were your own. When researching, it is all too easy to note down/cut and paste whole phrases and sentences from a source, and to incorporate these, advertently or otherwise, into your own writing. This is malpractice, and the penalties are potentially severe.

Bibliography: keeping notes and references

For both the investigation report and your media text, you will need to include a comprehensive bibliography of sources consulted. So whenever you consult a source of information, whether print-based or online, you need to keep careful notes. This means:

■ noting down the author, title, publisher and date of any publication you consult

■ noting down the full web address of any online source and the date you visited it

■ in your notes, if you are quoting/copying directly from the source, *always* showing this with speech/quotation marks

■ reproducing this information in your bibliography when you write your final texts.

Whatever sources you are using, don't forget to use them *critically*: check out the credentials of the author, the webpage or publication, and note the date when the material was compiled, to assess whether it is still valid for your research. As an example, consider the discussion below on the validity of Jenny Cheshire's Reading research in 1982.

■ **Secondary source:** The sociolinguist Jenny Cheshire published a study in 1982 based on recordings and interviews with teenagers in Reading. She claimed they revealed that boys and girls differed in the way they used local, non-standard speech forms, and that there was evidence of social class differences in the language use of groups of children with different backgrounds and values.

■ **Commentary:** Cheshire's study was based on primary data and there is good evidence for her findings, that could be systematically compared with your own research into the area. The study is more than 30 years old and not only may differences in gender behaviour have been eroded further, but trends in non-standard regional speech could also have changed. The idea of interviewing and recording boys and girls from a similar social background to investigate possible gender differences remains a useful model for a potential investigation, though you may wish to extend the focus beyond the question of the use of non-standard forms.

Link

There is more information about bibliographies and sources in the Coursework preparation and practice topic at the end of this section on page 171.

Classroom activity 8

Give the same sort of treatment to the secondary source described below, that of Otto Jespersen's research on language and gender from 1922. As above, evaluate the possible value and credibility of the source and discuss the potential of the source as a starting point for a new language investigation.

■ **Secondary source:** The respected linguist Otto Jespersen claimed in a work on language and gender published in 1922 that women 'shrank from coarse and gross expressions' and preferred 'veiled and indirect expressions'. Limited empirical evidence was presented in support.

Methodology: collecting your data

Starter activity

To give you an idea of the range of ways you could set your study up, look back at previous investigations. These can be research examples you have come across in your exam preparation, or past investigations that your college and the exam board will be able to provide you with.

Your data is the key to a productive investigation, and you should not underestimate the time and effort required to gather 'good' data. This means that as well as being ethical and valid, it is sufficiently rich to support detailed linguisitic analysis.

Some ethical issues

All research is inevitably constrained by ethical considerations, and when planning your investigation you need to bear these in mind. As a general rule, it will probably not be acceptable to undertake investigations involving:

- the use of offensive or indecent material
- any activity that is potentially harmful or illegal
- covert surveillance and recording.

Always follow these guidelines.

- When recording 'live' speech, always obtain permission from your participants before recording them, and confirm this with them again afterwards. Assure them that the recording is being made for academic purposes only and that confidentiality is guaranteed.

- When transcribing speech, delete from the transcript all names, places and other references that would enable the participants to be identified, replacing these with numbers or initials.

- With written materials, make sure you have the permission of the owner to use and quote from the texts. As with the transcripts, if necessary remove any personal references that might compromise the anonymity of the source.

- When investigating children's language, permission from either the school or the parents should be obtained.

- If in doubt, consult your supervisor.

The following two examples of student investigation proposals include a commentary on the ethical issues involved in each and the sort of advice a supervisor would give each student.

Table 6 *Ethical issues in investigation proposals*

Student investigation proposal	Commentary on ethics
Fathema is proposing to investigate the language of voice messages by collecting and transcribing all the messages left on her home phone over a period of several weeks.	Fathema would need to seek permission from the people leaving messages wherever possible, especially in the case of private friends or family members. She would also need to assure the householder that all messages would be rendered anonymous by substituting any names or other references that would allow them to be identified.
Gillian visits a primary school regularly for work experience and proposes to film a group of children engaged in a collaborative learning task.	Gillian would need to secure the written permission of the school to use any material produced by the children, and where filming is involved, the school is likely either to refuse or insist on parental permission being obtained. Although video is generally preferable as a source, in this case Gillian is likely to encounter fewer possible objections by sticking to audio recording.

Classroom activity 9

Here are some further ideas for investigations proposed by students. For each of them, identify any ethical issues involved and suggest what, if anything, the students might do to make their investigation ethically sound.

1 Alice is interested in comparing different accent forms over time in particular regions. She has found recordings of suitable speakers on YouTube, the British Library and BBC Voices websites, which she would like to use as her data. She plans to transcribe speech from them and provide a brief profile of the speakers that states their known or approximate date of birth, the region they come from, and their gender.

2 Gabrielle wants to investigate her own father's language repertoire by recording examples of his interactions at work (with colleagues and customers) and at home (with his wife and their children).

3 Michael has discovered a number of diaries and personal letters passed down through his family from his great-grandparents. He is interested in examining them for evidence of change in the language and style of personal communications since the early 20th century.

Study tip

It can take time to collect good data, so start off early. You will probably be introduced to the investigation at the end of your AS year, and the summer vacation is an excellent time to gather data, particularly if you are working with spoken data, or sifting through large amounts of written text. Starting early will also give you the opportunity to collect further or new data, if your initial material doesn't offer much potential.

■ The observer's paradox

Given the prohibition of covert recording, there is an immediate problem with any spoken data: as soon as our volunteers are aware they are being recorded, the 'natural' quality of spontaneous speech can be lost. Also, awareness of being recorded, and worse, of the study itself, can lead to **demand characteristics**, where people no longer behave naturally but 'perform' in a way they think they 'should', or would prefer to be, seen. In certain circumstances, this can also affect written data. Hence the so-called **observer's paradox** – we can only study our material by observing it, but the very act of observing it changes the very thing we are trying to study.

There are a number of ways in which you can try to take this into account in spoken recordings in particular.

1 Do not participate in the situation, and leave the room with the recording device running.

2 Limit yourself to data recorded from reality TV shows, radio or other sources.

3 Obtain permission from the volunteers to make recordings at unspecified times and check with them afterwards that they are happy for the data to stand.

4 Disregard the first section of any recording and only use material produced when the participants have started to 'forget' they are being recorded.

Unfortunately, each of these strategies can have its own pitfalls.

In the first strategy, unless the investigation depends on interviews with subjects, it is usually good practice for the investigator not to be a participant in the data; it would be all too easy for them to influence what was happening. However, it may not always be possible to leave your volunteers unattended, as in the case of young children.

In the second instance, data from reality TV shows may strike you as ideal, as the participants are all willing 'victims' and after days at a time we might assume they begin to 'forget' the presence of the cameras. However, the situations created by shows such as *Big Brother* are so abnormal that this is an unsafe assumption, and unless you record from the unedited coverage, you may also be at the mercy of skilful editing. It might be possible to find some better material, from radio phone-in shows or similar.

■ Key terms

Demand characteristics: unnatural features of people's behaviour and language use when they think they are being recorded for a particular purpose.

Observer's paradox: the difficulty of gaining examples of real language data, when the presence of an observer or a contrived situation might change the way people would normally use language.

Fig. 8 *One way of avoiding observer's paradox ... but is it ethical?*

Fig. 9 *A representative group of interviewees?*

Fig. 10 *Where and when an interview takes place can affect results*

■ Obtaining a representative sample

All investigations must, by definition, be based on 'samples' of data, as it is never possible to study every available example of language use. It is therefore important to ensure that the samples you collect are indeed reasonably typical of the vast amounts of material which cannot be studied. If so, you can legitimately start to **extrapolate** from your data. For example, one student decided to study the variations in writing standards of children in a Year 4 class. A sensible plan would be a selective sampling of the best and weakest examples (according to specified criteria) of a particular piece of work, with perhaps two or three in between.

■ Some data collection methods

There are several ways to set about collecting data and you will need to think carefully about the most appropriate method to get close to the data you need. Look at the details of five main types of data collection below, with an example of past research that has used each method.

Surveys and questionnaires

Tony Thorne published the findings of research into student slang use at King's College London (KCL). This involved an ongoing **survey** from 1995 onwards where students at KCL and other London universities submitted examples of slang terms in current use, together with an explanation of each term's meaning and use. By the year 2000 around 4,500 terms had been gathered and some semantic analysis had been carried out to place the terms in a range of categories.

Obviously you would not be able to conduct a survey over many years, although you could use this methodology in miniature very effectively. Alternatively, it might be possible to make use of an existing survey to help provide data for your investigation.

In addition to using a survey to capture actual language use, you might want to use an attitudinal survey to gain insight into the opinions that people have surrounding language use. These can then be used to put your findings into context, or perhaps to select the people you obtain data from.

Interviews

An A Level student, Tobias, wanted to gather some data on opinions towards the representation of males and females in popular magazines, to support his analysis of written data taken from a selection of male-targeted and female-targeted magazines. He used interviews with fellow students who represented part of the target audience of the magazines he was analysing, recorded them and took notes from the recordings to compare with his findings.

You can make use of interviews both to provide the main data for your investigation, if you are seeking to work with spoken transcripts, and to provide additional insight into your research.

Ethnographic study

An **ethnographic study** is one in which a researcher finds an opportunity to observe people using language in as close to a natural, real-life setting as possible. Jenny Cheshire undertook research in Reading that compared the use of certain non-standard grammatical variables by different groups of boys and girls. She got to know a group of children and observed them interacting and playing over time, whilst recording their use of the linguistic variables her research focused on.

The distinctive features of an ethnographic study are not so much the way that you record the data (this could be recorded in transcription, or a survey table) but in creating a situation where the language used is happening as 'normally' as possible, meaning that you avoid the observer's paradox.

Experiment

An **experiment** is in some ways the direct opposite to an ethnographic study in that a deliberate situation is set up in order to test a particular aspect of language or see what happens to language use in a particular circumstance. Howard Giles carried out a linguistic experiment when he tested people's attitudes towards Received Pronunciation and regional dialects using a **matched-guise** approach. He arranged for students to observe presentations on capital punishment by speakers of each of these language varieties, asking their views for and against capital punishment before and after the presentation, as a way of measuring the effect of the different accents upon them.

Although they take some thought and design, experiments can produce some excellent data, particularly if you are looking to create an investigation that tests something or seeks to find out people's attitudes – rather than one that tries to describe a particular form of language in use.

Corpus analysis

A significant amount of recorded, real language data is known as a corpus – and once it has been collected any number of tests and analyses can be carried out on it. As an example, an A Level student, Christobel, copied the text from 20 different web-based news reports on her favourite sport, the equestrian events, from the London Olympics. Half of her reports were from specialist sports sites, and half from popular, general interest sites. She pasted the reports into a word processor and used it to quickly find and record the use of specialist lexis related to equestrianism, and the way that key nouns in the event had been used and modified.

A **corpus analysis** can be used with spoken or written language sources – the difficult part is putting one together, as this may well be too time-consuming for the timeframe you will be working with. However, there are corpuses available online and electronically which you could base an investigation on. Computers and the internet make it possible to get hold of many electronic texts quickly and easily (for example on websites like the British Library), and these could lend themselves to this kind of methodology.

When it comes to applying one or more of these methodologies to your own research, you will find that several could be purposefully used – and perhaps even a combination, in certain stages, would work well. For example, if you were following an investigation into the differences between the ways girls and boys use language to interact with each other in a Year 8 secondary school classroom, in order to gain authentic data of children interacting, some sort of ethnographic study would be ideal, recording their language use for later transcription and analysis. Follow-up interviews or surveys with the children would also add value to the methodology of the investigation, although the crucial part would be the spoken data gathered by the ethnographic approach.

For some investigations, the data already occurs 'naturally' and the only practical task is for you to arrange to collect it, ensuring it is both ethical and valid. For other studies, however, you may need to create a context or stimulus which will enable the data to be produced.

Key terms

Experiment: an artificial and controlled situation or activity designed to test a specific idea or hypothesis.

Matched guise: a research method used for investigating attitudes towards language varieties. Similar material is presented to listeners, but delivered by speakers with different accent or dialect characteristics, and research is then carried out into the way each speaker was perceived and received. Studies can use actors to reproduce different speakers, or speakers from particular regions or backgrounds.

Corpus analysis: conclusions and findings drawn from running tests against a fairly large body of language material, often stored and assessed electronically.

Link

There is more information about the quantitative results from Cheshire's research on page 161.

Fig. 11 *Experiments can be set up to test aspects of language use*

Study tip

There are two ways of dealing with your methodology: at the beginning or at the end of your investigation. First, decide upon your methods for gathering your data. However, the 'Methodology' as a section of your written investigation report is best produced at the end of this process, when you can describe exactly what you did.

Classroom activity 10

Read the description of the following two different kinds of investigation and decide what sort of data-gathering methodology you think would be most appropriate for each. Make a few notes in each case, using the different methodologies set out on pages 150–151.

1 An investigation into the way in which the language of a Jane Austen novel has been incorporated within a film adaptation.

2 An investigation into the way that people of different ages use text messages to communicate with others.

Look at the investigation proposal in Table 7, set alongside an appropriate methodology and commentary on why this would fit well.

Table 7 *Applying an appropriate methodology*

Investigation proposal	Method	Commentary
To test some received ideas about differences between how males and females use language to negotiate, argue and persuade.	Set up a 'ranking' exercise in which you instruct your volunteers to reach agreement as a group on a task you provide. Examples might be: placing in order of merit a number of films/TV programmes/activities discussing a rank order of merit for the following holiday activities: sunbathing, watersports, visiting museums, outdoor pursuits, visiting funfairs/theme parks, sightseeing.	This kind of ranking exercise can be an effective way of eliciting many kinds of interaction. As far as the participants are concerned, you are mainly interested in the result of the discussion, perhaps as part of some kind of opinion survey; as the experimenter, of course, you are much more interested in how your participants arrive at it.

Classroom activity 11

In the table below are some more examples of student investigation proposals and suggested models for experimental data collection. They are jumbled up, and your task is to match up each investigation proposal with one of the numbered methods that you think might be suitable.

Investigation proposals	Methods
A. To investigate evidence of change in language and style in oral narratives produced by local residents of different ages.	1. Invite your volunteers to respond (orally or in writing) to a stimulus you provide – it could be pictures, statements, or objects.
B. To investigate the development of social talk among 5- and 6-year-olds.	2. Invite your volunteers to take part in a game (or other activity) that involves verbal communication.
C. To test some received ideas about possible differences in the ways males and females use colour vocabulary, vulgarism and non-standard constructions.	3. Invite your volunteers to relate (orally and/or in writing) a particular memory, anecdote or story. You might ask: ■ Tell me about an incident from your childhood when you were really scared. ■ Can you describe your earliest memories of Christmas?

■ Transcribing spoken language data

Making an accurate transcript of recorded speech is an important part of many investigations, but it can be a frustrating and time-consuming process. You will probably have recorded a lot more material than you can analyse in detail, so first you will need to select the extracts to transcribe. You may only be able to do justice to two or three minutes' worth of material in all.

The most basic transcriptions simply provide a record of the words spoken by the speakers with pauses and turn-taking clearly shown. If you intend to analyse a range of phonological features (such as the significance of prosodic features, or the distinctive pronunciation of some speakers), a more sophisticated transcription is required. Similarly, if you wish to comment on specific pronunciation/accent features, you could make selective use of the International Phonetic Alphabet to transcribe just the individual words concerned, or just make use of phonetic spelling to reproduce non-standard pronunciations.

You can explain the level of detail you have chosen to use in the methodology section of your investigation report. There is a brief introduction to transcription conventions at the start of this book (on page v), but the following example of a transcript shows you something of the range of transcription conventions that you could use.

K:	HEYA (.) you coming out tonight
G:	yeah (1.0) have you seen ↑Tommo↑
K:	↑mm↑ (.) what happened *(coughs)* to you│th. │
G:	│went to football│ │*(laughs)* │
K:	│?? │
K:	any good (2.) did you WIN=
G:	=yeah (.) four nil (1.) it was GO::::D stuff

Key:

HEYA	using capital letters to show an emphasis of louder volume
heya	**phonetic spelling** of the pronunciation of a word
(.)	a **micropause** of half a second or less
(1)	a longer pause, with the amount of seconds given as a number
↑mm↑	raised pitch
[*coughs*]	**paralinguistic** features like laughing, coughing, etc.
│went│	vertical lines show simultaneous speech
th.	a full stop showing a word clipped short
??	inaudible speech
=	running on from one speaker to another without pause
GO::::D	elongation of a sound

Fig. 12 *Making accurate transcripts of recorded speech can be frustrating and time-consuming!*

Study tip

There are many ways to represent speech phonetically. Don't feel you have to use IPA, but do work on selecting a consistent and accurate way of capturing the speech sounds that you need for your investigation analysis.

Key terms

Phonetic spelling: a way of writing down speech to show the way it was pronounced by using letters and symbols to represent single sounds.

Micropause: a pause of about half a second or less.

Paralinguistics: aspects of speech in addition to the actual words and word-sounds said.

Extension activity 6

Record a short clip of you talking with your friends – just 30 seconds to a minute will be fine. Then use it to play and replay and practise creating a transcript of a few utterances.

Looking ahead

Transcription and IPA are good examples of the sort of technical angle that English Language studies can take, which you could pursue further in linguistics courses and units at university.

Analysis: exploring your data

Study tip

Make sure that your analysis addresses a range of linguistic features and that it shows some real depth within the methods that you are using. A strong analysis section is important to all investigations.

Key terms

Anomalies: strange, one-off or unexpected results in your data.

Starter activity

One of the most important things to decide on when starting to analyse your data is the order in which you will tackle and present it. You will have several possibilities, depending on what you are investigating. For example:

- analysing the female data first, then the male

- taking the lexical aspects first, then the grammatical

- taking a different piece of data one after the other, in chronological order

- testing one hypothesis at a time.

Experiment with the different ways you can break down your data and decide which one will give you the most logical and effective sections of analysis.

The importance of the analysis

The analysis section is the most important part of your investigation, and should be approximately half of the overall word count. It is an objective presentation of the features that you find in your data, following the structure of analysis that you set out in your aims.

It is a good idea to think about the style of writing in your analysis in a similar way to the advice you will have been given for your language analysis essays in the examination: that is, to keep a three-fold analytical structure in mind of evidence, linguistic description and explanation of meaning or effect. This way, you might like to think of producing 'analytical paragraphs' when you write up your analysis and ensure that they contain these three elements.

Once you have collected and assembled your data, you can start to get down to the really important work – the close scrutiny and analysis of the material. It's a good idea to make a couple of copies of the data so that you can keep a clean set free of notes and annotations to include in your final submission.

The exploratory process that you will go through will be guided by the aims you have set out, but whatever that is, you will be looking to get an overall feel for what your data is presenting, whilst at the same time carrying out more detailed, systematic analysis.

Getting a feel for your data involves looking for emerging patterns and trends that seem to stretch across your data as a whole, or perhaps even **anomalies** that need to be understood or explained later, that you perhaps were not expecting.

A good way into analysing your data is to write an overview of the data (in just a few sentences) which sums up what you find interesting about it, and what issues it raises in relation to your stated investigation aim. Then go on to give a detailed initial line-by-line commentary on its significant features, either in the form of annotations/bullet points or continuous prose. The example that follows deals with this treatment of a 1930 car advertisement from the following investigation.

■ **Area for investigation:** Student interested in the changing styles of advertising language during the 20th and 21st centuries.

- **Focus question/hypothesis:** How has the language of advertising, as reflected in print-based car adverts, changed in the 20th and 21st centuries?
- **Key ideas/issues/contexts:** Informalisation (and trend towards more colloquial registers). Move from print-based to visual culture. Status/democratisation of car ownership. Changing car driving technologies. Discourse structure of adverts (Desire – fulfilment? Problem – solution?).
- **Methodology:** A set of six adverts for Ford saloon cars collected from non-specialist magazincs from thc 1930s to the 1980s, one from each decade.
- **Data source:** This is the earliest of the six pieces of data: from *Punch Magazine,* 30 July 1930.

Here is a **facsimile** of the original printed advertisement.

PUNCH, OR THE LONDON CHARIVARI.—JULY 30, 1930.

THE NEW FORDOR SALOON (3-WINDOW) £225, AT WORKS, MANCHESTER

GROWING PRIDE OF OWNERSHIP

MEN WHO ARE owners of new Ford cars appreciate their advanced, modern design — also the unusual uses of fine steels — for strength and safety.

Men like the robust chassis of the new Ford car. The strong steel bodies. The practice of avoiding seasonal models. The policy of building the cars to last a long time.

Men like the new Ford's low petrol consumption, low insurance and depreciation costs.

Women, perhaps even more than men, appreciate the ease of handling and steering the new Ford. The little need of gear changing in traffic. The ease of parking when shopping.

Women like the new Ford's positive four-wheel brakes with stop light. The quick acceleration and speed with safety. The unsplinterable glass windscreen. The protecting steel bumpers and steel running boards.

Women, especially, like the pleasing choice of colours. The graceful low streamlines. The everlasting brightness of the rustless steel lamps, radiator shell and hub caps. They like the quality of the upholstery. The roominess and comfort of the car.

We recommend that you study the new Ford cars at your dealer's. Then, in one of the new closed or open body styles, enjoy a trial run to-day.

Prices (investigate low Ford insurance charges): Tourer £180; Tudor Saloon £195; Coupé £215; Cabriolet £225; Fordor Saloon (3-window) £225; De Luxe Fordor with sliding roof £245. All prices at Works, Manchester.

FORD MOTOR COMPANY LIMITED, London & Manchester

LINCOLN Fordson

Key terms

Facsimile: an exact copy of a text, as if it has been photocopied, showing all graphological and orthographical elements in their original form.

Here is a transcription of the printed text.

Growing pride of ownership

Men who are owners of new Ford cars appreciate their advanced, modern design – also the unusual uses of fine steels – for strength and safety.

Men like the robust chassis of the new Ford car. The strong steel bodies. The practice of avoiding seasonal models. The policy of building the cars to last a long time.

Men like the new Ford's low petrol consumption, low insurance and depreciation costs.

Women, perhaps even more than men, appreciate the ease of handling and steering the new Ford. The little need of gear changing in traffic. The ease of parking when shopping.

Women like the new Ford's positive four-wheel brakes with stop light. The quick acceleration and speed with safety. The unsplinterable glass windscreen. The protecting steel bumpers and steel running boards.

Women, especially, like the pleasing choice of colours. The graceful low streamlines. The everlasting brightness of the rustless steel lamps, radiator shell and hub caps. They like the quality of the upholstery. The roominess and comfort of the car.

We recommend that you study the new Ford cars at your dealer's. Then, in one of the new closed or open body styles, enjoy a trial run to-day.

Prices (investigate low Ford insurance charges): Tourer £180; Tudor Saloon £195; Coupé £215; Cabriolet £225; Fordor Saloon (3-window) £225; De Luxe Fordor with sliding roof £245. All prices at Works, Manchester.

Ford Motor Company Limited, London & Manchester.

Study tip

When comparing texts from different eras, it can be useful to try to get a copy of the original source, including the way it was laid out and printed or written. This will allow you to consider the graphological elements and the way they might have influenced the language features that you analyse.

An overview of this item would be that the 1930 advertisement makes its appeal in terms of the 'pride' of owning one of the new Fords, but is most noticeable for its hand-designed illustration, its relatively 'wordy' text and its differentiated gender appeal. However, like some modern ads, it focuses keenly on technical, safety and aesthetic features.

The initial scrutiny for a written text like this would be best carried out by annotating a copy, to identify useful features and issues in the language use, as shown in Table 8.

Table 8 *Analysis of Ford advertisement*

Ford advertisement text	Analytical notes
The new Fordor Saloon (3-window) £225, at works, Manchester	Pun/blend – Ford/door
	Pic hand-drawn/print – juxtaposed with a horse-drawn vehicle Town v. country? – male driving – farmer admires/envies – status? Separation from text: 50:50 text/image split

Growing pride of ownership	Slogan? Focus on 'pride'/status symbol. **Minor sentence** Font – quite formal, serious, serif, caps	**Key terms**
Men who are owners of new Ford cars appreciate their advanced, modern design – also the unusual uses of fine steels – for strength and safety.	'who are owners of new Ford cars' – relative clause Focus on men – semantics/connotations – strength (steels, safety). Polysyllabic – 'appreciate'	**Minor sentence:** a phrase punctuated as a sentence but without the minimum requirement of a subject and verb in it. **Parallellism:** use of similar syntax for deliberate effect, for example repeated phrases or sentence lengths.
Men like the robust chassis of the new Ford car. The strong steel bodies. The practice of avoiding seasonal models. The policy of building the cars to last a long time.	Connotations of strength continued (robust). Register – continued polysyllabic phrasing – 'practice of avoiding …' Listing – parallel minor sentences – the practice of…the policy of…	
Men like the new Ford's low petrol consumption, low insurance and depreciation costs.	**Parallelism** – 'men like…' – synonymy – appreciate men – economy (semantics) – repetition – 'low' – specialist lexical field	
Women, perhaps even more than men, appreciate the ease of handling and steering the new Ford. The little need of gear changing in traffic. The ease of parking when shopping.	Gender issues – pragmatics – lexical repetition – 'appreciate'. Implies gender roles: men cautious, sensible, practical, save money; women – weak ('ease of handling … little need of gear changing'), spend money (assumes not working!)	
Women like the new Ford's positive four-wheel brakes with stop light. The quick acceleration and speed with safety. The unsplinterable glass windscreen. The protecting steel bumpers and steel running boards.	Tech – were 'brakes with stop light' a big deal? semantics – stress on safety – implies protectiveness. Unsplinterable/rustless – negative prefix/suffix – implies faults in other makes of car	
Women, especially, like the pleasing choice of colours. The graceful low streamlines. The everlasting brightness of the rustless steel lamps, radiator shell and hub caps. They like the quality of the upholstery. The roominess and comfort of the car.	Implies women preoccupied also with appearance and domesticity (upholstery/colours). Stereotype? Detailed noun phrases – 'the pleasing choice of colors' etc.	
We recommend that you study the new Ford cars at your dealer's. Then, in one of the new closed or open body styles, enjoy a trial run to-day.	'We' – 1st person plural – voice of Ford? Formal, sales tone in 'recommend' 'study'	
Prices (investigate low Ford insurance charges): Tourer £180; Tudor Saloon £195; Coupé £215; Cabriolet £225; Fordor Saloon (3-window) £225; De Luxe Fordor with sliding roof £245. All prices at Works, Manchester.	Model names: 'Tudor' – connotations? Cf modern names Derivations – borrowings ('De Luxe') and coinage 'Fordor'	

Classroom activity 12

Use the investigation brief and sample data below to carry out the same process of overview and initial analysis as that performed for the car advertisement. Make a note alongside each row of data to suggest an interesting feature.

- ■ **Area for investigation:** Student interested in the development of his twin brothers' reading skills.
- ■ **Focus question/hypothesis:** What does **miscue analysis** of 5-year-old readers reveal about the process of learning to read?
- ■ **Key ideas/issues/contexts:** Early literacy studies and 'phonics' debate
- ■ **Methodology:** Brothers recorded reading aloud from the same part of a book aimed at their stage of development called *Silly Pig*. Transcription of about 1 minute of data per child. Investigation to focus on miscue analysis.
- ■ **Data source:** *Silly Pig* by Laura Rader (Sterling, 2005) provided by researcher. Subjects recorded at home.

Table 9 *A side-by-side comparison of transcriptions of the two readers*

Source text: *Silly Pig*	Child X's reading	Child Y's reading
This is Silly Pig. Everyone calls her Silly Pig because she does silly things!	this silly **pig** everyone calls her silly pig (3) because they (1) she doesn't silly **things**	this tha this is silly **pig** everyone calls him silly pig because he says silly **things**
'You silly pig!' said Horse. 'Pigs don't put flowers on their head!'	(2) you **silly** pig (.) said (.) **horse** (.) pigs don't put things **flowers** on their heads	(3) you silly pig said pig pigs (2) don't put flowers on their heads
One day, Silly Pig had an idea. She went to tell the other animals about her idea.	(1) one day silly pig had an **idea** (1) she went to (2) tell the other animals about her idea	(3) one day silly pig had an idea (1) she went to the (2) tell the other animals about her **idea**
'I'm going to look for treasure on the farm,' she said. 'I'm going to find lots and lots of treasure.'	(.) I am going to look for **treasure** on the farm (.) she said (.) I am going to find lots and lots of **treasure**	(2) I am going to look for things (3) treasure_and the farm see she said (1) I am going to (2) feed (1) find lots and lots of **treasure**
'You silly pig!' said the other animals. 'You won't find treasure on the farm.'	you silly pig said (3) the other animals you won't find treasure on the **farm**	(2) you silly **pig** said the other animals you (2) won't find (1) treasure on the **farm**
Silly Pig set off to find treasure. She went out to the farmyard and up the lane.	(3) silly pig (3) tha set off to look for **treasure** (5) she went on out of the farm gate (3) and up the hill urm (2) **lane**	(4) silly pig shi set off to find (1) look for treasure she went out the farm (1) yard but (1) and up the lane
Suddenly Silly Pig stopped. She saw something sparkling in the tree.	(4) suddenly silly pig (4) **stooped** (1) she saw something (1) **sparkling** in the tree	(5) suddenly said silly pig (7) she saw something (3) spa (4) **sparkling** in the tree
'Ooh, I can see a sparkling necklace in the tree. A sparkling necklace is treasure. I shall put it around my neck.'	(2) ooh no I can see a (4) sparkling **necklace** in the tree (1) a sparkling necklace is the **treasure** (1) I will put (1) it around my neck	(1) ooh I can see a sparkling (2) **necklace** in the tree asked (5) a sparkling necklace is the **treasure** (1) I (2) shall put it round my neck
But the sparkling necklace wasn't really a necklace. It was a spider's web.	(3) but the sparkling necklace doesn't wasn't (2) really a necklace it was a spider's web	(.) but the sparkling necklace (.) wasn't (2) really a necklace it was a spiders **web**
The web was sparkling with raindrops. Spider was very cross.	(1) the web was sparkling with (1) rain drops (2) the spider was very cross	(2) the web was sparkling with (1) raindrops spider was very cross
'What a silly thing to do,' he said. 'You silly pig!' Silly Pig felt very silly. She set off up the lane.	(1) what a silly pig (1) thing to do he said you silly pig (2) silly pig (2) felt very silly she set off up the (1) lane	what a silly thing to do you silly pig_silly (1) pig felt very silly she set off up the lane

Source text: *Silly Pig*	Child X's reading	Child Y's reading
Suddenly Silly Pig stopped. She saw something sparkling in the hedge.	(3) suddenly silly pig stooped (1) she saw something sparkling in the (1) don't know that word	(3) suddenly silly pig (1) sto stopped (1) she saw something **sparkling** in the bushes
'Ooh, I can see sparkling earrings in the hedge,' she said. 'Sparkling earrings are treasure. I shall put them on my ears.'	(2) ooh no I can see sparkling ears **earrings** in the hedge (1) she said (1) sparkling earrings are the treasure I *(inaudible)*	(1) ooh I can see something (1) sparkling earrings in the hed (1) she said (1) sparkling earrings are **treasure** I sha shall put them (1) on my ears

◥ Developing a structure for analysis

There are many different ways to break down your analysis into sections. Doing this will help you to tackle your analysis systematically, make your findings more easily accessible to an examiner or any other person reading your report, and also help you to be in control of the range and depth of analysis you achieve.

The nature of your investigation, hypothesis, question and data will shape the best way to tackle your analysis, but consider the following approaches, to help you settle on a good method for your own work. You might even find a combination of methods will fit your data well.

■ **By text:** using the separate pieces of data as subheadings and tackling each in turn. For example: *FHM* magazine extract; *Cosmopolitan* magazine extract, etc.

■ **By theme:** your hypothesis or question might have thrown up more than one area of enquiry. For example, virtuous errors in child speech, parent use of child-directed speech, etc.

■ **By method:** a popular choice is to focus on one particular linguistic method at a time, for example lexis, grammar, semantics; or topic-specific areas like pronunciation, dialect words, non-standard grammar. This should be an integral part of the aims and methodology you have set out, and not simply a list. You could develop this approach further by using specific features you have identified, for example noun modification, sentence function, etc.

■ **By chronology:** your data may have been collected over a period of time, or from different historical periods, or may be enough to warrant simply tackling it from beginning to end. Here you can use sections that describe particular parts of the data in order, for example Early Modern English letter, 1540; Late Modern English letter, 1790; contemporary English letter, 2008.

Using a numbered system (e.g. 1.1, 1.2, etc.) of sections and sub-sections helps you to keep sight of the overall structure of your analysis – and also breaks down the task into manageable units of work which you can have the satisfaction of 'ticking off' as you go along.

Here, for example, is how one student decided to organise his analysis of his car advertisement as a hierarchy of sections and sub-sections. Within each section and sub-section he would go on to discuss all pieces of data:

Analysis structure

1 *Visual and graphological aspects*

    1.1 Text: Image ratio

    1.2 Nature and implications of image in relation to text

    1.3 Text font/size

Fig. 13 *'This is Silly Pig. Everyone calls her Silly Pig because she does silly things!'*

Study tip

Breaking your analysis down into different sections is very important, rather than presenting it as a continuous 1,000+ word essay.

Study tip

2 *The nature of the appeal: pragmatic and discourse aspects*

    2.1 Discourse structure and organisation (inc. paragraphing)

    2.2 Implied values of car and audience – lexis/semantics/pragmatics

3 *Style and register*

    3.1 Lexical formality

    3.2 Technical lexis

    3.3 Evidence of lexical and semantic change

    3.4 Sentence type and length

■ Informing your analysis: background reading

At this stage you will need to boost your understanding and knowledge with some background reading related to the data you are studying and the issues it raises. For example, the miscue data raises questions like the following.

■ What are the mental and physical processes involved in reading?

■ What methods are used to teach children to read?

■ What can we learn from a 'miscue analysis' of a child's reading aloud about the reading strategies a child is learning to use when reading?

■ How are children's reading abilities measured, and what standards are they expected to achieve by the age of 7?

■ Analysis techniques

Once you have your analysis structure in place, you can concentrate on just one aspect of the data at a time. However, there is a difference between the analytical technique you might use in a routine essay, and the approach needed in a more scientific investigation.

Overall, it is important to establish a more objective and measurable way of analysing the data – which is where the use of quantitative analysis comes in. This means not setling either for subjective observations or just looking for one or two random examples to illustrate a point, but surveying the data comprehensively to establish if there really is a pattern or trend.

Quantitative and qualitative analysis

Qualitative and quantitative analysis are the two main approaches you can use when analysing the data you have collected. A sound approach is often to blend the two – setting out a statistical view of your data using quantitative methods, and then qualitatively examining individual instances that represent your figures. For example, if you are trying to define formality in a text, you could analyse the following specific features.

■ What proportion of the open-class words used are monosyllabic as opposed to polysyllabic?

■ What proportion of the lexis is from the common register and what proportion from a specialised or technical register?

■ How frequently are phrasal verbs used instead of their single-word equivalents (e.g. 'go in' or 'enter')?

■ How often are contracted forms like 'we're' preferred to the full-length 'we are'?

■ How frequently are slang/idiomatic phrases used?

■ How frequently is non-standard language used?

Many of these criteria can, of course, be measured quantitatively. This kind of quantitative work is not an end in itself, but can be used as a starting point for meaningful comparisons and more qualitative analysis which tries to explain and understand the findings it has revealed.

Look at the following examples of the two different kinds of analysis in use from the work of some of the linguists mentioned earlier on.

An example of quantitative analysis is Jenny Cheshire's presentation of the frequency of non-standard grammatical features by the children she was observing in her Reading study. Cheshire classified the girls into two groups: Group A expressed negative attitudes to 'deviant' behaviour including swearing and minor criminality, while Group B approved of such things.

Table 10 *Extract from findings of Cheshire's Reading study*

Non-standard variable	Example of non-standard use	Group A girls	Group B girls
Non-standard –s	They calls me all the names under the sun.	25.84	57.27
Non-standard has	You just has to do what the teachers tell you.	36.36	35.85
Non-standard was	You was with me, wasn't you?	63.64	80.95
Negative concord	It ain't got no pedigree or nothing.	12.50	58.70
Non-standard never	I never went to school today.	45.45	41.07
Non-standard what	Are you the ones what hit my friend?	33.33	5.56
Non-standard come	I come down here yesterday.	30.77	90.63
Ain't = copula	You ain't no boss.	14.29	67.12

Adapted from **Jenny Cheshire**, Variation in an English dialect: a sociolinguistic study, *1982*

Here, Cheshire has calculated percentages to show the frequency of each use of non-standard English by two groups of girls she gathered data from. Using this form of data, it is possible to identify larger patterns, **trends** and anomalies in the overall data.

The following example is from Joanna Przedlacka's work on Estuary English and shows a qualitative approach, discussing specific instances of certain vowel pronunciations based around the /u/ and /oo/ sounds. Przedlacka's data consisted of recordings of speakers from four towns outside of central London, to test how far Estuary English was being used in those places.

> Vowel **fronting**: The word 'blue' uttered by a speaker from Buckinghamshire, has a front realisation of the vowel, while other front realisations can be heard in 'boots', pronounced by a Kent female and 'roof' (Essex female). A **central vowel** can be heard in 'new', uttered by a male teenager from Essex. **Back realisations** of the vowel, as in 'cucumber', uttered by a Kent teenager are infrequent. The vowel in 'butter' has a back realisation in the speech of an Essex speaker, but can be realised as a front vowel, as in 'dust' or 'cousins', both uttered by teenage girls from Buckinghamshire.

www.phon.ox.ac.uk

Data response exercise 2

Look at Cheshire's quantitative data. Compare the percentages given for Group A and Group B girls.

1 What patterns can you see emerging from the figures?

2 Are there any possible anomalies in the data?

Key terms

Trend: patterns in data that seem to show something in particular tending to happen.

Fronting: moving the place in which a vowel is pronounced towards the front of the mouth.

Central vowel: a vowel pronounced roughly in the 'middle' of the mouth cavity.

Backing: moving the place in which a vowel is pronounced towards the back of the mouth.

Although this is phonological, it is the sort of analysis that would complement the quantitative statistical table used in Cheshire's extract, by bringing out individual instances found in the data, for closer qualitative analysis and discussion.

Another example of the sort of qualitative analysis you might employ comes from Mark Sebba's investigation into London Jamaican, where quotations from data are brought into the analysis.

> Of particular interest are J.'s questions *im did phone you?* and *did 'im give you what you a look for?* Both are obviously intended to be Creole, as shown by the form of the subject pronoun (*him*) and the phonology. The first of these, *im did phone you?* would certainly pass for Creole in Jamaica, as it uses the same word order as the corresponding statement. The tense marker *did*, which corresponds to other Jamaican forms like *bin* and *en*, has to be treated with Jamaican Creole grammar as an invariant particle, not the past tense of an auxiliary verb *do* as in English. However, *did 'im give you what you a look for?* seems to be modelled on the English *did he give you* … with subject-auxiliary inversion moving *did* to first position.

Mark Sebba, Contact Languages, 1997

This might be the sort of analysis that you are more used to carrying out in language analysis essays. However, the important thing to remember is that both quantitative and qualitative approaches can benefit your investigation, especially if they are blended.

You can, and should, test and explore many of your initial ideas about your data by carrying out some quantification. In general, if you find yourself writing about a feature that 'often', 'sometimes' or 'always' occurs; if you are tempted to suggest that there are 'many', 'few', 'several' or even a 'vast number' of examples; or if you use phrases such as 'a majority of' or 'mainly' – then the chances are you should be justifying your claims by providing the appropriate statistical and quantifiable evidence. You can then go on to interpret and comment on the trends revealed by your quantification. A common approach will be to set out some quantitative findings in tables, and then to bring out individual examples of quoted evidence from your data, to analyse linguistic features more deeply – helping you to achieve both range and depth.

Surveying, listing, classifying and tabulating

Another way in which an investigation differs from a traditional essay is in the use of lists and tables to survey, sift and sort through the data. For example, in the case of the Ford advertisement, you might decide to investigate the adjectival pre-modification used in the text.

A traditional essay might begin to touch on this topic like this.

> As an advertisement, the Ford text uses a range of pre-modifying adjectives both to convey factual information about the product (such as 'four-wheel brakes' and 'steel bumpers')and to persuade potential purchasers of its desirability ('quick acceleration … pleasing choice of colours').

However, an investigative approach might start by listing *all* noun phrases in the text, showing the pre-modifying adjectives/adjectival phrases used alongside the head noun they describe (determiners omitted here), as in the example in Table 11, for the Ford car advertisement.

Table 11 *Noun phrases appearing in the Ford car advert*

Number	Pre-modification	Head noun
1	n/a	men
2	new	Ford cars
3	advanced modern	design
4	unusual	uses
5	fine	steels
6	n/a	strength
7	n/a	safety
8	n/a	men
9	robust	chassis
10	new	Ford car
11	strong steel	bodies
12	n/a	practice
13	seasonal	models
14	n/a	policy
15	n/a	cars
16	long	time
17	n/a	men
18	new	Ford
19	low	petrol consumption
20	low	insurance and depreciation costs
21	n/a	women
22	n/a	men
23	ease of	handling and steering
24	new	Ford
25	little	need

Number	Pre-modification	Head noun
26	gear	changing
27	n/a	traffic
28	ease of	parking
29	n/a	women
30	new	Ford
31	positive four-wheel	brakes
32	stop	light
33	quick	acceleration
34	unsplinterable glass	windscreen
35	protecting steel	bumpers
36	steel	running-boards
37	n/a	women
38	pleasing	choice of colours
39	graceful low	streamlines
40	everlasting	brightness
41	rustless steel	radiator shell hub caps lamps
42		quality of the upholstery
43		roominess and comfort
44	new	Ford cars
45	new	Ford cars
46	new closed or open	body styles

Now we can go further by organising these listed examples into categories of your own, that will allow you to offer a full qualitative and quantitative analysis of the major trends and patterns of pre-modification. You should always ensure you use paragraphs to discuss further the points of analysis your quantitative data raises. For example, Table 12 develops the initial pre-modification data and is followed by a paragraph detailing its significant features.

■ Classroom activity 14

Identify as many interesting or significant patterns and trends in the pre-modification data as you can, quantifying any of your observations as appropriate. Start by counting how many head nouns are pre-modified and how many are not, and make notes on the effect of those most heavily modified.

Table 12 *Trends and patterns of pre-modification in the Ford car advert*

Factual pre-modification		Subjective/opinionative pre-modification	
Associated with men	*Associated with women*	*Associated with men*	*Associated with women*
(not) seasonal models	four-wheel brakes	advanced, modern design	ease of handling/steering
low (?) petrol consumption	glass windscreen	unusual uses	little need of gear changing
low insurance	steel bumpers	fine (or factual?) steels	ease of parking
	steel running boards	robust chassis	positive brakes
	low streamlines		unsplinterable windscreen
	rustless (?) steel lamps		protecting bumpers
			pleasing choice of colours
			graceful streamlines
			everlasting brightness

These trends help to reveal the differentiated approach to the marketing of the car to men and women. The factual pre-modification related to men focuses on economical factors, whereas those aimed at women stress either safety or aesthetic concerns. Interestingly, the word 'low' is used differently, applying to costs for the men and the 'streamline' of the car for the women. This expectation that men, not women, would be concerned with financial matters may reflect the very different ideas about gender roles in society at this time. Similarly, the more subjective, persuasive pre-modifiers (which significantly outnumber the factual ones) differentiate between the semantics of strength, toughness and modernity (targeting men) and effortlessness, attractiveness and security (aimed at women). Here again we can see reflected in the data some contemporary stereotypical assumptions about gender roles.

■ Systematic analysis in practice

Looking back at the miscue analysis data in Table 9, focusing on the pauses as a particular variable can lead to the following blend of quantitative and qualitative analysis, to answer specific aspects of language use.

- ■ How often do pauses correspond with **sentence boundaries**?
- ■ How often are pauses associated with a 'difficult' word?
- ■ How often are pauses associated with other miscues?

The following is an example of a write-up of each of these lines of analytical enquiry.

Pauses corresponding to sentence/clause/phrase boundaries

Child X paused at sentence boundaries on 21 out of 30 possible occasions, whereas Child Y paused on 17. Both children show some security in recognising the syntactic function of full stops, but Child X is significantly more confident, with Child Y tending to rush over these towards the end.

■ **Key terms**

Sentence boundaries: marking sentences with capital letters and full stops, question marks or exclamation marks.

Fig. 14 *Children's early reading can make an excellent topic for a language investigation*

Pauses associated with 'difficult' words

The only individual words that really seem to cause Child X to pause are 'because', 'stopped', 'sparkling', 'farmyard' and 'raindrops'. He pauses after substituting 'farm gate' for 'farmyard', before substituting 'stooped' for 'stopped' and after suggesting 'something' for 'sparkling'. Two further pauses of 4 and 1 seconds precede the next two occurrences of 'sparkling' in the text, but the word is read without difficulty after that. Child Y also has trouble with 'sparkling', pausing before and after its first occurrence, and again after encountering the word a second time, and with stopped/stooped; he also pauses before other polysyllabic words such as 'treasure' (he pauses for 3 seconds after recognising his substitution of 'things', but deals with the word without difficulty on each subsequent encounter), 'farmyard' (a pause between the two parts of the word suggests the child may recognise each word separately but not as a compound) and 'raindrops' (another pause before a compound).

Pauses associated with other miscues

On three occasions Child X pauses between making an incorrect **substitution** and then making the self-correction (for example, 'up the hill urm (2) lane'), suggesting an active self-monitoring strategy. Interestingly, he pauses again before the second occurrence of 'lane', but this time avoids the substitution, clearly learning from his earlier self-correction. On at least one occasion a pause occurs after the self-correction has been made (for example, 'doesn't' – 'wasn't') and also immediately after a sentence boundary has been ignored – a trend much more noticeable in Child Y, who does this on three occasions (e.g. 'you silly pig said the other animals you (2)…') as if the failure to note the beginning of a sentence has interfered with his ability to read ahead. Child Y also pauses on 12 occasions immediately after making a substitution and prior to making a self-correction ('pig' for 'horse', 'the' for 'tell', 'things' for 'treasure', etc.). This also shows a self-monitoring process working effectively which allows him to check his reading against both sense and context. On just three occasions a pause occurs before a miscue (such as before his substitution of 'bushes' for 'hedge'). It seems that on the whole, Child Y prefers to 'have a go' and correct errors as he goes along, but is somewhat less accurate and fluent in his reading.

Table 13 *An example of a row of quantitative analysis comparing pause and sentence boundary correlation*

	Child X		Child Y	
	Frequency	Range	Frequency	Range
Pauses on sentence boundaries	21	(2) you silly / (.) pigs don't / (1) one day / (1) she went / (.) I am / (3) silly pig / (5) she went / (4) suddenly silly / (1) she saw / (2) ooh no / (1) a sparkling / (1) I will / (3) but the / (1) the web / (2) the spider / (1) what a / (2) silly pig / (3) suddenly silly / (1) she saw / (2) ooh no / (1) sparkling earrings	17	(3) you silly / (3) one day / (1) she went / (2) I am / (1) I am / (2) you silly / (4) silly pig / (5) suddenly said / (7) she saw / (1) ooh I / (1) I / (.) but the / (2) the web / (3) suddenly silly / (1) she saw / (1) ooh I / (1) sparkling earrings

Conclusion and evaluation

In this topic you will:

■ learn what your conclusion section is for

■ learn how to finish off your investigation in the evaluation.

Starter activity

Before putting your conclusion and evaluation on paper, share your data and analysis with someone else and explain to them how it all went: the things you found out, the challenges you faced, and what you think your findings mean. Writing the conclusion is all about identifying the overall meaning that can be taken from your work, so this would be a good way for you to think of it, before drafting it.

Reflecting on what you have learned

After carrying out your analysis, the conclusions section that follows allows you to provide a summary of what you have found, and reflect on how this relates to the original quesion or hypothesis you set out. In the evaluation, you are also able to put your investigation into context and suggest what future research could be done as a result of your findings.

Conclusion

The balance between your conclusion and your analysis can be difficult to strike, as there will be things that you find could be sensibly placed in either section, if given the right treatment. However, the following guidelines may help you decide what should be in your conclusion:

■ Use your hypothesis, question and aims to help structure your conclusion by commenting on your findings in relation to the points you raised at the start of your investigation.

■ Don't repeat points already made in your analysis – if you find this happening, look carefully at the analysis and decide where that particular point should go.

■ Be prepared to deal with anomalies thrown up by your data and put forward some suggestions as to why these appeared.

■ Remember, your findings can only be considered as **provisional** and qualified. Place your investigation in context and be realistic about what you have found only being relevant to the particular data you were able to collect. You can speculate about what your findings mean in the wider context, but show an awareness of the difference between the two.

■ If your investigation has gone largely against your hypothesis, that doesn't make what you have done invalid, or even jeopardise its ability to be a strong piece of coursework. However, you must present what you found and deal with it in just as systematic and objective a way as if you had found what you expected.

Evaluation

Your evaluation gives you the opportunity to foreground your successes – and challenges – and place your work into a wider context. It is also important to end your investigation strongly. If you evaluate well, you will be able to leave your reader feeling that you have understood your

Key terms

Provisional: refers to the fact that your results are only a small-scale example, and cannot be regarded as comprehensive or 'proving' anything for certain. All research results are provisional in the sense that they can only provide a snapshot of a particular range of data.

Study tip

Make sure that you don't waste your evaluation by stating things that are obvious and too general. Make points that are distinct to your investigation and based on specific experiences and ideas you had. In particular, avoid slipping into writing a wishlist of 'If I had more time/ money/data …'.

work and have achieved something worthwhile. Your evaluation should include:

- a reflection on the success of your methodology and investigation design, discussing any alterations you had to make
- observations about how your findings and work might fit in with that of other linguists and research, especially any you mentioned in your introduction
- a consideration of how your findings fit into the context of wider English language use
- suggestions for relevant further research – either improvements to your own investigation, or ideas for entirely new lines of research to develop what you have found.

Study tip

Think about the most logical order to write your investigation up: it's not simply a case of writing from the introduction to the evaluation! For example, at the beginning you will have set out your aims and hypothesis. After that, it makes sense to write your analysis up, followed by the conclusions you draw from it. You can then produce an account of your methodology, before writing an introduction to the whole piece and an overall evaluation of your project. Then you only have to present the piece, making use of a cover page, contents, bibliography and appendices, which are explained in the next topic.

Coursework preparation and practice

Fig. 15 *The presentation of your investigation report is very important*

Study tip

Remember to keep the balance of the different parts of your investigation report. The Analysis is by far the most significant section and should constitute at least half of your overall write-up.

Once you have gone through the stages described, it is time to put your investigation together as a whole. This is a process in which you will aim to make your work communicate its ideas as clearly as possible, proofread and edit your material and submit it correctly and on time.

How to present your investigation

The report of the investigation that you submit for assessment should be presented as professionally as possible, using the appropriate style and conventions of academic documents. Think of your audience not just as your teacher/supervisor, but the wider academic community of specialist teachers and students with expertise and interest in the topic you have been studying.

Below is a summary of what each section of your report should contain.

■ **Cover page:** The title and scope of your investigation, and your name.

■ **Contents:** A list of the main section headings and page numbers.

■ **Acknowledgements:** Briefly acknowledge the sources of your data, thanking people who have given permission for you to use materials, and any other assistance you have received in the preparation of your investigation.

■ **Introduction (guide 400 words):** Explain the background and context to your investigation, including your reasons for choosing to explore the topic you have, and the aims and focus of your investigation, including your initial questions/hypothesis.

■ **Methodology (guide 300 words):** Explain how you decided on what data you needed to collect, and the methods you used to collect/sample it. Note here also any limitations or difficulty you experienced with the collection of the data.

■ **Analysis (with sub-sections, guide 1,400 words):** The bulk of your investigation. You will need to create sub-section headings according to the different levels of analysis you are carrying out. These headings may correspond to different frameworks/questions.

Use this section to present analysis of the data in detail, identifying and presenting the evidence for patterns, then interpreting and explaining them in terms of the relevant linguistic and contextual factors. As well as full verbal analysis and explanation of the data, you may wish to use statistical and diagrammatic forms, such as tables, bar charts and any other graphic devices which seem appropriate.

Remember, it is not enough to offer an observation with an odd example – in a scientific investigation you need to test your ideas rigorously by thorough surveys of the data. The quality of your analysis and explanation will largely determine the mark your investigation receives.

■ **Conclusion and evaluation (guide 400 words):** As you started your investigation by asking some questions about your data, or by setting out to test a theory or hypothesis, your analysis should lead you towards some answers to these queries.

You should also reflect on your findings – was there anything surprising in your findings, and if so, what might explain them? Remember, a good scientist will keep an open mind about the investigation, not allowing prior assumptions to influence the conclusions you come to. It is quite likely that you will find something surprising, or even inconclusive. Don't worry. Remember, it is the quality of the process of investigation which matters. So, in drawing your conclusions:

- be open-minded: don't make the data fit your preconceptions
- be cautious: how true a sample, and how representative of all the possible material you could have collected is your data?
- be tentative: use expressions such as –
  - there is a tendency for …
  - on the whole, this seems to be …
  - we can perhaps conclude …
- be self-critical: how effective and revealing have your chosen methods of analysis been?
- explore what is next: suggest ways in which your investigation could be developed or extended given the opportunity.

■ **Bibliography:** As noted earlier, a comprehensive list of all print- and web-based sources consulted.

■ **Appendices:** Present your data, clearly labelled and with the sources clearly identified and dated. It is useful, also, to provide line numbers for ease of reference in your analysis sections. These should be clean copies free of your working annotations.

🔍 Using an academic register

AO1 requires you to 'communicate relevant knowledge using appropriate terminology and coherent, accurate written expression'. Think of your investigation report as a formal, academic document with a specialist audience – teachers, researchers and students with a strong interest in and prior knowledge of language studies. This means they will expect you to use the shared, technical language of experts in the field – so there's no need to explain or define the terms you use (though this will be a different matter when you come to write your media text). The nature of the task also presumes that you will use a reasonably formal register of Standard English, and 'coherent, accurate, written expression' implies a high level of accuracy and precision in your writing.

Let's consider two versions of an extract from the analysis section of an investigation arising from our sample data on the Ford text.

■ **Version A:** In my opinion, the first piece of data is very old-fashioned– no-one would accept an advert like that today. It appeals to sexist snobs who just want to look down on people who can't afford cars, and who think all their wives are good for is going shopping. But I do think it is interesting that the adverts does think of women driving at all.

The language is all very formal and nothing like the modern adverts with their witty slogans and colloquial language. There is too much text and no-one nowadays would bother to read all of that print, as they would expect just to look at a glamorous photograph.

There are many describing words in the text. These are called adjectives. When adjectives are placed with nouns we call these noun phrases.

Study tip

Although you do not have to send off the actual recordings you made and used with your folder, you must make sure that you keep them safe. It is possible that the exam board may want to hear or watch them, and you should be able to make them available if necessary.

■ **Version B:** The first piece of data seems to reflect the values and contexts of its day. Its stress on the abstract nouns 'pride' and 'ownership' reminds us of the prestige of the car industry at a time when this was the preserve of an affluent minority. Although the gender values it encodes strike a modern reader as sexist, as it implies that women are preoccupied with appearances, consumption and protection, not economy and practicality, it is nevertheless interesting that they are still acknowledged as potential drivers, if not owners. The register tends towards formality and verbosity, with a very low frequency of more colloquial lexis that would come to dominate the more image-oriented advertisements of the future.

Classroom activity 16

Highlight or make a list of the words and phrases in each version that you think fit under the following headings: linguistic terminology; precise and articulate vocabulary. Compare your findings for each version and discuss with a partner which example satisfies AO1 most sucessfully, and what helps to achieve this.

Link

Look back at page 132 for a breakdown of the focus and balance of different assessment objectives for the investigation coursework.

The criteria for achieving the upper mark bands also refer to 'suitably tentative' conclusions. The academic register is characterised by caution; beware of making sweeping generalisations, overstating and exaggerating, and claiming over-emphatically the truth of what you are saying. Instead, begin your points from definite evidence, like the frequency of a particular linguistic feature in your quantitative analysis, before going on to suggest possible interpretations of your findings. After all, you are carrying out your study based on a tiny fragment of data, so you really will not be able to claim many earth-shattering discoveries.

Study tip

Make sure the connection between your data and the points you make is clear. There are a number of ways of doing this (quoting, tables, line number references), but don't just leave these things out, make unsupported statements and hope the moderator will make the link for you.

Classroom activity 17

Look at the following extract from a conclusion written by a student who had investigated the language used by employees in different parts of a restaurant. Rewrite it in a more suitably academic register and comment on the reasons for your changes:

'In the restaurant, I found that just about everybody used loads of questions which there was only a couple possible answers to, whereas the ones in the kitchen were always more open. This must be because the waitresses really needed to know stuff like where their plates were etc. I also found that there was loads of slang used in both places. I guess this was to create a friendly informal atmosphere with the customers. I noticed a vast number of cases where there was lexical repetition; waiters did this a lot when taking customers' orders, obviously to check they had taken the order down right.'

Looking ahead

Practising the use of conventions such as writing in an academic register and acknowledging source texts is a key skill for all kinds of university study.

■ Quoting from your data

You will need to make a good deal of reference to your data throughout your investigation – in the analysis and conclusion sections particularly. There are several conventions that you can use to make this efficient, help you to make a range of different points quickly, and to make your investigation clear to any reader. Look at the following tools that you can make use of, and think about which will be most useful in your own data handling.

■ **Line references:** If you are working with continuous spoken or written data, numbering the lines will help you to be able to refer to particular sections quickly and easily in your write-up, particularly if you want to refer to larger sections or passages of data.

■ **Short quotation and extracts:** You can use the standard essay-style method of directly quoting language from the data you have collected.

■ **Statistical:** Including quantitative analysis of your findings gives your investigation an additional dimension and allows you to use tables and graphical forms of presentation to make some strong overall points and comparisons about data.

■ **Appendices:** You should provide copies of all the data you have collected and refer to it in the appendix of your investigation, and number the pieces. In this way, you will also be able to refer to particular supporting data or information quickly by referencing the specific part of your appendices.

■ **Footnotes:** Sometimes footnotes can be used to add information and references to particular data. These are notes that support a point you are making in the main text but are placed at the bottom of a page, or at the end of a section.

As with many of these different approaches, it is often best to use several of the different forms available to tailor to the particular needs of your project.

Extension activity 8

Look for examples of these different conventions being used in your wider reading, whether in books, articles or webpages. When you have come across several different uses, apply the ones that you think will help you in your own investigation.

■ Bibliography and sources

There are various accepted methods for identifying any sources you refer to or quote from in an academic study, but the most commonly used is the Harvard referencing system.

As your research proceeds, compile your bibliography by listing sources according to author (listed alphabetically), date of publication, title (and source if referring to an article in a magazine, newspaper or journal). Don't forget also to include the details of websites you visited. It will begin to look something like the example below.

A. Browne, 2001, *Developing Language and Literacy* (2nd edition), Paul Chapman

D. Crystal, 1988, *Rediscover Grammar*, Longman

M. Whitehead, 2002, *Developing Language and Literacy with Young Children*, Paul Chapman

www.mantex.co.uk/ou/resource/lit-term.htm, 2004 (Checklist of literary terms)

As long as you have listed a source in your bibliography, whenever you quote or refer to it in your text all you need to do is to place the author and date of publication in brackets immediately after the reference; so if the student in the example above wanted to reference *Developing Language and Literacy with Young Children*, she would just have to put 'Whitehead (2002)'.

Study tip

You should include in your bibliography any websites that you used to obtain data, for example, YouTube. In this case, give the entire URL of the page that contained the video or audio you used, and the date you accessed it, as sometimes they move or are removed from websites.

■ Applying the assessment criteria

Your work will be assessed according to how successfully it satisfies the assessment objectives set by the exam board: use Table 14 for reference at every stage of your work.

Table 14 *Assessment criteria for the investigation report, with commentary and advice*

	Assessment criteria	Commentary and advice
AO1	Select and apply a range of linguistic methods, to communicate relevant knowledge using appropriate terminology and coherent, accurate written expression (5%)	In your investigation report, write clearly, accurately and in depth about your data; go into considerable detail, using the areas of language and terminology you need to be precise and rigorous in your analysis. This should represent the best writing you are capable of at the end of two years of Advanced Level study, and show lots of evidence of the learning you have been engaged in throughout the course.
AO2	Demonstrate critical understanding of a range of concepts and issues relating to the construction and analysis of meanings in spoken and written language, using knowledge of linguistic approaches (5%)	Show in your report that you have studied and understood the main theoretical ideas about language relevant to your investigation, and applied these using suitable methods of linguistic analysis. You need to show you can analyse and discuss the most interesting aspects of language using the ideas and terminology you have learned over the previous two years.
AO3	Analyse and evaluate the influence of contextual factors on the production and reception of spoken and written language, showing knowledge of the key constituents of language (2.5%)	Show in your report that you have understood the importance of various contextual factors in influencing how language is used in the particular situation you have investigated. You also need to demonstrate knowledge of different linguistic methods and apply these productively to your data.

A full breakdown of the AOs and marks can be found in the Language B Specification on the AQA website, but the maximum possible marks that can be scored for each AO in your language investigation are as follows.

■ Maximum total marks for AO1 – 20 marks
■ Maximum total marks for AO2 – 20 marks
■ Maximum total marks for AO3 – 10 marks
■ Maximum total for language investigation – 50 marks

Some extracts from Clare's investigation report are set out in Table 15. She chose to explore how four texts from a child's reading scheme (The Oxford Reading Tree) systematically introduced children to an increasingly challenging range of language. The section reprinted here focuses on the increasing degree to which the lexical content of texts introduces irregular spelling patterns.

The following extracts from her investigation are matched up to an assessor's comments, making use of the criteria of the assessment objectives and showing plus (+) and minus (–) points.

Table 15 *Extracts from a student's investigation with assessor's comments*

Investigation report extracts	Assessor's comments
Section 2.2 Lexical Range: Phonemic Predictability Even though we only have 26 letters in our alphabet there are actually 44 sounds that we use in our speech. When reading, the child has to make the links between graphemes and the phonemes they represent. Some words are easily predictable because their phoneme and grapheme correspondence is very close (e.g. 'red' = /red/). Words get more difficult as this correspondence becomes less obvious, making the process of deciphering longer. We have features such as silent letters, digraphs and unusual grapheme: phoneme correspondence.	+ AO1/2: Sound intro to section: shows understanding of relevant concepts and uses relevant terminology accurately. + AO1/2: Uses relevant knowledge (phonetic spelling) effectively to analyse her data.
Text A Being the first stage we would not expect any unpredictable words so the ones that are featured can easily be 'sounded out' from their graphemic form. One word which may cause a problem, is 'Who'. The digraph 'wh' is common but is sounded differently in different words. 'Where' is an example where it represents /w/ whereas in 'who' it represents /h/. Introducing this very common word at this stage is a good idea, as all 'wh' question words are regularly found in books and so this will be the basis for their knowledge in the area.	– But could demonstrate predictability of other words by examples. + AO3: sensible comments re context (early stage of reading development).
Text B The English spelling system is not particularly phonemic and has many anomalies and irregularities so the scheme soon starts to introduce more unusual sets of phoneme: grapheme correspondences. This stage involves the words 'bought', 'statue' and 'said' which are less straightforward. The use of the four letters 'ough' is a new challenge because if you tried to spell them out separately as you came across them in the word, you would not get the correct word at all. In 'bought' this group of letters represents /-aw/. Here, it is used twice within the same text to help embed it. The word 'statue' shows that /u:/ can be represented by the two letters 'ue' though the same sound is represented differently in more common words such as 'moon' and 'do'. By including 'statue' alongside words like 'balloon', 'new' and 'blew', the child is exposed to different ways of spelling the same sound idea. 'Said' = /sed/ is also another common word in books and so this is the best time to expose a child to it, as it isn't the easiest word to know how to spell and recognise as 'ai' does not often express the sound /e/.	+ AO1: sub-sections show highly systematic approach to analysis – effective. Expression is coherent and accurate.
Text C The amount of words with a close relationship between spelling and sound is still high but the proportion of more 'difficult' words has risen now at stage 5. Six words are less conventional for children: 'Read', 'laughed', 'laugh', 'photographs', 'believe' and 'watched'. Once again the author has picked up on a certain sound /f/ and is repeating it in different digraph forms 'gh', 'ph' to allow the child to become familiar with it.	+ AO3/2: Insight into how context (i.e. the position of the text in a graded reader scheme) has affected selection of lexis and phonemic patterns. Good understanding of relevant concepts. + AO1: some attempt to quantify data here – systematic.
Text D This text is now able to use words from a large vocabulary list because the child will have built up an adequate dictionary in their minds. There are a number of phonemically unpredictable words whose graphemic state and phonemic sound are quite distant: machine engine right knocked captain However due to the steady way in which the *Tree* introduces these types of words the child has the set basis to make knowledgeable guesses about their sound.	– But what is the proportion, exactly? + AO2: Perceptively observes patterns which illuminate data. + AO1: fair observations on data. – AO1: but not analysed here. Could note –ine pattern, for example.

■ Further reading

General

Articles at www.emagazine.org.uk (subscription required)

Bragg, M. *The Adventure of English*, Hodder and Stoughton, 2003

Crystal, D. *Encyclopedia of Language*, CUP, 1997

Crystal, D. *Encyclopedia of the English Language*, CUP, 2003

Crystal, D. *How Language Works: How Babies Babble, Words Change Meaning and Languages Live or Die*, Penguin, 2007

Fromkin, V. and Rodman, R. *An Introduction to Language* (7th edition), Thomson, 2002

Jackson, H. and Stockwell, P. *The Nature and Functions of Language*, Continuum, 2010

The Oxford English Dictionary online (www.oed.com)

Thorn, S. *Mastering Advanced English Language*, Palgrave, 2008

AQA English podcasts website (www.theenglishfaculty.org)

Language investigation

The Advertising Archives website (www.advertisingarchives.co.uk)

British Library website, accents and dialects (http://sounds.bl.uk/accents-and-dialects)

British National Corpus (www.natcorp.ox.ac.uk)

Carter, R. *et al. Working with Texts: A Core Book for Language Analysis*, Routledge, 2008

Engelmann, S. *Teach your Child to Read in 100 Easy Lessons*, Simon and Schuster, 1986

Freeborn, D. *From Old English to Standard English*, Macmillan, 2006

Garfield, A. *Teach Your Child to Read: A Phonic Reading Guide for Parents and Teachers*, Vermilion, 2007

Goddard, A. *Researching Language*, Heinemann, 2000

Jager Adams, M. *Beginning to Read*, MIT, 1994

Keith, G. and Shuttleworth, J. *Living Language*, Hodder and Stoughton, 1997

Langford, D. *Analysing Talk: Investigating Interaction in English*, Macmillan, 1994

Leith, D. *A Social History of English*, Routledge, 1997

McDonald, C. *English Language Project Work*, Macmillan, 1992

Sealey, A. *Researching English Language: A Resource Book for Students*, Routledge, 2008

■ **Looking ahead**

The investigation is a very detailed piece of work that will prepare you well for degree-level study, if you are thinking of going to university. Reading widely in a subject is also an important part of this, and excellent practice for higher education where you will find it is essential for the more focused and independent nature of study involved.

Introduction

- consider the range of media texts open to you to write

- understand the different assessment criteria for the media text.

You have already been conducting research and analysis in your chosen area of language, and have been producing an academic report for a specialist audience of fellow language experts. The second text you are required to produce must be in the same area of study and should be designed to inform your audience about a particular aspect of language. It should be between 750 and 1000 words, and could take a variety of forms. Popular examples are:

- an article for a newspaper or magazine

- a pamphlet for general information and distribution

- a script for an audio medium, such as radio or podcast

- a script and handouts/slides for a 'live' presentation.

Although you do not simply have to represent and rewrite the material of your language investigation report, it is likely that you will wish to make use of the research and reading you have done to produce a text that presents the topic you have been studying for people with little prior specialist knowledge.

Think of the media text task as a lively and accessible spin-off in which you find an interesting angle on your chosen topic, which will have a wide appeal. If the investigation report draws on many of the concepts and skills developed through Units 1 and 3, to satisfy the assessment objectives for the media text you will be developing many of the skills you practised in Unit 2.

AO4: Demonstrate expertise and creativity in the use of English in a range of different contexts informed by linguistic study (7.5%).

What this means is that when you write your media text, you should adopt a suitable approach and style to re-present the subject you explored in your investigation in an interesting and accessible way for a wider non-specialist audience. As with the texts you produced for your Unit 2 AS Level coursework, this means you have to:

- select, organise and present material appropriately

- research and study suitable style models

- adopt the relevant genre conventions for your text

- write in a style that is lively and engaging as well as informative

- produce a text that is genuinely 'original' and creative

- produce a coherent text with very high standards of expression and accuracy

- present your work as professionally as possible.

The nature of the media text you will write will clearly be quite different from the document you produce as your language investigation report. It is in a different **genre** (which you will decide), will be published in a different **medium**, will have a different kind of **audience**, and will have a different **purpose**, as it needs not only to inform but also to engage the interest of and perhaps even advise or entertain its readers.

Study tip

Remember, there should be a clear link between your investigation and media coursework pieces. This could be a very close connection, for example if you have conducted an investigation on rhetoric, power and reader positioning in charity advertisements, you might then go on to produce a media text on how charity advertisements persuade their readers. Or, more indirectly, you could pursue something that is more broadly within the study of language and power, for example a media text on how MPs negotiate power in the House of Commons.

Preparing to write

Fig. 1 *Reworking and drafting your writing will help produce something you're happy with*

Study tip

You don't need to come up with all of the material for your media text yourself. Although the final piece will be your own original writing, the ideas in it will usually be wider, existing linguistic debates and you are given credit for understanding these well through your own reading and synthesising them in your writing.

Starter activity

One of the best ways to prepare for writing your media text is to read widely among the sort of things you might want to produce, so you can have a clear image of what you are trying to achieve. And don't forget, 'reading' might include listening to radio podcasts, or watching video clips in this section, as these are media forms that you can reproduce as well.

Finding a 'style model' in this way need not mean that all of your reading has to be on the same topic as your investigation – it need not even be about English language. Sometimes it is more helpful to find a piece in the right genre, with the sort of tone and look you are after, which is not closely related to what you are doing, so you have to translate the way it is put together into your own idea, rather than risk copying something too closely.

When you tackle your media text in earnest, there are a few things that might help you to keep the right sort of approach in mind. Whether you find it difficult to start writing a language production piece, or you find it difficult to make it sufficiently linguistic, or you don't find it comfortable producing 'creative' writing, the following points should help you.

■ **Value originality**: Go with your own ideas and try to keep what you write lively and varied. Once you've typed it out, it is easy to rework it, get second opinions and generally shape what you've got – so make what you've got raw and experimental, and then hone it. If you start off with cautious writing, there won't be so much you can do with it.

■ **Remember that drafting is your friend**: Don't agonise over 'first sentences' or 'the right word' to the point that you come to a complete standstill. Try to get writing and sustain it. The way you will create a really strong piece is through honest and thoughtful drafting of your material.

■ **Think 'process' not 'perfect'**: This sums up both of the previous two. Embrace your media text as a writing process and don't get hung up on it being perfect in the first couple of drafts.

💡 Finding an angle

To produce a successful text that really engages a more general audience you will need to find a particular aspect of language within your area of study that raises thought-provoking issues and connects with interests your audience already has. Let's take the two investigations we were working with in Unit 4, Section A (car advertisements and child reading miscues) as examples.

1 If you had been working on the changing language and style of car adverts in the 20th century, you might write an article for a magazine about the changing styles of adverts, possibly for readers with an interest in cars but no prior specialist knowledge of language. Or, you could produce a text that details the way technology has changed language over time.

2 If you had been studying the development of reading skills in twin brothers, you could produce an article for a parenting magazine, or a pamphlet to be given away by nurseries, or even the script for a presentation to be given to the parents of 3- to 4-year-olds, about the importance of shared reading experiences for the development of children's reading. Alternatively, you could write a newspaper article contributing to the debate about the merits of phonics-based teaching methods.

Some more suggestions that might arise from some of the investigations suggested earlier are offered in Table 1.

Table 1 *Some suggestions for media texts*

Topic area	Language investigation	Possible angles for media texts
Language varieties	Studies of broadcast and/or print-based news media.	Article for newspaper/magazine about contrasting styles (and bias?) of the news. Is it being 'dumbed down'? Is it truly neutral?
	Studies of persuasion in spoken/written texts.	A *Times Educational Supplement* article advising teachers and students on language strategies for effective public speaking.
	Studies of teacher talk and/or classroom discourse.	Article about teaching styles and the language of the classroom, possibly for your own school or college magazine. Could be lively and amusing but also ask questions about teaching and learning.
	Studies of the language of humour, for example *Have I Got News For You* or *Mock the Week*.	The script for an item on the BBC Radio 3 programme *The Verb* informing the audience of the most effective linguistic strategies employed by stand-up comedians.
Language and gender	Studies of male and female language use.	Newspaper feature (perhaps for the weekend magazine section) about the myths and reality of language and gender. Are men really from Mars and women from Venus, or do they just *talk* like they're from different planets?
Language and power	Studies of pragmatics, status and power in conversational discourse and/or written texts.	An article about the hidden meanings, codes and power games that exist beneath the surface of everyday conversations – perhaps for your fellow students.
Language and technology	Studies of the evolution of language conventions in new technologies.	A script for a talk or presentation you might give to parents and teachers who are worried about the apparently harmful influence of new technologies on standards of literacy.
Language acquisition	Studies in the development of literacy.	A newspaper article that contributes to the current debate about approaches to the teaching of reading.
Language change	Studies in the change reflected in 20th- and 21st-century spoken and written sources.	A weekend newspaper or magazine article reflecting nostalgically on changing times and our changing language.
Topics arising from individual interests	Studies in individuals' language use at work.	An article for the 'Business Magazine' section of the British Council website, entitled 'Impressing your clients: successful language for business people', informing its audience about research into effective business communication.

Classroom activity 1

For each of the following investigations, suggest an angle for a possible media text that might arise.

1. A study of the language used in a reality TV show.

2. A study of how males and females describe themselves and their ideal partner in an online dating site.

3. A study of the differences between the styles of radio and television sports commentaries.

4. A study of the language development of a child between 2 and $2\frac{1}{2}$ years.

🔍 Looking at style models

Not only is your media text going to be significantly shorter than your investigation report, it will, in many other respects, provide a new kind of writing challenge. It will differ in terms of:

- layout and presentation
- degree of linguistic detail

Fig. 2 *When producing your media text, it is useful to observe how the professionals do it*

Looking ahead

If you are interested in a career in journalism of any kind, working with style models can be a good way to explore the range of professional writing available out there, and to start experimenting with your own distinctive style.

■ tone and style
■ use of specialist terminology.

Classroom activity 2

Consider how each of the bullet-pointed areas above will be different in your media text from your investigation report.

An excellent way to approach creating your own original media text is to look carefully at the way professional writers manipulate language in their published and broadcast pieces. If you find some texts that appeal to you, you can use them as a style model to learn the conventions of that particular genre, and get some ideas for generating subtle effects like humour or creating a debate.

The following extracts showcase this kind of lively, original way of presenting a linguistic topic to a non-specialist audience. Remember that you have the opportunity to produce a text of a spoken or written mode in your media piece, and these extracts will provide you with an example of each.

Mind your language

I was relaxing in an Old Compton Street café when the waiter jogged my elbow, sending a hot stream of cappuccino up my nose. As I gave him a piece of my mind, he announced to the floor, 'God, she is soooo butch!' and whisked away, chortling. I was irked by this poisonous retort, but my gay friend was reassuring.

'He doesn't mean you're dykey. Butch is Polari for upfront, strong,' he said. 'It's the lingo, innit? Like "vada the bona casa". Or "get a load of her lallies."'

He could have donned a bowler hat and spoken in Droog for all I understood, but Polari did strike me as something novel and, well, fantabulosa (a useful Polari adjective). Paul Baker, a research associate at Lancaster University who is writing a PhD on Polari, has noticed something of a revival of interest in Polari in certain circles, as well as increasing interest in gay linguistics among academics …

Peter Gilliver, associate editor of the Oxford English Dictionary, tells me that Polari is actually more than 200 years old, and that the roots of some words are older still. Reference to the verb 'troll' (to take a walk) is to be found in a 14th-century text (although Polari gave us the derived noun 'trollette'). The ubiquitous 'bona' (good, attractive) was absorbed into English as long ago as Shakespeare's Henry IV Part II, where it appears as 'bona roba' (a wench, apparently, one wearing a lovely dress).

*An extract from 'Mind your language', **Beverley D'Silva**, The Observer, 10 December 2000*

D'Silva's piece provides some excellent examples of how it is possible to blend original writing with informative linguistic content. It is based on the language variety of Polari, used by homosexual men in the mid-20th century, and uses details from the research carried out by Dr Paul Baker. The commentary in Table 2 picks out some of the main techniques and features that achieve this combination of flair and linguistic depth.

Table 2 *Commentary on main techniques and features used in 'Mind your language'*

Technique/feature	Commentary on effect
1. Dropping in examples of language use related to your chosen subject. Examples: 'soooo butch', 'vada the bona casa', 'lallies', 'fantabulosa', 'the derived noun "trollette"', 'bona roba'.	With an area that offers as much inventive vocabulary as Polari, D'Silva uses words from its lexicon like 'vada de bona casa' (probably 'look at the lovely house' in this context) and 'lallies' (legs) to set an informal, lively tone, but also to interest a non-specialist audience with words that are unfamiliar and exotic. This also shows a depth of knowledge of the subject.
2. Using original wider references for effects or depth. Examples: *Oxford English Dictionary*, 'could have donned a bowler hat and spoken in Droog', Shakespeare's *Henry IV Part II*.	By referencing such bastions of the English language as the *OED* and Shakespeare, D'Silva lends a weight of credibility to her article. However, she also makes a subtle and less well-known **allusion** to Anthony Burgess's novel *A Clockwork Orange*. This works particularly well as it has much in common with Polari as they both occurred largely in London; use their own invented vocabulary; and are about anti-language and **subculture.**
3. Employing varied, articulate and distinctive vocabulary. Examples: jogged, cappuccino, announced, whisked, chortling, irked, poisonous retort, donned, novel, fantabulosa, revival, ubiquitous, absorbed.	D'Silva creates a number of effects with her vocabulary choices. They range from an informal, entertaining register ('jogged', 'chortling') through to a formal, academic one ('donned', 'ubiquitous') which helps the piece gain credibility in each of these purposes. She also makes use of Polari-specific vocabulary herself, not just to exhibit it, but also incorporating it in her own style, as in the use of 'fantabulosa'. There are also some clever references: 'cappuccino' is Italian-derived, like much of Polari, and 'donned' perhaps alludes to the world of universities and PhDs that appear in the paragraph it is in. All of these make the piece work well, but also show a depth of linguistic awareness behind the writing.
4. Showing depth of knowledge in your chosen area of language study. Examples: Polari, Paul Baker, Lancaster University, gay linguistics, Peter Gilliver.	D'Silva makes it clear to her audience that Polari is a subject that has undergone recent academic study by using a term like 'gay linguistics' and name-dropping Paul Baker. She also adds range with Peter Gilliver, by placing Polari into the wider context of the English language.

The following text is an extract from the script for an episode of BBC Radio 4's *Word of Mouth* programme, presented by Michael Rosen and contributed to by Ian Peacock.

The problem with prepositions

Michael Rosen: And now WITHOUT any further ado, we arrive AT the contentious issue OF English prepositions UPON which Ian Peacock has disturbingly strident views which are somewhat OFF the wall, OVER the top, and BEYOND the realms of sanity. Frankly, Ian's opinions drive me UP the wall and ROUND the bend. In fact I suspect he may be OUT OF his depth and OUT OF his tree. And possibly OFF his face and OFF his rocker ...

Ian Peacock: That is the sort of introduction up with which I will not put. To what do you think you're up? You've no idea through what I've been. Anyway: welcome to ... aboard ... into this feature on ... about ... regarding prepositions and issues around them, by means of and as a consequence of which you may feel a little confused.

Under ... in the circumstances ... I went out-and-about and to-and-fro and hither-and-thither, over-and-above the call of duty and set off erelong, in a good mood and a taxi, sitting abaft, athwart the back-seat, betwixt Scylla and Charybdis, pondering prepositions we no longer use.

[...]

> **Key terms**
>
> **Allusion:** a subtle reference to a story or factual aspect outside of the text.
>
> **Subculture:** a cultural pursuit engaged in that happens outside of the mainstream, accepted values of society.

> Gosh. It's almost time to quickly wrap up ... up with which quickly to wrap ... which brings me to TIME prepositions. Just for the record ... the clock does not stand still at ten BEFORE three, nor ten AFTER three. Nor is it logically possible to arrive at 6.30 FOR 7. I refuse to work Monday THROUGH Friday or to do anything ACROSS the weekend. I suspect we got these expressions off of the Americans. They're certainly completely different than ... from ... to ... the grammar up with which I was brought.

Michael Rosen and *Ian Peacock*, Word of Mouth, *BBC Radio 4, 2007*

In discussing the use of prepositions in the English language, this piece also makes use of original phrasing and specific linguistic content, and it is interesting to compare how a more explicitly spoken mode piece goes about this in comparison to D'Silva's largely written mode text. The commentary in Table 3 looks at the way Rosen and Peacock make use of the same four strategies:

Fig. 3 *Michael Rosen, the presenter of BBC Radio 4's* Word of Mouth

Table 3 *Commentary on main techniques and features used in* **Word of Mouth**

Technique/feature	Commentary on effect
1. Dropping in examples of language use related to your chosen subject. Examples: 'WITHOUT' and other prepositions used, 'abaft' and other **archaic** prepositions.	Rosen makes repeated, even exaggerated, use of a range of prepositions, like 'without' in his introduction to the topic, which is entertaining, as well as showing good knowledge of the range of use of the word class. This is given depth by putting the prepositions used in common idioms, and by Peacock later distinguishing archaic prepositions like 'abaft'.
2. Using original wider references for effects or depth. Examples: 'in a good mood and a taxi', Scylla and Charybdis.	Peacock sets a certain scene with his phrase 'in a good mood and a taxi', painting a kind of **word picture** of his surroundings and continuing a lively, informal narrative style. He also uses a **classical allusion** to the mythical monsters of Scylla and Charybdis, which works subtly as it refers to being stuck between two difficult problems that require you to find a balance between them – much like the problem of preposition use being defined.
3. Employing varied, articulate and distinctive vocabulary. Examples: ado, contentious, disturbingly strident, sanity, off his rocker, to-and-fro, athwart, pondering prepositions.	Because this is a broadcast piece, rather than in print, the sound of the words can be used to even greater effect. Rosen and Peacock's text therefore strikes a balance between an informal/formal register with contrasting phrases like 'off his rocker' and 'disturbingly strident'. Preposition phrases are also used to good effect to double up the entertainment and linguistic purposes of the script. An example of the sound of words being foregrounded comes in Peacock's use of alliteration in 'pondering prepositions'.
4. Showing depth of knowledge in your chosen area of language study. Examples: Ian Peacock, 'To what do you think you're up?', 'ten BEFORE three', 'the Americans. They're certainly completely different than ... from ... to ... the grammar up'.	Both Rosen and Peacock make wide use of prepositions and related phrases, but Peacock takes this a step further by including some non-standard phrases like 'ten before three' to illustrate his knowledge of the potential prescriptivist debate over such use. Peacock himself is included as a contributor as he has done some specialist work in the field, and he develops his point further by linking preposition use to the wider debate about **Americanisms** and their influence on British English usage.

Extension activity 1

Take each of the strategies listed in turn and apply it to the language area that you are working in. Come up with your own bank of words and phrases for the four techniques below that you can work into your media piece as you draft it.

1 Dropping in examples of language use related to your chosen subject.

2 Using original wider references for effects or depth.

3 Employing varied, articulate and distinctive vocabulary.

4 Showing depth of knowledge in your chosen area of language study.

■ Editorial skills

Once you have a clear idea for your media text and have found some style models to work with, the writing process will involve exercising a range of editorial skills. You will be aiming to make your media text achieve many different things: address a non-specialist audience, provide a convincing and subtle focus on a linguistic topic, and create an original style, written with flair.

Language around you activity 1

There is an almost limitless range of different kinds of media text that you could produce. Read widely in newspapers, magazines and online, and keep copies of anything that appeals to you and gives you a good idea of the layout and style.

Genre conventions

In addition to these, it will be important to produce an authentic version of the particular genre of text you are writing. Different genres can be identified by the conventions and features they use, which can involve graphological elements, particular textual segments, as well as the style of language and content. Look at Table 4 for a guide to the conventions for some of the media texts you might write.

Key terms

Archaic: a word from an earlier period of English usage that is rarely used in the modern contemporary language.

Word picture: a feature of radio broadcasting where a presenter will put forward a visual scene using verbal narrative description.

Classical allusion: a reference to a character or event in classic Greek or Roman mythology.

Americanisms: examples of language use distinct to American English speakers.

Table 4 *Conventions and features of various genres*

Media genre	Conventions and segments	Style and content
Newspaper article	Bold, large font in main title Use of bold or italics for emphasis Images with captions Text layout in columns Title, subtitles and main text	Objective approach Use of factual information Summary and interpretation of main concepts Integration of short quotation
Editorial	Bold, large font in main title Photo of writer Images or supporting graphics Email address or website for readers to send comment to	Lively, discursive style Generation of debate Contains opinion and subjective material Use of wordplay, humour and figurative devices
Webpage	Use of colour and font style variation Images and graphical elements Website menu Website banner Advertisement boxes and panels	Style can vary widely depending on nature of text Quotations and statistics from reader contributions Hyperlinks to related subjects, previous pages, video and audio

Study tip

The language of your media text is ultimately the most important aspect. You can improve the overall cohesion and impact of it by crafting the graphological and structural elements.

■ Key terms

Anaphora: repeated syntactical structures for effect, for example, a sequence of sentences beginning in the same way, or a list of things using the same phrase form.

Litotes: deliberate understatement for rhetorical effect. This can be in the form of euphemism or of multiple negation, for example, describing someone who is older as 'not as young as he was'.

Synecdoche: a figure of speech where something is referred to by just a part of itself, or where something is referred to by a larger thing or idea it is part of. Examples include calling a police officer 'the law' or the violins, viola and cello in an orchestra 'the strings'.

Effective writing and rhetorical techniques

Never lose sight of the fact that writing effectively and inventively is at the heart of your media text production piece. Outside of the use of style models and preparing good linguistic content, you might remind yourself of some basic techniques that can go a long way to helping you write an original text. Here are some tips.

■ Keep in mind the importance of variety. This should be evident in your punctuation, paragraph and sentence structures and vocabulary.

■ Make use of specific rhetorical devices and effects, for example: alliteration, assonance, metaphor, simile, **anaphora**, **litotes**, **synecdoche**, tripling, and others you have encountered.

■ Experiment with register by using a range of spoken and written mode features, varying manner elements like formality for effect.

■ Think of the impact of your text across the frameworks. This means trying to make sure that you show originality in terms of your choice of lexis, semantic and phonological effects, grammatical structures and layout and graphology.

■ Extension activity 2

Revise your knowledge of the language devices you can employ. Use the table below to record as many different kinds of device as you can. You can select ones most appropriate to your text type – or perhaps identify those appearing in your style model.

Table 5 *A range of different stylistic devices you might select from to bring your media text to life*

Discourse devices	Latching on,
Grammatical devices	Adverb fronting,
Graphological devices	Italics,
Lexical devices	Coinage,
Phonological devices	Sibilance,
Pragmatic devices	Humour,
Rhetorical devices	Tripling,
Semantic devices	Simile,

Coursework preparation and practice

In this topic you will:

- learn how to present your media text

- learn how to reference your work

- apply the assessment criteria to examples of students' work.

Fig. 4 *Make sure you've checked off everything you need to do before submitting your media text*

Study tip

A bibliography is not there to catch you out. Including a large or small number of texts in your bibliography won't give you a worse or better mark. But it must be an honest account of what you have used. Remember that when you submit your coursework you will sign to declare the work is your own. If you are found to have plagiarised, the consequences are serious and can have an impact on all the qualifications you are taking, and not just this particular English unit, or the English course.

Now that you have explored a range of techniques for putting your media text together, this topic will provide a few tips on how to complete and submit your media text coursework piece, as well as presenting you with the assessment criteria that your piece will be judged against, with a worked example of a final piece being assessed.

How to present your media text

The media text is a relatively simple piece to put together and submit. Here is a checklist for you to use as you enter the final stages.

- Is the topic link to your investigation clear?
- What is the word count – is it between 750 and 1,000 words?
- Have you typed up your piece and formatted the text?
- Do you have a record of the style models and source texts you used?
- Are you sure you have 'transformed' the language of the style models and source texts and avoided any risk of plagiarism?
- Have you stated a specific genre, text type and audience for your piece? For example, 'A special report for the *Daily Mail*'s 'Femail' supplement magazine, aimed at mothers with pre-school children'.

Bibliography and sources

Just as you did in your investigation, you will need to give a record of the sources that you used to help you with your media text. It may well be that some are 'doubled up' from your investigation, but you should provide a brief bibliography either immediately after your text, or on a separate, titled sheet, detailing any books, articles or webpages you used, either as a style model, or as a source for the information in your piece.

Applying the assessment criteria

Only one assessment objective (AO4) is used in assessing your media text, and it is worth 30 marks in total. Although it is only a single AO, it covers several threads in your piece, including:

- showing expertise in your writing, by controlling your accuracy and expression
- recreating a particular genre of text convincingly
- exhibiting creativity and originality in the stylistic choices that you make
- maintaining a focus on a relevant language topic.

Table 6 *Assessment criteria for the media text, with commentary and advice*

	Assessment criteria	Commentary and advice
AO4	Demonstrate expertise and creativity in the use of English in a range of different contexts informed by linguistic study (7.5%)	When you write your media text, adopt a suitable approach and style to make the subject of your investigation interesting and accessible for a wider non-specialist audience.

Table 7 *Assessment criteria and breakdown of marks for the media text*

Mark	AO4: Demonstrate expertise and creativity in the use of English in a range of different contexts informed by linguistic study.
28–30	Originality in the deployment of the structures and conventions associated with media texts. Sensitive and convincing manipulation of register to meet demands of audience and purpose. Successful, effective and convincing new text; demonstrates ingenuity and finesse in the use of original materials and ideas.
26–27	Confident, controlled deployment of the structures and genre conventions. Appropriate control of register, demonstrating sophisticated awareness of the demands of audience and purpose. Effective and sustained adaptation of original materials; sources manipulated and integrated into entirely new text.
22–24	Sustained deployment of appropriate structures and genre conventions; strong clarity and control of writing. Coherent register, secure writing style – effective for audience and purpose. Effective adaptation of original materials for new audience and purpose.
19–21	Competent deployment of structures and genre conventions – good clarity and control of writing. Growing sophistication in control of register – article likely to be effective for audience and purpose. Largely effective adaptation of original materials for new audience and purpose.
16–18	Demonstrates control of genre requirements; good clarity and control in writing. Effective register, demonstrating the ability to adapt writing to engage and interest audience. Source original materials shaped to suit new audience/purpose – some lack of control at times.
13–15	Language choices generally effective and appropriate, demonstrating increasing control; some awareness of structures and genre conventions. Register mainly appropriate; some ability to adapt writing to engage and interest audience. Partly effective transformation; attempts to shape original materials for new audience/purpose.
10–12	Some ability to control genre requirements for audience and purpose – likely to be inconsistent. Mainly appropriate register – possibly oversimplified at times or overly complex. Some transformation – demonstrates awareness of the need to shape original materials for new audience/purpose.
7–9	Knowledge of genre, and purpose demonstrated; oversimplified audience awareness. Beginnings of appropriate register – likely to be inconsistent across writing. Some transformation for new audience/purpose, likely to shadow original materials.
4–6	Some limited understanding of audience, purpose and genre. Some limited control over writing – attempts to develop appropriate register. Some limited attempt to transform original materials, though not very successfully; very dependent on original sources.
1–3	Little understanding of writing activity – inappropriate content; limited awareness of genre, audience and purpose. Ineffective register; imprecise language choices, little control over writing. Little transformation of original materials leading to inappropriate content for task.
0	Nothing written/totally inappropriate for tasks.

It is a sensible idea to familiarise yourself with the contents of Table 7 in order to get an accurate impression of the quality of text expected.

Classroom activity 3

The following text is the opening of a media text that might arise out of the car advertisement investigation, focusing on the language of slogans in advertising.

With a partner, discuss the following points.

■ Define an appropriate audience, purpose and context for this piece, as specifically as you can.

■ Decide on the strengths of the piece, for example, the use of language to create certain effects, and evidence of detail and linguistic knowledge.

■ Apply the AO4 criteria in Table 7 and make notes on the sort of bands you would place this work.

Then, individually, research and write a continuation of this piece. Try to sustain the successful material you identified, and to develop it further to bring in your own ideas and produce a complete piece that matches the audience, purpose and context you established. When you have both finished, compare your pieces and discuss what you tried to achieve and the different ways you went about it.

Probably the best slogan in the world?

James Smythe on how advertising's catchy phrases conquered the globe.

Slogans appear to be an inescapable part of the backdrop to the modern world. Towns and cities have become galleries for the corporate masterpieces of the advertising era, with constantly changing exhibitions of the latest works from the easel of Sony or Nike or Volkswagen. And, as we walk around the aisles and take it all in, our radios, televisions – even our friends – provide a running commentary of the latest adspeak. From 'Every Little Helps' (Tesco) to 'Where do you want to go today?' (Microsoft) the reassuring voices of advertising are everywhere – but just how do these mantras, bon-mots and one-liners make such a lasting impression on us, and why do we keep coming back for more?

Apparently, the word 'slogan' is derived from a couple of ancient Gaelic words for host, 'sluagh', and cry, 'gairm', that realised they were made for each other and gradually sidled up closer to become the word we know and love today. In the original Gaelic setting, 'sluagh-gairm' was a full-throated battle cry – a far cry now, perhaps, from the subtler, if no-less-powerful stealth of the world's marketing departments. And so, we now live in the world of 'The World's Online Market Place' (eBay), where 'Life's Good' (LG) and 'The Future's Bright, The Future's —' (Orange, right?).

Classroom activity 4

The following piece is an extract from a media text arising out of the other investigation idea from the first section, on the language use of young children. It is the first part of a leaflet (again approximately 25–30 per cent of the overall piece) to promote the value of shared reading between parents and young children. It would be aimed at the parents and would appear in public places like local libraries, nurseries and schools.

Read it carefully and use the assessment criteria from Table 7 on page 184 to 'mark' the piece. Make notes of particular things it achieves and the band you think each is described by, and also any problems you can see.

Extension activity 3

Your school or college will have examples of media text coursework pieces from the examination board, and from previous students, which you will be able to read and analyse. Many of these pieces may also have teacher or moderator comments available, so you can see how marks have been awarded. Gather a selection of different pieces and make notes on the most successful techniques used, beginning, if possible, with those identified by the person who marked the piece initially. Share your findings with others in your class, and pool the tips you have picked up for writing a strong media text.

Reading together

How to share books with your child

Reading with your children is one of the most important and enjoyable things you can do with them. As your child grows older, being able to read well will help them a great deal in their schooling and life – as well as being good fun! Sharing books is worth doing at any age, even with very young babies, and this leaflet will give you a few tips on how to do it well, and why it is so valuable.

The value of reading

Reading is great for growing children for many reasons:

• It introduces young babies to the sounds of words and language.
• Stories give lively young minds lots to think about and enjoy.
• Sitting together reading is a lovely time to bond with your child.
• Reading from an early age helps develop your child's literacy skills.

Some tips for shared reading

Sitting and reading with your child will probably come very naturally. Here are some tips to help you both get the most from it:

• Let your child choose books he or she would like to read.
• Visit the library or the bookshop together every week or so.
• Reading can happen at any time, but try to build in a regular slot each day.
• Encourage your child to talk about books and stories and ask questions.

■ Further reading

General

Articles at www.emagazine.org.uk

Bragg, M. *The Adventure of English*, Hodder and Stoughton, 2003

Crystal, D. *Encyclopedia of Language*, CUP, 1997

Crystal, D. *Encyclopedia of the English Language*, CUP, 2003

Crystal, D. *How Language Works: How Babies Babble, Words Change Meaning and Languages Live or Die*, Penguin, 2007

Fromkin, V. and Rodman, R. *An Introduction to Language* (seventh edition), Thomson, 2002

Jackson, H. and Stockwell, P. *The Nature and Functions of Language*, Continuum, 2010

The Oxford English Dictionary online (www.oed.com)

Thorn, S. *Mastering Advanced English Language*, Palgrave, 2008

Media text

Clark, U. *Introducing Stylistics*, Stanley Thornes, 1996

Cook, G. *The Discourse of Advertising*, Routledge, 2001

Freeborn, D., Langford, D. and French, P. *Varieties of English*, Macmillan, 1993

Goddard, A. *The Language of Advertising*, Routledge, 2002

Morkane, S. *Original Writing*, Routledge, 2004

Russell, S. *Grammar, Structure and Style*, OUP, 2001

Feedback on the activities

Unit 3, Section A Language acquisition

Developing speech

Classroom activity 1

Stage	Lexis/semantics	Phonology	Grammar	Pragmatics/discourse
Pre-verbal		Vocal skills are vital to producing phonemes. Combining sounds to produce recognisable words is practised.		By practising pitch, intonation and volume, children prepare themselves for conversation and rehearse ways to make meanings clear in their speech acts.
Holophrastic/ one-word	At the proto-word and holophrastic stages, the lexical process is under way.	With only one word, phonology is still important to conveying meaning.		
Two-word	Successfully joining words and phrases involves understanding the meanings of words (semantics).		Once two words can be combined, then syntactical and grammatical advances can be made.	Discourse skills such as turn-taking develop as conversations become possible and politeness skills encouraged by parents may appear.
Telegraphic	More words are needed to combine together, so vocabulary is likely to be developing rapidly.		Grammatical ability will become more important at this stage to combine words together in the correct order.	Discourse and pragmatic awareness become more sophisticated as children learn to interpret other people's speech and meanings.
Post-telegraphic			More complex utterances are created accurately. Skills being refined and practised.	

Classroom activity 2

There is no feedback for this activity.

Classroom activity 3

Plosives form most of the first sounds produced by 24 months, but the sounds produced are mainly those created by using the tongue and teeth (n, m) and the lips (p, b). These sounds mostly fall into the 'stop' consonants and voiced categories, with their voiceless counterparts (f, s) produced later. Fricatives appear later because physical control of speech organs is needed, especially a more delicate control of the tongue and the lips; children often replace fricatives with stop consonants in early sounds. Understanding the order in which children acquire consonant sounds, and the ways the sounds are produced, helps in interpreting the typical phonological 'errors' they make.

Classroom activity 4

There is no feedback for this activity.

Classroom activity 5

Some ways in which you may have grouped the words include the following.

Proper nouns: 'Jasper', 'Daddy', 'Laa-Laa', 'Nana', etc.

Food/drink words: 'juice', 'jam', 'biscuits', 'cup', etc.

Social words: 'bye-bye', 'hello', 'hiya'

Politeness words: 'ta', 'please'

Requests: 'cuddle', 'wassat', 'more'

Animals: 'duck', 'quack', 'woof', 'cat'

Interestingly, you were probably able to group them quite easily, which shows that there are patterns to first words. These may be influenced by social interaction and the contexts (situations) of children's development. Notice amongst the first 50 words here are 'Laa-Laa' (from the television programme *Teletubbies*) and 'book', displaying Rachel's early cultural experiences.

Classroom activity 6

There is no feedback for this activity.

Classroom activity 7

Example	Meaning relation
More cat	Recurrence
Daddy sit	Agent + action
No dolly	Negation
Brush hair	Action + affected
Mummy key	Possessor + possession
Ball big	Entity + attribute
There Jack	Nomination
Biscuit floor	Entity + location
Sit buggy	Action + location
Drop juice	Agent + affected

Classroom activity 8

This data does not support Skinner's views about imitation. Here, the child wants to say 'another spoon', but expresses this request using two determiners ('other one'). The message is unclear to the father, who tries to correct the child's speech by breaking the phrase into separate words. Despite the correction the child continues uttering the same noun phrase ('other one spoon'), which seems to support Piaget's view that thought influences language development and that this child has not grasped the concepts surrounding the varieties of determiners that can suggest quantity etc. But, for Chomsky, this child has engaged with a key syntactical rule, i.e. that determiners are used before nouns in order to make a more precise message, even if they have not fully mastered this yet.

Classroom activity 9

There are no right or wrong answers to some of the utterances because you don't have the full context and can't see or hear the children. Here are some conclusions you may have made.

Utterance	Context	Halliday's function	Dore's function
Look at me, I superman	Child playing	Imaginative	Requesting
Mummy	Mummy returns home from work	Representational	Labelling or greeting
Want juice	Child is thirsty	Instrumental	Requesting

Put down	Father is holding child	Regulatory	Requesting or protesting
Me like that	Child looks at toy in a shop	Personal	Answering or labelling
Why?	Child asks why she has to get her shoes on	Heuristic	Requesting action (i.e. response to question)
Night night daddy, love you	Being put to bed	Interactional	Answering or repeating
No	Child wants to stay at the park	Personal	Protesting

Classroom activity 10

Gender could be argued to determine the children's roles and activities. In the mixed-gender interaction, Hollie and Ewan role play shops. Ewan clearly wants the role of shopkeeper, perhaps because he sees this as more powerful, and Hollie seemingly happily takes the customer role. Yet Hollie's understanding of the discourse of shopping is evident in the field-specific lexis she uses, her grammatical constructions and her instructions to Ewan as to his behaviours and language in his role. With the single-sex interaction, Anya and Keri role play mummy and baby bedtime routines and also want to dress as princesses, perhaps supporting the view that socialisation into more stereotypical female roles has occurred.

Hollie's politeness and communicative competence in the exchange might be perceived as more typical of women's language. Anya's modifier ('lovely') and the positive address terms ('baby', 'princess', 'fairy') also seem more characteristic of women's language.

Many theories and issues surrounding gender and language could be applied here. For example, Deborah Tannen's six contrasts of male/female language use could be applied to Hollie and Ewan's interaction. Hollie illustrates *support* as she coaches Ewan into the correct discourse and seeks assistance from Laura to play too. This is counterbalanced with Ewan's desire for *status* in both his choice of role and asserting himself with his comments on 'real' scans and his use of declaratives. Hollie also offers *proposals* for Ewan's turns, modelling the language used in real-life shopping interactions. In Keri and Anya's play, there is also evidence of *proposals* in the suggestions for the direction of the play and in Keri's suggestions for Anya's actions.

Lakoff, too, could be applied relevantly as Hollie demonstrates the modal forms she associates with the shopkeeper/customer discourse ('would you like cash back') and Anya uses empty adjectives ('lovely'). Hollie's communicative competence is particularly evident as she manipulates the play and undermines Ewan in his role. Keri and Anya also vie for dominance, with Keri (like Hollie) being quite subversive in her attempts to not allow Anya the upper hand in her mother's role.

Classroom activity 11

In Text A the mother repeats utterances ('what a noise', 'it is a long time') and uses lexical repetition ('dear'). She uses the present tense ('is it a long time', 'let's go') and her utterances are simple sentences ('are you hungry') with simple verbs such as the copula ('is') and other verbs ('get', 'let', 'are', etc.). Yes/no interrogatives ('are you hungry', 'you're all right aren't you') simulate imagined responses from the baby, modelling discourse structure in adjacency pairs – despite his inability to apply this at this early developmental stage. The mother treats the baby's sounds as responses to her utterances, teaching Michael that communication is two-way (dyadic). Surprisingly, she doesn't use the baby's name and uses few concrete nouns, perhaps because the baby is young and she is responding to sounds that represent his basic food and comfort needs.

The mother's linguistic choices in Text B support the view that CDS adapts as the child develops. She constructs more sophisticated interrogatives ('how many chickens are there') requiring a more developed response. Her discussion of chickens expands the conversation, asking Tom to count how many, and recalls their earlier experience of seeing chickens and his actions of stroking the chicken. Here the mother uses lexical repetition more consistently ('Pascale', 'chicken', 'stroke') than Michael's mother to help Tom learn new labels and terms to describe his actions.

For Classroom activity 12, see page 190.

Developing reading

 ## Classroom activity 13

First books do not resemble adult books. They are often made of soft material, thick card or even plastic, and exploit the tactile and physical nature of children's early experiences. Interactivity is important in children's books because reading is usually shared with adults. Children actively engage with reading books by pointing to objects in the text, lifting a flap to reveal the words and images underneath, or guessing rhymes.

Sound effects, and other phonological/poetic devices, are common features. Children delight in the sounds of words and the effects of rhythm and rhyme. Books also offer explicit learning, both of language itself, and of the world around them; they can be used by carers to support – or to use Bruner's term 'scaffold' – development of the spoken word by giving young children new lexical terms for objects around them and to describe their feelings and experiences.

These books also assist children's social and pragmatic development, modelling the handling of real-life situations. Books also encourage children's imagination and their use of play to represent their understanding of the surrounding world.

Classroom activity 14

These examples are not exhaustive and you may have considered other, equally valid, onsets with the rimes given.

Onset	Rime
b/m/r/gl/bl/	-ow
b/c/m/r/t	-ake
l/gl/sh/m/cl	-ove
r/t/en	-ough

Both -ow and -ake appear more straightforward and follow sound patterns. You can see that -ove can be pronounced differently (as in 'move', 'clove' and 'glove'), showing some of the possible problems with completely phonic approaches.

For Classroom activity 15, see page 191.

Classroom activity 16

The book has a traditional narrative structure with the setting clearly stated in the first sentence, providing a recognisable context for a school-age child. However, unlike story books there is little descriptive language, and plot development relies on the use of direct speech. Recapping the storyline is a key, as characters repeat sentences and lexical features ('race') as a way of foregrounding both the stages of the story and the new vocabulary being introduced; this means that there are fewer deictic references than would appear in naturally occurring speech. Although simple reporting clauses ('asked', 'said') are usually used, here the speech tags suggest the prosody of speech ('shouted'). Inverting reporting clauses only occur when a noun is used (as in 'shouted Mr March').

The lexical choices are context-dependent, forming a sports-day related semantic field. Colloquial lexis is included ('dad') and contractions ('it's') add to the informality. Nouns and verbs are repeated as they are new words introduced in this book ('race', 'gym' and 'train'). Pronouns ('he') are used anaphorically once a proper noun ('Ben', 'dad') has been introduced; this makes the text cohesive and helps the child to connect the noun and pronoun. Simple and compound sentences are used, and the repetition of sentences reinforces new vocabulary and creates predictable patterns. Graphologically, the sentences are laid out mainly on one line, running on only after a conjunction ('and', 'but'); children already recognise that these function as linking words. Pictures visually represent the words and allow children to 'cue'.

Classroom activity 12

Possible links you may have explored to create your paragraph linking AO1 and AO2 are as follows.

Examples	Concept/Theory	Comment
this is a cup of tea [*brings it to her father*]	Vygotsky/Snow	The whole interaction is an example of the child's role-play using the 'prop' of a tea set to simulate adult actions and experiences.
D: this is a cup of tea [*brings it to her father*] F: mm (.) that's not a cup of tea (.) that's (.) a teapot D: do you want a teapot (.) do you want a tea (.) cup (.) cup F: teapot D: do you want a teacup (1.0) here [*hands over teapot*] F: say teapot	Behaviourism/imitation/reinforcement	Some negative reinforcement is given as a way to correct Dora with 'that's not a cup of tea'. Dora then imitates him with 'teapot' but does not understand the difference. She attempts to correct herself with the right lexical item 'teacup' (perhaps hinting at cognition and Piaget here, that could be explored). Although we don't know if he is going to be successful, the father's imperative 'say teapot' is a request for Dora to imitate him.
there aren't any cup of teas	Bellugi's negation stages	Dora uses the adverb 'not' correctly in the contracted verb phase, the third stage of negation.
do you want a teapot (.) do you want a tea (.) cup (.) cup	Stages of question formation	Dora inverts the syntax, using the auxiliary 'do' to create the interrogative.
I get one (1.0) [*goes back to tea set and picks up a plastic teapot*] look here's a cup of tea (2.0) this is a cup of tea	Imaginative/interactional Halliday's functions of language	The whole interaction is based on Dora's imaginative function, but within this she uses interactional language with the interrogatives and the representational function as she gives information to her father.
there aren't any cup of teas	Innateness/LAD/virtuous errors/overgeneralisation/wug	Attaching the plural inflection 's' to 'tea' is wrong in this context and is a virtuous error. She is treating the noun phrase 'cup of tea' as a single morphological unit (as in Brown's MLU), so she pluralises it as a single item, rather than the headword, with the prepositional phrase as a post-modifier. She is overgeneralising the 's', in a sense and is constructing a sentence that an adult would not say (Chomsky). The 'wug' test could be explored in relation to young children's understanding of pluralisation.
Teacup for teapot	Overextension	Dora overextends the noun 'teacup' for 'teapot' and is beginning to package items and network build (Aitchison) in her attempts to differentiate between the objects.
Dora are you making tea can you make daddy a cup of tea there aren't any cup of teas/teapot	CDS	Typical CDS strategies are the use of names and speaking in the third person ('daddy') instead of using pronouns. Repetition is another feature, used both to repeat the request for an imaginary tea and Dora's utterance. The correction of Dora's lexical mistake over 'teapot' is interesting as it supports findings that parents correct lexical content but not grammatical, as shown by the father not correcting Dora's 'cup of teas'. Vygotsky's 'ZPD' and Bruner's 'scaffolding' could also be used to explain the father's contributions to the discourse.

Classroom activity 15

Some of the advantages and disadvantages that you might have discussed include the following.

Method	Advantages	Disadvantages
Whole-word	Children learn visual methods to read words. Good for beginners, mirroring the ways children learn their name.	Children don't have strategies for working out new words. Not all children have good visual memories.
Phonics	Children: ■ become good spellers ■ tackle new words effectively by breaking them down into smaller units ■ can self-teach by applying rules they have been taught.	Not all English words fit patterns neatly.
Analytic phonics	Children: ■ learn the patterns and rules of English spelling and sound/grapheme correspondence, applying these to unseen words ■ can use the rhymes of words to read and spell unfamiliar words, comparing their knowledge of similar word patterns ■ develop an excellent sight vocabulary for both reading and spelling ■ benefit from having phonics combined with other teaching methods and exposure to reading books.	It takes time to learn all the sounds/letters and combinations of vowels and consonants. Not all children have good rhyming skills. Not effective if children can't apply their knowledge to unfamiliar words and words that are not accompanied by a picture.
Synthetic phonics	Children: ■ benefit from the speed at which they learn all phonemes, encouraging reading and spelling skills immediately ■ can apply knowledge to unseen words quickly as the blending of sounds is taught early on.	Existing research has not found any disadvantages.

Developing writing

Classroom activity 17

The written text summarises the story viewed on television into a compound sentence using adverbials ('one day', 'on a trip', 'in the Tardis'). He has captured the main plot elements and uses words lexically relevant to Dr Who. He has not elaborated on the story descriptively, using pictures to show the stages of the story and help the reader visualise the events. Cameron's graphological choice of a storyboard is interesting. It is unlikely he has been taught this; perhaps he has used his cultural experiences of watching or reading comic-strips and cartoons. This supports researchers' links between cultural experience and literacy. Cameron shows awareness that different representations of the same information are possible by using other symbol systems; the text is still multimodal and the images support the text's meanings, adding cohesion.

Understanding of writing processes is demonstrated in his use of a title ('Doctor Who Story') and claiming authorship at the bottom of the text. Cameron understands lineation and directionality. His writing is fairly neat and letter formation is generally secure, including some understanding of both upper- and lower-case letters. Some mirroring of letters ('d'/'b') is evident. Typically of an early learning stage, his separation of letters and words is inconsistent, possibly reflecting his mental re-composition of the story. For an audience, he has not presented his message clearly enough and the transliteration is required for it to make sense to someone who was not present when he wrote this.

His spelling shows phonetic awareness, indicating that he knows some strategies for guessing unfamiliar words. He has to spell 'Shakespeare' because it is polysyllabic and has many separate sounds that cannot be replicated phonetically. This will require further knowledge of English spelling rules to produce accurately. Importantly, he has created a complete text but has yet to progress in writing an extended piece of discourse with cohesive links.

Classroom activity 18

The first text 'Our trip to Chatsworth Farm' is a 4-year-old's recount of a school trip to a farm. Because of the child's age, the orientation is typed at the top by the teacher. The child structures their recount into simple sentences, following a subject, verb, object pattern. It has a list-like layout, with each sentence beginning with the first person pronoun ('I') on a new line. You might question whether it meets Rothery's definition of a recount as chronological, as it is difficult to conclude whether this is the order of the child's experiences or everything that they recalled about their trip. You might perceive that the child's use of the adjective ('favourite') is an evaluation of their experience.

This choice of adjective along with other descriptive lexis suggests that 'My favourite place' is an observation/comment genre. Although it could have evolved into a report-type task, this was obviously intended to allow the child to explore and evaluate their experiences, suggested by the extensive use of modifiers ('warm', 'lovely', 'delicious', 'most wonderful').

'Hedgehogs' fulfils some of the genre criteria for a report, being factual and not sequencing the events chronologically. The dynamic verbs ('eat', 'wander', 'curl') describe the hedgehog's actions, demonstrating the child's understanding that these, rather than any descriptive lexical choices, are more relevant for the task. The 8-year-old's graphological choices show awareness of the appropriate layout for a report, seemingly into bullet points and separate paragraphs. She has edited her writing, crossing out her statement ('because I like them') which reveals that she knows that you don't need this evaluative comment in a report.

Classroom activity 19

Imogen's poem uses a variety of genre conventions, showing her awareness of poetic forms despite her inexperience with language. She gives the poem a title ('Trees'), creates a recognisable quatrain stanza form, uses parallelism in the first two lines and rhyme (if only of the same word 'brez'). Not only does she use these conventions, she also acts like a poet in choosing language for effect, varying the verbs ('sway' and 'russl') to create the visual image for the reader.

Similarly, Oliver's poem demonstrates an understanding of stanza form and he attempts a rhythm with the grammatical patterning of noun + verb ('lions roar'). He, too, has chosen his verbs carefully to reflect the animal he is depicting. Interestingly, he also has a sense of the need for a concluding message to his poem with the coordinating clause 'and we sleep' introducing the human world. The title, like Imogen's, is literal and summarises the topic of the poem. Both children add authorship, just as poems would be attributed to their writer.

Both children are given scaffolding through the graphology, adding a visual aid to help them focus on the topic. Other scaffolding may have been given in the lesson to help them with the typical genre features and appropriate vocabulary for their topic.

Classroom activity 20

Child's spelling	Actual spelling	Type of spelling error(s)
suddnly	suddenly	Omission of salient sounds
peculier/ perculiar	peculiar	Phonetic
cloke	cloak	Phonetic
kitchin	kitchen	Phonetic
discusting	disgusting	Phonetic
(golf) corse	course	Omission/phonetic
shale (shall)	shall	Overgeneralising/ phonetic
exspensis	expensive	Phonetic/salient sounds
twincling	twinkling	Substitution/phonetic

butifull	beautiful	Omission/ overgeneralising
kitins	kittens	Phonetic
fraindly	friendly	Phonetic/transposition
becuase	because	Transposition
correg (meaning bravery)	courage	Phonetic/over-generalising
bissnis	business	Phonetic/over- and undergeneralising
chearful	cheerful	Overgeneralising
intelgent	intelligent	Salient sounds

Your findings indicate that children make a range of errors based on their phonetic, grammatical and visual memories. There is usually a logical reason for these errors, making them 'virtuous' rather than random.

Classroom activity 21

The teacher's use of metalanguage (the language used to talk about the English language and learning) is focused on the child's achievement of certain literacy criteria, such as the use of paragraphs. Adjectives like 'super' and praise phrases 'well done' and 'good work' all offer positive reinforcement and feedback, and the teacher's use of the child's name adds to the reinforcement. The ticking of the child's use of structural devices such as paragraphs and the content 'details' reward the child with a recognisable symbol of achievement.

The suggestions for improvement are couched within a question that the teacher does not leave as rhetorical but offers a suggestion. However, the question mark after 'the caravan' makes it seem only a suggestion, rather than what the child could have done to make it better.

The teacher is most likely using the National targets and literacy strategies to determine the child's achievement, but only comments and not grades are given here. For younger children, interrogatives rather than imperatives appear to be used.

The personal opinions of the teacher 'I think' personalise it and pragmatically indicate the teacher's engagement with the child's work, and exclamatories add an enthusiastic tone.

Other concepts and ideas from acquisition that could be applied usefully are Vygotsky (ZPD) and Bruner (scaffolding). Vygotsky's idea is that when a student is at the ZPD for a particular activity, providing the appropriate assistance (scaffolding) will help them to achieve the task. So here, the teacher gives them a 'boost' with feedback to apply to the next similar literacy task, and once they master features like paragraphing the scaffolding can be removed and the children will then be able to complete the task by themselves. Applying Bruner, the teacher acts as facilitator to the child's learning by commenting on what was done well and making suggestions for future improvements. Both Bruner and Vygotsky agree that learning is a social experience, with others needed to scaffold this. These teachers perform this role in a formal learning environment but take the age of the children into consideration with their comments, being positive and complimentary.

Data response exercise 1

1 The student response addresses AO1 and AO2 throughout, but does not explicitly address contextual factors (AO3).

2 Good awareness of the importance of AO1 is shown with the range of language terms used and accurate examples given. The response is heavily focused on grammatical features, which are well selected from the data. Regular and salient links to concepts (stage, CDS, Piaget, power, gender, Skinner) demonstrate that the students know that AO2 is the second most important AO. The lack of AO3 comment shows that the student understands that this is not as important, but overlooking it could affect their overall grade.

3 It is systematic in the ways the student identifies features, exemplifying and analysing these. So, the point, evidence, analysis (PEA) model is used effectively, but some of the paragraphs could be arranged more systematically. Starting with the child's developmental stage is good, but the paragraph is brief and the student returns to the stage with more evidence in paragraph four.

4 Some points are developed more securely, as in paragraph four where there is engagement with Tom's use of the progressive and the link to the idea that he is moving through the telegraphic stage, and the effective comment about Tom's imitation of his mother as evidence for Skinner. There are some opportunities to explore further the CDS strategies used by the parents, perhaps comparing their language use.

5 This is a very competent answer, but the main improvements would be to ensure that contextual factors are linked to language, ensuring that paragraphs are structured logically (i.e. CDS and stage observations are placed together). This might have been achieved if the essay had been planned carefully before it was written.

Data response exercise 2

Key contextual factors for this data are the environment and activity: the home setting as different to school, reading as a homework activity and opportunity to practise skills learned at school and develop confidence. Other important contextual factors are the role of the parent. In this activity, the parent acts as teacher, offering support and encouragement, and as a reading companion to encourage the child to use their knowledge of reading and the world. In addition to the roles the parent and child play, the book itself is important. It is designed to help the child learn to read rather than being purely for entertainment.

By looking at the final paragraph you can see that the student does not always give examples of the features they say are in the text, making more assertions than offering analysis and evaluation. Exemplification is needed for simple sentences, the minimal use of speech, the monosyllabic lexis and the use of punctuation to aid the child. Also, the discussion of the miscue could have been more precise, as the current wording is a little descriptive.

Unit 3, Section B Language change

Changes in context, lexis and semantics

Classroom activity 1

Word	Origin	Word	Origin
poncho, hammock, mosquitoes, guitar, tortilla	Spain, or South America	marmalade	Portugal
anorak, parka, igloo, kayak	Arctic Region/Inuit	shish kebab, sherbert	Turkey
dungarees, pyjamas	India	sushi, kamikaze	Japan
ski	Norway	tea	China
chocolate	France	moussaka	Greece
knapsack, cruise	Holland	safari, trekked	Africa
tobogganing	Canada	barbecue, cannibal	Caribbean
anonymous	Greece	tattooed	Polynesia
pow-wow	North America	assassin	Egypt
zero, coffee	Arabic origin		

From this you can see just how wide-ranging English borrowing has been, as this passage only represents a few. Some clues lie in the consonant combinations used more commonly in other languages ('kk'). The words seem to fall into semantic fields: clothes ('poncho', 'anorak') and food ('tortilla', 'coffee') being the main ones. These would indicate the influence of travel and different cultural experiences, which English did not have existing words to describe.

Some have been borrowed because of colonisation and empire-building, such as the Indian words 'dungarees', 'pyjamas'. Mainly we use their native, non-anglicised form as loan words using the relevant orthography ('ski', 'kamikaze'), but sometimes we anglicise them in both spelling and pronunciation ('chocolate' instead of 'chocolat').

This exercise has introduced the importance of etymology, the study of the origins and history of words and their meanings. This helps us understand how speakers and writers have used English over time and is vital when analysing historic texts in a detailed and informed manner.

Classroom activity 2

Blend	Blended words	Blend	Blended words
motel	motor + hotel	skort	skirt + short
brunch	breakfast + lunch	Oxbridge	Oxford + Cambridge
Wikipedia	Wiki + encyclopedia	labradoodle	labrador + poodle
docusoap	documentary + soap	boxercise	box + exercise
guesstimate	guess + estimate	netiquette	internet + etiquette
Chunnel	Channel + tunnel	confuzzle	confuse + puzzle

Blends are based on the idea of merging objects together ('labradoodle', 'skort', 'Oxbridge'). Another technique is to use the first letter from one word with the majority of another ('motel', 'brunch'). Sometimes whole words are blended with parts of others ('guesstimate', 'boxercise').

For Classroom activity 3, see page 195.

Classroom activity 4

	1747	1852	1998
neologisms			nutrition, calories, protein, carbohydrate
borrowings/ loan words	currey		wan kai thai-style curry, soy sauce, mangetout
compound	tea spoonful, sauce-pan, stew-pan	table-spoonfuls, piled-up	supermarkets, non-stick
archaism	enough	broth, fat pot	
narrowing	fowls, shovel	liquor	
broadening	scum		'in'
conversion		salt	

Classroom activity 3

Word	Semantic change	Word	Semantic change
doctor	**Narrowing** The word once referring to teachers, now mainly used for the medical profession and academics	web	**Metaphor** Now most commonly used to refer to the internet, metaphorically suggesting ideas of thin, invisible, interlinked webs. Still has its existing meaning, so arguably has also broadened
gay	**Pejoration** Originally meaning 'happy', it ameliorated, and used metaphorically, in reference to homosexuality. In current slang it now refers to something defective or unfashionable, e.g. 'that's gay'	mouse	**Broadening/metaphor** As well as the small animal, the meaning now includes the object used to interface with the computer
virus	**Metaphor/broadening** Once only associated with an illness transmitted from people, but now also refers to the infecting of computers by bugs	a domestic	**Euphemism/narrowing** Now used euphemistically to refer to arguments between spouses, probably a shortening of a longer phrase such as 'a domestic incident'
guts	**Amelioration** Once referred to animal/human entrails and now is more positively associated with courage	friendly fire	**Euphemism** A phrase used to refer to killing allies accidentally in a war context
punk	**Broadening/semantic shift** Used to mean a prostitute. In US slang it now means a petty criminal or thug, as well as a coward. In UK use it is now associated with a music sub-culture	hoodie	**Metaphor/broadening/pejoration** Refers to an item of clothing, the colloquial term for a hooded top. However, it is now associated with the type of person wearing it and the associated anti-social behaviour
vulgar	**Pejoration** Used to mean popular and now means in rather bad taste	starve	**Narrowing** Once meant to die, and now refers to death by not eating

Changes in written style

Classroom activity 5

The earliest text shows surprisingly few differences from modern spelling, with the only unusual orthographical representation being the letter 's'. The short 's' appears at the ends of words ('companies', 'delicious') and the long in the initial or medial position ('ʃlave', 'taʃk').

Dorothy Wordsworth's journal shows more variation, perhaps because it was originally handwritten rather than printed. Use of the –e at the end of words is different from modern usage (it is used in 'sate' but not in 'headach'). Both spellings are used consistently but don't follow yet the rule for long and short vowel sounds.

The 2004 message shows many features of non-standard spelling: phonetic ('foreva', 'iz'); vowel deletions ('wy', 'thnk'); substitutions ('faze', 'dis'). These give the message a more informal and conversational tone, but are still based on certain evolving conventions of text usage despite their non-conformity to Standard English.

Classroom activity 6

Font	Connotations
Graphology is important	Comic Sans creates a playful and informal font
Graphology is important	Fonts such as Times New Roman and Arial can be used to connote a more academic and traditional style
Graphology is important	The bold perhaps creates a sense of the text's importance, but the style contradicts this and suggests a light-hearted message
Graphology is important	The handwritten effect connotes a friendly font and would suit a more personal message

Classroom activity 7

Punctuation

When reporting direct speech, Stedman uses speech marks on every line on the left of the page only, as well as to open and close the speech tag ('said he'). Other noticeable differences are that the semicolons mark subordinate clauses 'into this hospital'; 'where I beheld'…) and before the translation ('dogo tay Tamara; The sun is just going to sleep'). Punctuation is inconsistent in these cases as the determiner ('The') is capitalised in the second example. The first sentence is much longer than would be typical now, using semicolons, colons and dashes to add further clauses in the first paragraph.

All sentences begin with the same adverb ('here'), arguably because this is a 'real' account, rather than a literary, fictional representation and so stylistic variety is not important.

Mary Kingsley's travel writing from the late 19th century suggests that the use of semicolons and colons had declined. However, many commas still separate clauses, often being used to convey her opinions ('I should say', 'however much I may deplore') and the majority of sentences are complex. Both texts show that capitalisation had been standardised to proper nouns only. Punctuation in the 2008 travel blog has become more non-standard with missing apostrophes ('cant', 'its'), use of the slash ('on/off') and the use of brackets adds the humorous tone and afterthoughts for the audience, a feature Mary Kingsley also employs. Commas divide clause elements but are used less frequently in the text and there are more simple and elliptical sentences ('Time to go I thought').

Graphology

The use of italics for place names and other languages is an interesting graphological feature; in the 2008 blog capital letters are used for a speech-like emphasis ('WRONG') rather than to signal important information. The placing of one word on the last line ('morrow') is typical of the time and the word would be repeated on the next page to provide cohesion for the reader.

Orthography/spelling

The long 's' is still evident in 1796 and has clearly died out by the 1897 piece. Number and letter homophones ('U' '4') in 2008 reveal the influence of text/online chat styles.

Classroom activity 8

He told me in our journey…	Prepositions
She was small of her age	
She say you to the day?	Auxiliary verbs
She doubted not…	
It is a nothing of a part…	Articles
To be taken into the account…	
Fanny shrunk back	Irregular verbs
and much was ate…	
I am so glad we are got acquainted.	Tense usage
So you are come at last!	

The properest manner…	Comparative/ superlative adjectives
The richest of the two…	
Will not it be a good plan?	Contractions
It would quite shock you…would not it?	
I stood for a moment, felling dreadfully.	Adverbs
It is really very well for a novel.	

Classroom activity 9

There are many examples of the subjunctive, mainly using the same syntactical structure 'if he be'. The subjunctive appears used in connection to the potential wishes of the superior and as part of the advice to ensure that it is the higher-ranked person's desires that must be anticipated in order not to cause offence.

Pronouns used are the third person ('he' and 'she') when referring to the lord or lady and the second person pronoun 'you' to direct the advice at the reader. The pronoun 'whom', used here for the objective case, is becoming an archaic grammatical form. Interestingly, 'your self' is written as two separate words, suggesting that compounding had yet to occur for the reflexive pronoun.

As it has the genre of an advice guide, modal verbs appear to give the reader instructions about their behaviour. 'Must' and 'will', deontic modal verbs, appear frequently to tell the reader how they should act with those of higher rank. Clearly, genre conventions have not changed, although the topic of this book would appear outmoded in a more socially equal society. Other verb forms of interest, from a language change perspective, are the progressive aspect being used in 'reading, writing or studying'.

Other noteworthy features are the non-standard capitalisation of nouns, a feature of both Early Modern English and Late Modern English pre-standardisation, and the spellings of 'Physick', where the consonant cluster 'ck' has now been reduced to the 'c' alone, and 'jole', probably reflecting the pronunciation of the time.

Classroom activity 10

All three extracts have a female audience, but use pronouns to create different relationships.

'Summer Preview' adopts an instructional tone, offering the writer's expert opinion to her audience through the use of the first person. ('I think we can all manage', 'I have'). The instructional and informative advice is given in imperatives using direct address ('give you', 'help you'), although some inclusive pronouns ('let's') present a more equal relationship. Patronising as it seems to us, it appears that access to fashionable clothes couldn't be taken for granted in this post-war period.

'Beauty is where Beauty is' is written from the reader's perspective. The contractions ('let's', 'don't'), the speech-like interjections ('oh') and the dashes suggesting the writer's personal asides ('– well, my chat –') are in an informal register. Other interactive features are the rhetorical interrogatives, often introduced as non-standard sentences beginning with conjunctions ('And how about pretty chocolate boxes for stockings and hankies?'). Although written in the first person ('I'), direct address ('you') is used; this is intended in a matey style to highlight the writer's shared experiences with the reader. Indeed some language choices hint at an existing relationship between the writer and reader ('like I always do'). The pronoun choices support the pragmatics, as in the inclusive pronouns ('we all use hair rollers' and 'let's face it'); here the shared knowledge centres on the awfulness of 'hair rollers' to 1960s girls. Some lexical choices, like the compound ('hair rollers'), seem dated today, as do some of the ideas offered – again showing how attitudes and language change. Apart from the pronouns, adjectival repetition ('pretty') reinforces the writer's engagement with the audience.

The problem page letter is different; it doesn't just entertain, but advises not only the individual addressee but, pragmatically, the wider readership, who have similar problems. 1970s' attitudes to girls' work and educational opportunities seem old-fashioned to us and the writers' pronoun choices appear patronising ('we sympathise, but we think that you should look at it from your parents' point of view', 'we hope you appreciate it'). The direct address ('you') is repeated, emphasising the advice offered, and the plural pronoun ('we') is not used inclusively, but to show the writers' joint perspective.

 Classroom activity 11

The purpose of this letter is to address the receiver's concerns on behalf of the estate that the sender has not acted properly in some recent business transactions. Given that this is a sensitive issue and bears both on the sender's local reputation and the possible consequences for his relationship with the powerful landowners, you can see why he adopts such a polite tone. There is some evidence of positive politeness with the deliberate attention to the receiver's wants established in the sentence such as 'I find it is your wish'. This conveys the writer's cooperation as he owns up to having deceived the estate. The final topic of the dairy maid and her mother's illness meets Brown and Levinson's suggestion of small talk and shared group interest as another positive politeness marker. However, the writer uses many negative politeness strategies. A pessimistic tone is created through the auxiliary verb used for negation in 'I cannot think of troubleing him' and apologies are apparent in the admission of wrongdoing in many examples ('it wd have been a greater Crime in me', 'as the whole human race are liable to errors', 'I hope this will not be an unpardonable one in me', and 'It is not my wish to secret'). The writer begs for forgiveness in 'I should have made you acquainted with the last time I had the pleasure of seeing you'. Finally, as a marker of negative politeness, the sign off 'I am Dr. Sr.' shows his deference to the receiver, although this would have been a convention of the time given the different status of the writer/reader of the letter.

You could introduce some power ideas from AS in interpreting this letter. It may be that, in 18th-century society, the landowners had instrumental power over workers for the estate or their tenants. Certainly, the receiver of this letter holds practical power over the writer with his ability to offer or deny him financial support for his business and to influence how others view his reputation.

Other conventions of texts from this time include punctuation features such as the capitalisation of nouns ('House'), contraction of verbs ('receiv'd') and the use of dashes. Grammatically, complex sentences, with possible multiple subordination, are evident. Because of the dashes, sentence demarcation is not entirely clear, and those that do seem separate are mostly compound-complex owing to the high frequency of coordinate clauses in the piece. The subjunctive ('you will pray be so obliging'), and non-standard uses of conjunctions ('and' and 'but') are other grammatical features that illustrate language change and are prior to the influence of grammarians and grammar books. Lexically, 'an other' is written as two separate words rather than the modern compounded form.

 Classroom activity 12

Handwriting the letter means that changes can't be made, but also, as the writer can't send letters regularly and instantly like email, he has to add to his letter until ready to send it – hence the letter spanning five days. With modern electronic communication, the soldier would have sent his update daily and received feedback, whereas a letter is one-way communication.

The solider mentions another problem with sending letters, especially during war time, and that is the unreliability and his lack of knowledge as to whether his letters are reaching their destination. There also seems to be a hierarchy of importance in letters, and this social communication seems less important than more military communications.

The soldier uses a very elliptical style, typical of more modern forms of communication, perhaps used here either because of time constraints, paper restrictions or reflecting a soldier's style of only using important content words and omitting function words such as '[I] hope it reaches home'.

Changes in speech style

 Classroom activity 13

The convict's language shows his dialect and social class, with lexical choices suggesting his accent. Instead of 'victuals' (an archaism for food), the convict offers an alternative word ('wittles'); Dickens presents this using eye dialect for his audience's interpretation. This could also suggest assimilation in the sounds typical of his accent or his lack of knowledge. The use of elision ('em') also reinforces his mode of speech. The verb choice is also interesting ('lookee'), possibly elision of 'look' and 'thee', suggesting the archaic pronoun used in some dialectal forms. Dickens chooses to make the distinction between the speech of the boy and the convict, showing the divergence between them. Note the boy's polite reply, using the pragmatics of polite speech with the conditional ('if'), modal auxiliaries ('would') and an adverb to suggest possibility ('perhaps'). This hesitancy shows the boy's fear but also marks him as more educated.

Why does language change?

 Classroom activity 14

Swift uses very emotive lexis to describe his fears ('corruptions', 'abuses', 'absurdities'). His worries centre in this extract on young male university graduates, who presumably enjoyed high social status at the time, who wanted to use the popular and fashionable colloquial language of the day not only in their speech but also in their writing, in order to be seen as both funny and clever. Although his criticisms are specific, his negative view of youth sociolect and slang seem very familiar!

Johnson, on the other hand, realised that he couldn't fix meanings in a prescriptive way – by stopping them changing – and could only reflect current ones (a more descriptive approach to how words were being used at that time). This still resonates with us now as dictionaries are continually updated.

■ Classroom activity 15

Non-standard English	Standard English	Feedback
I didn't do nothing wrong	I didn't do anything wrong	Standard English views a double negative as forming a positive
Who are you going out with?	With whom are you going out?	Ending a sentence with a preposition is deemed ungrammatical
Can you borrow me this pen?	Can you lend me this pen?	Lexical confusion with the words 'borrow' and 'lend'
You was right, wasn't you?	You were right, weren't you?	In Standard English the second person agreement would be the plural form
That was sick.	That was very good.	The slang use of the word 'sick' is not recognised in Standard English
r u goin 2 james house l8er	Are you going to James' house later?	Words in the non-standard form are spelled phonetically or use number/letter homophones
Den im goin 2 da cinemas	Then I'm going to the cinema	Youth sociolect and instant messaging/text language choices are not recognised in Standard English

Some of these could be thought of as dialectal, as in the multiple negation and number agreement, and are probably left over from regional or historic usage. Other examples show how slang and youth sociolect have an impact on language use and the effect of text messaging and instant messaging chat on the phonetic spellings of words, the lack of punctuation and the use of number/letter homophones.

■ Classroom activity 16

Humphrys' language is highly rhetorical, with exaggerated comparisons between texters and the medieval Mongol warlord, Genghis Khan, well known for his violence towards his enemies. This semantic field of violence is reinforced in the tripartite ('pillaging', 'savaging', 'raping') and the military choices make the discourse more cohesive ('quiver', 'arrow'). It is also humorously self-effacing in the way he pokes fun at his own attitudes through the imagined direct speech of a texter ('granddad', 'quill pen'), appealing to the readers who agree with him by explaining the initialism ('SMS Short Messaging Service') and using the archaic pronoun ('one') to give a mock RP air. Humphrys use a conversion ('texters'), which perhaps shows his more modern use of lexis; he also uses the root word as an adjective to qualify the type of message ('text')!

Humphrys' lexical choices are interesting too for semantic change, as with the noun ('vandals') which once referred to an invading Germanic tribe and now means someone who destroys something, usually property. This example of an eponym has been used metaphorically and, perhaps, narrowed in meaning as the tribe no longer exists. The blend 'emoticon' (from emotion + icon) indicates Humphrys' knowledge of the new terms used in text language; and the 'smiley', although annoying to him, is evidence of a graphological (and typographical) style possible because of technology. Both emoticons and smileys are ways that graphology provides visual presentations of paralinguistic features in text messages.

The two orthographical choices ('answerphone', 'ansafone') visually portray the influence of text spelling choices based on phonetics and the desire to use fewer letters; both are unhyphenated compounds, showing how the words entered the language separately but have combined to describe a recent invention. Later in the article, Humphrys acknowledges that some people will say that 'language changes', but worries about the lasting effect on written language caused by text and netspeak.

Unit 4, Section A Language investigation

Focusing your investigation

Classroom activity 1

The focus in each of these investigations should be limited to just one or two stories.

1 An effective advertising investigation will usually focus on a single product – cars, cosmetics, chocolate or whatever – and if gender is the issue, then the adverts should be broadly aimed at people of a similar age and socio-economic group. So you could look at car/cosmetic/chocolate adverts in magazines with a primarily young male/young female readership (perhaps *Cosmopolitan* and *FHM*?). However, modern adverts in print media tend to have minimal text content so you may need to collect quite a few.

2 If you enjoy sport, this could be an attractive option: take the same game or event, pick out one or two specific incidents, and record and transcribe the commentary on radio and television. As the variable here is medium, try to avoid any other variations. Other commentary-related possibilities include comparing commentary styles of different commentators (same game, same medium) or even comparing professionals and amateurs – tape the 'fan zone' amateur commentaries which are a feature of some Sky TV broadcasts and compare with the professional version of the same match. Yet another alternative approach is to vary the sport and investigate the differences between the commentary on a darts match with one on a horse race, for example.

3 Magazine-based studies need to limit the scope and range of the data; you might stick to a single gender and magazine feature, perhaps comparing the advice page, true-life story, horoscopes or fashion tips found in publications aimed at boys (or girls) of different ages – say, *Sugar*, *J17* and *Elle*.

4 This kind of investigation is likely to appeal as the data is close to hand, but you will need to be clear about the focus of the study. You could take a single teacher who teaches the same subject to several different age groups, and record a similar *kind* of lesson, perhaps concentrating on the opening few minutes, or on a class discussion. An alternative might be to keep the age range constant, and focus on how a variation in the subject affects language choice – how, for example, a chemistry lesson differs from an English lesson.

Classroom activity 2

Three examples of the data required to tackle a question from the list are as follows.

- **How true is it that males use less phatic talk than females?** This would require working with spoken and then transcribed data from both male and female speakers. The data would need to be drawn from interactions, and it would be necessary to try to gather data that is as realistic as possible, and that involves a similar audience, purpose and context. It would also be important to decide if the investigation was going to focus on mixed or single-sex interaction, or include a comparison of the two. Ideally, data from at least three different speakers in each sex would be needed to provide some basis for comparison.

- **How does the language of legal texts convey power and authority?** At first glance this seems to be about written texts, although the investigation could compare or make use of spoken legal texts as well. In the case of written texts, a small corpus of texts would be useful, either ranging across legal genres, or narrowing the focus of the investigation to look at one particular kind of text.

- **Are texting and email more like speech or writing?** A range of authentic text messages and emails would need to be sourced, preferably ones that had been written without the investigation itself in mind. A decent amount would be needed to set up the sort of quantitative analysis that would work well in this kind of approach, so a minimum of four of each text type would be necessary – and more would be beneficial.

Classroom activity 3

- **Child speech development**: Any study of early reading materials is likely to be informed by the current debate about teaching methods and the influence of phonics-based approaches in particular. Sampling three or four texts from different stages of the Oxford Reading Tree would be one approach, or you could include a couple of examples of early 'readers' from the 1950s and 1960s for a potentially rewarding language change element in such a study. Working directly with children and asking them to read a short passage aloud is likely to produce a more interesting study; a miscue analysis – transcribing and analysing the results – can be one of the most productive of all studies in this area (see pages 158–159 for an example).

- **Child literacy studies**: Children's writing can be sampled and analysed in various ways – across the primary age range, for example, taking a couple of similar pieces from an 'average' child in each year, or sampling the ability range within a single class to gauge the variation in writing skills at a given age. There may even be interesting gender issues to explore here.

- **Language change**: The best approach to a study of changing report styles is to take a single type of report – a sports report, or crime, or major disaster – and find two or three examples from the same publication at perhaps 20-year intervals. (You can track down examples of historic newspapers online, or using the local archive – usually a department attached to the central library in major towns and cities – which usually has local and national newspapers stretching back to the 19th century.) The archive may also be able to help you turn up examples of other genres, such as children's literature. Other sources would also include online archives, such as that of the British Library, Project Gutenburg and the British Museum. Comparing television or film texts can work well, with good access to high-quality archive material available on DVD, or by acquiring second-hand VHS tapes. The only disadvantage can be the often time-consuming process of transcribing from a video source, although the advantage to this is that you can tailor the transcription to precisely the features that you would like to record on paper for analysis. In addition, scripts are widely available either published in books, or through internet sources, for example the Internet Movie Script Database, along with other enthusiast sites.

Data response exercise 1

Non-standard features that you might have identified in the Scouse transcript are:

- h-dropping in the word 'ow' and 'im'
- slang contraction in the words 'gonna' and 'ain't'
- possible dialect words in 'friggin'' and 'youse'
- g-dropping in 'friggin''
- non-standard verb form (3rd person instead of 1st person) used in 'knows'
- t-dropping or possible glottalling on 'wha''
- multiple negative construction in 'ain't never'
- ellipsis of auxilliary verb 'had' in 'you better'.

Classroom activity 4

This table shows the examples of both Standard and non-standard English that you might have identified in the Agard and Sebba texts.

	Agard's poem	Sebba's transcript
Non-standard language	ent, double negative, de, yu, mash up	double negative, /tek/, right, sneakup, wha, no, wearin', yeh, jean guy, 'n, 'er, bwo::y, no I never
Standard English	Queen's English, the story of my life, I don't need, to split up	you shouldn't take, sorry, you didn't want me to, you see, that's Nicolette, look at her, that's me, Valerie cut me off, must be the one in my bathroom, It's just my wardrobe, that's all

1. Agard's poem could be compared with poets writing in Standard English at a similar time, with an investigation into their distinctive styles.

2. Agard's poem could be compared with spoken data from speakers using Jamaican creole to see how far his poem has accurately reproduced it, or to provide evidence of how Jamaican creole has changed since the poem was written.

3. Agard's poem could be used alongside other black English forms to research attitudes towards these varieties and particular features.

4. Sebba's data could be compared with Cockney, Jamaican Creole and Standard English forms to investigate the balance of different language sources in London Jamaican, and the concept of code-switching.

5. Some of the words and phrases in Sebba's transcript could begin an investigation into the development of more modern urban language forms such as Multicultural London English, and Multi-Ethnic Youth Dialect.

Classroom activity 5

Some of the many possibilities for Mark include the following.

Details about Mark's life	Potential investigation ideas
Part-time job: Helps out on his dad's market stall on Saturdays.	The family market stall would be an interesting place to base an investigation into the interaction between stall holders and customers (in so-called 'service encounters') and the use of occupationally-specific sales talk.
Interests and hobbies: Football – plays for local team in Sunday league and supports Manchester City. Cars – has recently passed test. Music – plays guitar in a band with friends.	There are also many possibilities within the world of football: the banter between his fellow players in the dressing room before and after a match (how does winning, or losing, affect this?), or the manager's half-time team talk, for example. Then there's the colourful language of the terraces, or the contrast between fanzine language and that of the official programme. Mark may even be able to access match programmes from the distant past and make these the subject of a language change study. The online supporters' forum may also provide rich material for a study of e-discourse.
Media habits: Enjoys a variety of music; reads car magazines; contributes to online Manchester City supporters' forum. Favourite programmes: enjoys reality TV shows such as *I'm a Celebrity ...* and *Big Brother*.	Mark could compare the language associated with various kinds of music media – the speech of DJs live or on radio, the reviews of new music or gigs, or the contrasting styles and language of publications catering for specialist tastes, to suggest but a few. Mark's preferred television programmes do offer some interesting possibilities: reality TV allows us unproblematic access to an abundance of spontaneous speech, and can often yield rich material in terms of discourse and pragmatics.

Classroom activity 6

1. Here, the hypothesis provides a specific and well-informed point of departure for the investigation, as it refers to a well-documented trend in the style of reporting and defines three specific linguistic elements for the investigation.

2. This is a suitably 'open' question which would lead to a wide-ranging investigation, though the 'member' of the 'family' and the 'different contexts' would need to be specified, as would the aspects of 'talk' to be studied (Turn-taking? Dialectal/idiomatic/slang usage? Politeness features and observance of Grice's Maxims?)

3 The question here is too limiting: 'what do they have in common?' invites a simplistic response and seems to exclude discussion of a range of similarities and differences. A better question might be 'To what extent does Blair's oratory use similar rhetorical techniques to Churchill's, and to what extent does he depart from these?'

Classroom activity 7

The following table sums up the range of each proposal put forward by Maxine, with discussion below of the advice she would need.

Investigation criteria	Proposal 2	Proposal 3
1. Your link to, or interest in, the investigation area.	Favourite topic from AS.	Originally from Birmingham.
2. The sort of data you plan to collect – if you can provide a sample, even better.	Male and female descriptions of pictures.	Spoken language from three generations of family.
3. Where and how you plan to gather your data.	Show males and females a series of colourful pictures and ask them to describe what they see.	From immediate family.
4. The main linguistic frameworks and features you aim to work with.	Semantics in detail and also lexis.	Phonology in depth but also some other areas.
5. The question or hypothesis at the heart of your idea.	Testing out Lakoff's theory.	Comparing accents in the family against original Brummie accent to see how much it has changed.
6. Details of any related linguistic research or theories.	Robin Lakoff and women's use of language to describe colours.	Estuary English awareness.

Advice for proposal 2:

This sort of idea has worked well before, Maxine, and male and female data is fine and would be good to compare.

■ Bear in mind that exactly what sort of data you would collect needs to be defined more clearly. It could be spoken or written, for example.

■ The stimulus pictures would need to be carefully chosen to fairly test both male and female interests and knowledge.

■ Your link to Lakoff's theory is purposeful, although focusing on only the colour terms part might be too narrow to provide a full analysis.

■ Begin thinking about more specific language features that you would like to focus on from the frameworks that you mention, and think if it would be possible to extend the aims a bit to include some deeper grammatical data and analysis.

Advice for proposal 3:

This is a lively topic, Maxine, and there is a good research base you could make use of.

■ Remember that you should not analyse your own language – perhaps your sister could take your place as the data for the youngest generation.

■ You have good ideas about Estuary English, especially being based in London – look into Paul Kerswill's research as your investigation could look for evidence of Estuary English in each speaker.

■ Using spoken data would work well – although you need to think about how to obtain it reliably through recording and transcribing, so it might be time-consuming.

■ Phonology will be an important framework – it would be possible and useful to open the investigation out to include some analysis of non-standard lexis or grammar use. Start to think about the particular linguistic variables you would need to test.

Classroom activity 8

■ **Commentary**: Jespersen's status as a 'respected linguist' is somewhat offset by the lack of empirical evidence, and the date of the source (1922). Even if his observations were true then, much has changed in society in general and in gender roles in particular. Nevertheless, there are echoes of his ideas in more recent research-based discussions of language and gender, and the issues of taboo/vulgar and tentative expression remain interesting aspects of language study.

Methodology: collecting your data

Classroom activity 9

1 Publically accessible recordings from websites can be a very good source of data. However, it is important to think carefully about the different kinds of data they contain, and how to handle them. 'Official' websites like the British Library and BBC Voices will contain material for which consent will already have been granted, and which has gone through a process of editing to make sure it is suitable; for example, it will not be offensive, or refer to other people or institutions who may not wish to be involved. This material is often already part of a larger piece of research or language study, which the participants would have agreed to their speech being part of. In these cases, it is reasonable to assume that using these recordings for your own smaller-scale investigation is ethically sound. Websites where individuals can post privately produced and unprofessional recordings can be more problematic. The content may be inappropriate, the person may be very young, or may not have given consent for the recording to be made public. Although websites like YouTube do have systems for dealing with offensive content, it is possible that such videos can appear on them for a while, even if they are later removed. Such data may also be unreliable. Therefore, although it can be possible to use such data, it is important to evaluate these issues and reject any data you think may compromise any of these considerations of ethics or validity. For all data obtained online, you should carefully acknowledge the source of each piece you use: give the URL, state the time you accessed it (in case it changes), and the exact part of the recording you used, for example, from 2:17 (2 minutes, 17 seconds) to 5:34).

2 There are some problems with this potentially interesting investigation, mainly regarding the workplace-based conversations. Gabrielle needs to establish the ground rules for the home recordings, and then talk to her father about what kinds of conversations it may be admissible for him to record – with all the participants' permission.

3 In principle this sounds like potentially a very interesting idea, but just because the authors of the letters are dead doesn't rule out some possible sensitivities – especially if they contain very personal material. He needs to get full permission from his family, and promise to render the material anonymous.

Classroom activity 10

1 Working with the text of both the film and book would be essential here, so a kind of corpus analysis would be the most obvious candidate. If the film script could be found online and an e-book of the novel acquired, then some quite sophisticated searching of particular lexical patterns would form the structure of the investigation and help identify the most important parts of each text for more qualitative analysis.

2 This could be set up in several possible ways. Some sort of experiment could be devised where a group of people agree to respond to text messages from the researcher and their replies are then used as data. Alternatively, people could volunteer existing messages from the 'sent' box of their mobile phone and these could even be processed to form a kind of mini-corpus for analysis. A survey or interview would also be possible, although maybe these would be more appropriate as supporting methods to the first two, as they would be less likely to yield raw text message data for analysis.

Classroom activity 11

The matches, with commentary, are as follows.

- **1 and C**: Well-chosen visual stimuli – such as those featuring colourful items of clothing, or members of the opposite sex of varying degrees of attractiveness, can be effective in provoking responses which test received ideas about language and gender. Make the stimulus a series of controversial/outrageous statements like 'the death penalty should be re-introduced for paedophiles' and you may elicit a useful corpus of data related to the expression of opinion.

- **2 and B**: Games are useful for any age group, providing they require plenty of verbal communication. One student recorded a group of friends during a game of Monopoly to investigate the balance between game-focused and social talk, and to see whether the dynamics and style of the usual group 'banter' changed once clear 'winners' and 'losers' started to emerge. With younger children, engaging them in some kind of productive activity is a good way of overcoming their self-consciousness.

- **3 and A**: Whether confining your study to children, or investigating storytelling more generally, you need to settle on a specific task or stimulus. Inviting older people to reminisce about specific experiences can yield fascinating data, whether your focus is narrative skills or the use of regional dialect. Just don't tell them you're interested in their language – you could present your investigation as being about local history, for example.

Analysis: exploring your data

Classroom activity 12

Overview: Both children successfully negotiate the text provided without any prompting, demonstrating a number of competencies in terms of reading skills. This is interesting as the text uses a mixture of narrative and dialogue, and the young readers need to recognise the function of speech marks. However, there are many examples of hesitations and other miscues in their reading, and some interesting differences between these which indicate that the twins are using different reading strategies.

Please refer to the tables on pages 203 and 204.

Classroom activity 13

There is, of course, no single 'correct' way of organising the analysis, but the versions suggested here would certainly provide a robust structure for a comprehensive investigation.

Sample: Children reading

1 Pauses in reading
   1.1 Correct recognition of sentence boundaries and other phrase/clauses
   1.2 Pausing associated with 'challenging' words
   1.3 Pausing associated with miscues

2 Substitutions
   2.1 Resulting from visual miscue
   2.2 Resulting from semantic prediction

3 Analysis and explanation of omissions/deletions

4 Analysis and explanation of self-corrections

5 Analysis and explanation of false starts, hesitation (non-fluency)

6 Analysis and explanation of evidence from prosodic features (stress and intonation pattern of understanding)

7 Overall conclusions

Data response exercise 2

1 In general, the Group B girls show a trend of using non-standard language more frequently, with significantly higher percentages in the use of the non-standard '–s', 'was', negative concord, 'come' and 'ain't' features.

2 The most striking anomaly is in the Group B girls' frequency of use for the non-standard 'what' feature. This seems a very low frequency of use compared with the more general trend of the Group B girls to use a higher frequency of non-standard forms.

Classroom activity 14

Of the examples listed, the overwhelming majority of nouns (37/48) are pre-modified in some way; there are five cases of double pre-modification ('design', 'bodies', 'windscreen', 'bodies', 'streamlines'), three of which are concentrated in the description of features thought to appeal to women. Where this occurs, the pair of adjectives are semantically related, as with 'steel' and

'protecting' when applied to the 'bumpers'. We will explore the different kinds of pre-modification next; it's worth noting here that every time the word 'Ford' or phrase 'Ford car' appears, it is preceded by 'new' – six times in all, with a seventh when it describes the 'open or closed body styles': this repeats the association of the brand name with the modernity, supporting the theme of the image used.

The following tables relate to Classroom activity 12.

Initial scrutiny:

Child X	Analytical notes
this silly **pig** everyone calls her silly pig (3) because they (1) she doesn't silly **things**	Omits verb 'to be' and doesn't observe punctuation – micropauses for thought, not at punctuation marks – takes 3 secs to recognise visual shape of 'because'. Substitutes 'she' for 'they' after everyone – but self-corrects. Then negates – 'doesn't' for 'does'. Reading for sense?
(2) you **silly** pig (.) said (.) **horse** (.) pigs don't put things **flowers** on their heads	Micropauses possibly reflect recognition of speech marks? Substitutes 'things' for 'flowers' – makes syntactic/semantic sense – predictive reading, influenced by an echo from previous line?
(1) one day silly pig had an **idea** (1) she went to (2) tell the other animals about her idea	Recognises sentence boundary at 'idea' – pause + stress. Pause before 'tell' – reading ahead?
(.) I am going to look for **treasure** on the farm (.) she said (1.) I am going to find lots and lots of **treasure**	Confident recognition of 'treasure' – stress shows understanding. Again, micropauses recognise speech marks? Again – 'treasure' stressed – but sentence boundary not recognised here.
you silly pig said (3) the other animals you won't find treasure on the **farm**	Longer pause – reading ahead?
(3) silly pig (3) tha set off to look for **treasure** (5) she went on out of the farm gate (3) and up the hill urm (2) **lane**	Longer pause followed by miscue – that? Then? Predictive reading but self-corrects. Longest pause so far – sentence boundary – followed by three miscues – suggests reading ahead and spotting 'obstacles'. Substitutes 'on' for 'out', 'of' for 'to' and 'farm gate' for 'farm yard'. Gate/yard – semantically OK – visually similar (four letters, initial letter with descender, second letter 'a'). Filled pause marks self-correction of substitution – predicts semantically possible 'hill' (from collocation 'up the hill').
(4) suddenly silly pig (4) **stooped** (1) she saw something (1) **sparkling** in the tree	Longer pause (4) prior to miscue – substitution of 'stooped' for 'stopped'. Semantically/syntactically possible – visual confusion of 'stopped' and 'stooped'. Pauses before 'sparkling' on three occasions.
(2) ooh no I can see a (4) sparkling **necklace** in the tree (1) a sparkling necklace is the **treasure** (1) I will put (1) it around my neck	Longest of three 'sparkling' pauses before 'sparkling necklace' – word recognition. Insertion of 'the' – predicts syntax. Substitutes 'will' for 'shall' – more commonly used.
(3) but the sparkling necklace doesn't wasn't (2) really a necklace it was a spider's web	Self-corrects wasn't/doesn't – realises syntactic impossibility of 'the necklace doesn't really a necklace'?
(1) the web was sparkling with (1) rain drops (2) the spider was very cross	Insertion of 'the' – syntactically/semantically reasonable.
(1) what a silly pig (1) thing to do he said you silly pig (2) silly pig (2) felt very silly she set off up the (1) lane	Pauses/self-corrects after substitution, influenced by repeated collocation of 'silly pig'.
(3) suddenly silly pig stooped (1) she saw something sparkling in the (1) don't know that word	Longer pause correctly observes sentence boundary punctuation. Avoids earlier 'hill'/'lane' substitution. Repeats previous 'stopped' /'stooped' confusion – not really semantically OK here. Sense? Which word? Hedge? Or earrings? More likely – reading ahead.
(2) ooh no I can see sparkling ears **earrings** in the hedge (1) she said (1) sparkling earrings are the treasure I [*inaudible*]	False start – takes cue form beginning of word – self-corrects (semantically impossible).

Child Y	Analytical notes
this tha this is silly **pig** everyone calls him silly pig because he says silly **things**	Initial hesitation – then fails to observe punctuation at sentence boundary. Substitutes male for female pronouns. Substitutes 'says' for 'does' – both semantically/syntactically OK.
(3) you silly pig said pig pigs (2) don't put flowers on their heads	Substitutes 'pig' for 'horse'. Inserts plural suffix on 'heads' – logical concord with subject 'pigs'.
(3) one day silly pig had an idea (1) she went to the (2) tell the other animals about her **idea**	Gender pronoun OK now! Seems to jump ahead to 'the other animals' – self-corrects with 'tell' – suggests reading ahead. Secure recognition of sentence boundary by stress.
(2) I am going to look for things (3) **treasure** and the farm see she said (1) I am going to (2) feed (1) find lots and lots of **treasure**	Substitutes 'things' for 'treasure' – semantically possible – longer word, initial letter – but self-corrects. Substitutes 'and' for 'on' – sense? Phonetic confusion of 'she' and 'see' next to 'said' – tongue twist effect. Substitutes 'feed' for 'find' – triggered by initial letter recognition and semantic context (animals, farm).
(2) you silly **pig** said the other animals you (2) won't find (1) treasure on the **farm**	Slight hesitation on polysyllabic 'treasure'.
(4) silly pig shi set off to find (1) look for treasure she went out the farm (1) yard but (1) and up the lane	Hesitates – 'shi'/ 'set' – tempted to substitute subject pronoun. Inserts 'look for' alongside 'find'. Substitutes/self-corrects conjunction 'but' for 'and'.
(5) suddenly said silly pig (7) she saw something (3) spa (4) **sparkling** in the tree	Substitutes entire phrase 'said silly Pig' for 'Silly Pig stopped'. False start and pause before 'sparkling' – word recognition.
(1) Ooh I can see a sparkling (2) **necklace** in the tree asked (5) a sparkling necklace is the **treasure** (1) I (2) shall put it round my neck	Insertion of 'asked' (nb. check word class) followed by long pause – insertion of 'the'. Deletion of initial vowel of 'around'.
(.) but the sparkling necklace (.) wasn't (2) really a necklace it was a spiders **web**	Occasional micropauses but mainly observes sense and sentence boundaries.
(2) the web was sparkling with (1) raindrops spider was very cross	Pause before 'raindrops' (recognition?).
what a silly thing to do you silly pig silly (1) pig felt very silly she set off up the lane	Sentence boundary/punctuation not observed. Deletion of phrase 'he said'.
(3) suddenly silly pig (1) sto stopped (1) she saw something **sparkling** in the bushes	Correctly observes sentence boundary. Slight hesitation on 'stopped'. Substitutes 'bushes' for 'hedge' – semantic prediction.
(1) ooh I can see something (1) sparkling earrings in the hed (1) she said (1) sparkling earrings are **treasure** I sha shall put them (1) on my ears	Substitutes 'something' for 'sparkling' – influenced by previous sentence – self-corrects. This time correctly reads as 'hedge', though with deletion of final consonant. Slight hesitation on (unfamiliar?) 'shall'.

Classroom activity 15

Text	Child X	Self-corrects?	Cause of substitution?	Text	Child Y	Self-corrects?	Cause?
she	they	yes	Assumes 'everyone' is plural subject of sentence.	this	tha	yes	Visual miscue of 'this'/'that'?
does	doesn't	no	Adds negation – cause unclear.	she	he	no	Imposes expectation of gender.
flowers	things	yes	Semantic prediction.	does	says	no	Semantic prediction.
set off	tha	yes	They? Then?	horse	pig	no	Repeats previous word.
out to the farmyard	on out of the farm gate	no	Unfamiliar with 'farmyard'. Assumes journey begins by going 'out of'.	head	heads	no	Logical – assumes plural subject 'pigs' has plural object 'heads'.
lane	hill	yes	Semantic prediction.	treasure	things	yes	Semantic prediction.
stopped	stooped	no	Visual confusion of similar verbs.	she	se	yes	Phonic slip?
shall	will	no	Replaces less familiar with more commonly used modal verb.	find	feed	yes	Semantic prediction compatible with farm context.
wasn't	doesn't	yes	Visual miscue?	set off	she	yes	Predicts subject of sentence.
thing	pig	yes	Collocation? 'Silly pig' already used several times.	and	but	yes	Grammatical/lexical prediction of conjunction.
stopped	stooped	no	As above.	silly pig stopped	said silly pig	no	Discourse prediction.
earrings	ears	yes	Recognises first part of word.	hedge	bushes	no	Semantic synonym.
				sparkling	something	yes	Partial visual miscue (–ing)?

From the table we can see that both children make a similar number of substitutions, and both immediately self-correct about 50 per cent of the time. It is also clear that both children use a number of different strategies when reading, including making several creative but semantically sound predictions. Neither child seems to be 'sounding out' words in a phonics-influenced way, but some of the substitutions do suggest a reliance on visual recognition and 'reading for meaning'.

Coursework preparation and practice

Classroom activity 16

Version B is clearly much better as an academic text, for many reasons. Although there is no prohibition on the use of 1st person in your investigation report, there is nothing to be gained by using phrases like 'in my opinion' (Version A) and as a 'scientist', you should aim for a more impersonal style. The tone of condemnation and criticism in phrases like 'rather old-fashioned' and 'no-one would … today' is inappropriate; your task is not to judge, but to analyse and explain. The attack on 'sexist snobs' is also completely out of place – note how Version B deals with the issue of values and attitudes but in a much less emotional way. The comments in Version A about the register and style of the text are far too sweeping and simplistic ('all very formal'), and once again adopts an inappropriately condemnatory tone ('too much text'), as well as including lapses of style (no-one would bother to …). When using technical language, the writer explains unnecessarily the meaning of terms like 'adjective' and 'noun phrase' which can be taken for granted at this level.

Version B, on the other hand, uses an appropriate register – not particularly technical here, but with words like 'affluent', 'prestige', 'consumption' and even 'verbosity'. The discussion of language recognises that it is not all black and white, and suggests an alertness to subtlety and detail totally lacking from Version A.

Classroom activity 17

Original version	Suggested version	Commentary
In the restaurant, I found that just about everybody used loads of questions which there was only a couple possible answers to, whereas the ones in the kitchen were always more open. This must be because the waitresses really needed to know stuff like where their plates were etc. I also found that there was loads of slang used in both places. I guess this was to create a friendly informal atmosphere with the customers. I noticed a vast number of cases where there was lexical repetition; waiters did this a lot when taking customers' orders, obviously to check they had taken the order down right.	In the restaurant a large majority of staff tended to use closed questions, whereas those in the kitchen were generally open questions, quite probably because these expressed a genuine need for practical information on the part of the waitresses. There was significant use of slang, quite possibly to help create a friendly atmosphere with customers. The tendency towards significant amounts of lexical repetition noted was presumably due to the waiters' need to confirm the accuracy of the customers' orders.	No need for 'I'. 'A large majority' better than 'just about everybody'. Closed questions – use the terminology. No need to explain. 'Quite probably because' – more tentative than 'this must be'. Get rid of vague, casual expression – 'know stuff'. 'Significant use of' much better than 'loads of'. 'I guess' too personal/casual. 'Tendency towards' – much more tentative than 'vast number'. 'Presumably' more tentative than 'obviously'.

Unit 4, Section B Media text

Preparing to write

Classroom activity 1

1 One obvious option would be an article for a television listings magazine or television review page of a newspaper; it could focus on what the participants reveal about themselves through their language and conversational behaviour.

2 This topic would lend itself to a light-hearted look at the subject of gender differences in language for a school or college magazine.

3 An article aimed at sports fans, or even the script for a podcast from a newspaper or radio station like Radio 5 Live would be possibilities here.

4 The subject of early child language will be of interest to any parent or carer, and you could consider any genre that would reach this audience, such as an article for an appropriate magazine, an informative pamphlet available in clinics and surgeries, or the script for a possible talk/presentation to first-time parents.

Classroom activity 2

■ **Layout and presentation**: This will depend entirely on the genre/medium you choose. As with your work for Unit 2, you should study a suitable style model carefully and aim to emulate its distinctive presentational features.

■ **Degree of linguistic detail**: There will obviously be a lot less technical detail in your text, though you will still need to use suitable illustrations and quotations to enliven and illustrate your piece.

■ **Tone and style**: For a non-specialist audience, the tone needs to be less intensely serious; a lively, journalistic touch is needed, with the occasional light-hearted observation or anecdote.

■ **Use of specialist terminology**: As for terminology, you can no longer assume your readers will understand the more technical linguistic vocabulary; you may need to introduce a few useful terms, but it would be a mistake to bombard your readers with jargon.

Coursework preparation and practice

Classroom activity 3

This is a feature article. It is written by a single, named writer, and might appear in the business or comment section of a business magazine or national newspaper website, or perhaps in a printed magazine or newspaper supplement. It would appeal to an adult audience, familiar with popular culture and interested in discursive writing on language, cultural and business-related issues, especially people who work in a media-related industry. The purpose is to discuss the power and influence of advertising slogans and provide some additional, sometimes linguistic, insight into them. Articles of this kind are also designed to entertain the reader, often through the use of humour and tone.

The use of a headline and sub-headed introduction provides a clear opening and textual organisation. From there, vocabulary is varied and the tone set up is articulate. There is a purposeful use of metaphor to describe advertisements as 'exhibitions' in 'galleries', which is chosen and handled with some sophistication. The use of a question addresses the audience while establishing and developing a relationship with the reader. Etymological detail is given for the word 'slogan', which lends depth and weight to the material. Including quoted slogans shows evidence of research and knowledge of the chosen field. There are attempts at humour, although these may be a bit overexaggerated.

The piece provides evidence for the 19–21 mark band upwards. For example, there is 'good clarity and control of writing' and a 'largely effective adaptation' of the idea is begun. However, the use of 'appropriate structures' is evident, there is clear 'adaptation of original materials', and the piece appears to be 'effective for audience and purpose', all from the 22–24 band. There are also some aspects nearer the 28–30 mark band: there are contributions to the 'use of original ideas', and production of a 'convincing new text' in evidence.

Classroom activity 4

Overall, the piece seems to work well, with clear communication. Some specific achievements and problems are noted below, with reference to the sort of criteria that might be most relevant to them. Although the piece feels very competent, it could lack the flair and originality to get it into the top bands.

Achievements:

■ Very clear sections to the text, using headings and bullet points. (19–21 band, 'deployment of structures and genre conventions')

■ Convincing style and tone reads clearly and well. (19–21 band, 'article likely to be effective for audience and purpose')

■ Some overview of the value of reading to child language development given. (19–21 band, 'largely effective adaptation of original materials')

Some problems:

■ Some confusion of using pronouns to refer to the 'child' – on one occasion the plural 'their' is used. (16–18 band, 'some lack of control at times')

■ The subject and genre might limit the opportunities to show 'top band' flair in the language.

Glossary

A

accent: the distinctive pronunciation patterns used by a particular group of people.

allusion: a subtle reference to a story or factual aspect outside of the text.

Americanisms: examples of language use distinct to American English speakers.

anaphora: repeated syntactical structures for effect, for example, a sequence of sentences beginning in the same way, or a list of things using the same phrase form.

anglicised loan word: a borrowed word from another language that has been altered in its pronunciation or spelling.

anomalies: strange, one-off or unexpected results in your data.

anti-language: language that is used by a particular group to prevent others from understanding them.

archaic: a word from an earlier period of English usage that is rarely used in the modern contemporary language.

archaism: an old word or phrase no longer in general spoken or written use.

ascender: the typographical feature where a portion of the letter goes above the usual height for letters in any font.

assimilation: the influence exercised by one sound upon the articulation of another, so that the sounds become more alike.

B

backing: moving the place in which a vowel is pronounced towards the back of the mouth.

behaviourists: those who believe that language is acquired through imitation and reinforcement.

bound morpheme: one that cannot stand alone as an independent word, but must be attached to another morpheme/word (affixes, such as the plural '–s', are always bound, as is the comparative adjective inflection '–er').

C

care giver: the term used to refer to the main adult who looks after a child.

central vowel: a vowel pronounced roughly in the 'middle' of the mouth cavity.

child-directed speech: a distinctive form of language use employed by adults when interacting with young children.

classical allusion: a reference to a character or event in classic Greek or Roman mythology.

Cockney: a distinctive dialect spoken in the London area.

code-switching: a language skill that enables the user to change between different languages and language varieties while speaking.

cognitive theorists: those who believe that language acquisition is part of a wider development of understanding.

cohesion: the way in which a text appears logical and well constructed.

colloquialisation: where writing uses language more typically seen in spoken registers.

consonant: a speech sound that is produced when the vocal tract is either blocked or so restricted that there is audible friction.

content word: a type of word that has an independent 'dictionary' meaning, also called a lexical word.

convergence: a process of linguistic change in which people adjust their dialect, accent or speech style to those of others, often occurring to express solidarity and understanding.

corpus: a large, text-based collection of data, usually stored electronically so that it can be quickly analysed and searched.

corpus analysis: conclusions and findings drawn from running tests against a fairly large body of language material, often stored and assessed electronically.

covert prestige: refers to the status speakers who choose not to adopt a standard dialect get from a particular group within society.

creole: a language variety created by contact between one or more language forms and becoming established over several generations of users.

cueing: the strategies used to help decode written texts successfully.

cursive handwriting: handwriting in which the characters are joined in rounded and flowing strokes.

D

data: examples of any kind of language in use collected, sourced, or presented for analysis.

deixis: lexical items that 'point' to the time, place or situation, e.g. words like 'now' and 'there'.

derivational morphology: the creation of new words by adding prefixes and suffixes.

descender: where part of a letter goes below the baseline of a font.

descriptivism: an attitude to language use that seeks to describe it without making value judgements.

diachronic change: refers to the study of historical laguage change occuring over a span of time.

dialect: the lexical, semantic and grammatical patterns of language use distinctive to a particular group of people.

digraph: a graphic unit in which two symbols combine, or any sequence of two letters produced as a single sound, e.g. 'sh'.

diphthong: a sound formed by combining two vowels in a single syllable, where the sound begins as one vowel and moves towards another.

discourse: a stretch of communication.

divergence: when a person's speech patterns become more individualised and less like those of the other person in a conversation.

drift: a process of linguistic change over a period of time.

dummy auxiliary: the verb 'do' which is used to form questions and negatives or to add emphasis in a statement.

dynamic verb: a type of verb that expresses activities and changes of state, allowing such forms as the progressive.

E

economisation: where certain written genres (e.g. newspaper reporting) have resulted in compressed styles of writing in order to communicate information efficiently and sparingly.

egocentric speech: the running discourse style of speech used by children where no listener is directly addressed and the talk is focused on the child's activities.

emergent writing: children's early scribble writing, a stage of their literacy development.

emoticons: the online means of showing facial expressions and gestures.

empirical: work that comes from observation and experience, rather than pure theory.

enclitic contraction: where a separate word becomes part of the word preceding it.

Estuary English: a variety of English with its roots in the Thames estuary area, but seen to be spreading to many other parts of the UK.

ethically sound: this refers to the methods of gathering data and conducting an investigation that make sure it won't mislead or offend anyone.

ethnographic study: a research method involving observing the 'real life' behaviour of the people being studied.

euphemism: inoffensive word or phrase used to suggest something less pleasant.

expansion: the development of a child's utterance into a longer, more meaningful form.

experiment: an artificial and controlled situation or activity designed to test a specific idea or hypothesis.

extrapolate: to draw conclusions based on a sample of data which might apply more widely.

eye dialect: a way of spelling words that suggests a regional or social way of talking.

F

facsimile: an exact copy of a text, as if it has been photocopied, showing all graphological and orthographical elements in their original form.

fascicle: one of the divisions of a book published in parts.

free morpheme: one that can stand alone as an independent word, e.g. apple.

fronting: moving the place in which a vowel is pronounced towards the front of the mouth.

function word: a word whose role is largely or wholly to express a grammatical relationship.

G

grapheme: a written symbol, letter or combination of letters that is used to represent a phoneme.

H

holophrase: a single word expressing a whole idea.

homophone: a lexical item that has the same pronunciation as another.

hypernym: a superordinate, i.e. a word that is more generic or general and can have more specific words under it.

hyponym: a more specific word within a category or under a hypernym.

hyponymy: the hierarchical structure that exists between lexical items.

hypothesis: a statement of theory to be tested by research and data analysis.

I

idiolect: an individual's own 'linguistic fingerprint'.

idiom: a speech form or an expression of a given language that is peculiar to itself grammatically or cannot be understood from the individual meanings of its elements.

inflectional morphology: the alteration of words to make new grammatical forms.

influential power: power used to influence or persuade others.

informalisation: the way in which language is becoming increasingly informal in all areas of society.

instrumental power: power used to maintain and enforce authority.

interview: an interaction between two or more people for a specific purpose.

International Phonetic Alphabet: also known as IPA, this is a detailed system containing over 160 symbols to represent the sounds of spoken language.

L

Language Acquisition Device (LAD): the human brain's inbuilt capacity to acquire language.

Language Acquisition Support System (LASS): this refers to the child's interaction with the adults around them and how this interaction supports language development.

lexicon: the vocabulary of a language.

lexis: the vocabulary of a language.

ligature: the linking of two graphemes, once common practice in printing but now becoming less common.

linguistic variables: specific linguistic features identified as markers for possible variation in an investigation.

litotes: deliberate understatement for rhetorical effect. This can be in the form of euphemism or of multiple negation, for example, describing someone who is older as 'not as young as he was'.

London Jamaican: a distinctive variety of language blending Cockney, Jamaican creole and Standard English forms.

longitudinal study: a data-gathering exercise for investigation that takes place over a significant period of time, for example recording the same child's language use over several weeks or months.

M

matched guise: a research method used for investigating attitudes towards language varieties. Similar material is presented to listeners, but delivered by speakers with different accent or dialect characteristics, and research is then carried out into the way each speaker was perceived and received. Studies can use actors to reproduce different speakers, or speakers from particular regions or backgrounds.

mean length utterance (MLU): a measure of children's ability to produce stretches of language; the number of morphemes is divided by the total number of utterances to find the average length. A higher MLU is taken to indicate a higher level of language proficiency.

methodology: the design of an investigation and the stages it goes through.

micropause: a pause of about half a second or less.

minor sentence: a phrase punctuated as a sentence but without the minimum requirement of a subject and verb in it.

miscue: errors made by children when reading.

miscue analysis: a way of recording the errors in reading a passage of text aloud, particularly in young children.

mixed-mode: features of printed text combined with features expected in conversation.

morphology: the area of language study that deals with the formation of words from smaller units called morphemes.

multimodal texts: texts that combine word, image and sound to produce meaning.

N

nativists: those who believe that humans have an inbuilt capacity to acquire language.

negative reinforcement: when an undesirable behaviour is unrewarded with the intention that it will not be repeated.

non-anglicised loan word: a borrowed word from another language that has not been altered from its original form.

non-standard: language use of any kind that differs from standard grammatical, lexical, semantic, phonological or graphological uses.

O

object permanence: the awareness that objects continue to exist even when they are no longer visible.

objective: an unbiased, factual view of a subject.

observer's paradox: the difficulty of gaining examples of real language data, when the presence of an observer or a contrived situation might change the way people would normally use language.

obsolete: no longer having any use.

omission: the leaving out of a phoneme in a group of phonemes clustered together.

orthography: the study of the use of letters and the rules of spelling in a language.

overextension: a feature of a child's language where the word used to label something is 'stretched' to include things that aren't normally part of that word's meaning.

overgeneralisation: a learner's extension of a word meaning or grammatical rule beyond its normal use.

overt prestige: refers to the status speakers get from using the most official and standard form of a language. Received Pronunciation and Standard English are accepted as the most prestigious English accent and dialect.

P

paralinguistics: aspects of speech in addition to the actual words and word-sounds said.

parallellism: use of similar syntax for deliberate effect, for example repeated phrases or sentence lengths.

phoneme: the smallest contrastive unit in the sound system of a language.

phonemic contraction: the variety of sounds is reduced to the sounds of the main language used.

phonemic expansion: the variety of sounds produced increases.

phonetic spelling: a way of writing down speech to show the way it was pronounced by using letters and symbols to represent single sounds.

phonetics: the study of the sounds used in speech, including how they are produced.

phonics: a system of teaching reading and spelling that stresses basic symbol–sound relationships and their use in decoding words; a system used especially in the early stages of reading.

phonology: the study of the sound systems of language and how they communicate meaning.

political correctness: words or phrases used to replace those that are deemed offensive.

polysyllabic: words that contain three or more syllables.

positive reinforcement: when a behaviour is rewarded, including verbal praise to encourage this behviour to be repeated.

pragmatics: the factors that influence the choices that speakers make in their use of language – why we choose to say one thing rather than another.

prescriptivism: an attitude to language use that makes judgements about what is right and wrong and holds language up to an ideal standard that should be maintained.

primary data: spoken or written data collected by a researcher.

proclitic contraction: where a separate word becomes part of the word following it.

proposal: a document that sets out the main area of your investigation, and details about the question or hypothesis you want to test and the data you intend to collect.

proto-word: an invented word that has a consistent meaning.

provisional: refers to the fact that your results are only a small-scale example, and cannot be regarded as comprehensive or 'proving' anything for certain. All research results are provisional in the sense that they can only provide a snapshot of a particular range of data.

Q

qualitatative: data analysis that focuses on individual instances of language use and analyses them closely and in context.

quantitative: data analysis that summarises findings in larger sets of data and presents statistical findings.

R

recast: the commenting on, extending and rephrasing of a child's utterance.

received pronunciation (RP): the prestige form of English pronunciation, sometimes considered as the 'accent' of Standard English.

register: a variety of language appropriate to a particular purpose and context.

reliable: used to refer to data that is an accurate reflection of real language use.

S

scaffolding: the process of transferring a skill from adult to child and then withdrawing support once the skill has been mastered.

Scouse: a distinctive dialect spoken in Merseyside.

secondary data: data that has already been collected by another researcher, that is made use of in a new investigation.

semantics: the study of meaning.

sentence boundaries: marking sentences with capital letters and full stops, question marks or exclamation marks.

social interactionists: those who believe that child language develops through interaction with carers.

social variables: the ways in which the context of data differs by social factors like age, gender, ethnicity and social class.

sociolect: a defined use of language as a result of membership of a social group.

standardisation: making all variations of language conform to the standard language.

stative verb: verb that describes a state; stative verbs are not usually used in the progresive aspect, which is used for incomplete actions in progress.

subculture: a cultural pursuit engaged in that happens outside of the mainstream, accepted values of society.

subjective: a view of a subject that includes personal opinion.

subjunctive: a grammatical mood.

substitution: a word, sound or letter used to replace another in speech or writing. This is often due to errors in pronunciation, vocabulary or spelling.

survey: gathering data on attitudes or knowledge by asking many people to respond to questions and information through a questionnaire or some other method.

synchronic change: refers to an approach that studies language at the theoretical point in time without considering the historical context.

synecdoche: a figure of speech where something is referred to by just a part of itself, or where something is referred to by a larger thing or idea it is part of. Examples include calling a police officer 'the law' or the violins, viola and cello in an orchestra 'the strings'.

synonyms: words with very similar semantic value.

synoptic: bringing together a full range of skills and viewpoints.

syntax: the way words are arranged to make sentences.

trend: patterns in data that seem to show something in particular tending to happen.

typography: the study of the graphic features of the printed page.

underextension: a feature of a child's language where the word used to label is 'reduced' to include only part of its normal meaning.

universal grammar: the explanation that all world languages share the principles of grammar despite surface differences in lexis and phonology. Sometimes called linguistic universals.

virtuous error: syntactic errors made by young children in which the non-standard utterance reveals some understanding, though incomplete, of standard syntax.

vocative: a form (especially a noun) used to address a person.

vowel: a sound made without closure or audible friction.

word picture: a feature of radio broadcasting where a presenter will put forward a visual scene using verbal narrative description.

Index

Key terms and their page numbers, where they are explained in the margin, are in **bold**.